The
Prosperity
Paradox

ALSO BY CLAYTON CHRISTENSEN

The Innovator's Solution

The Innovator's Prescription

Disrupting Class

The Innovative University

The Innovator's Dilemma

The Innovator's DNA

Seeing What's Next

With Karen Dillon

How Will You Measure Your Life?

Competing Against Luck

The
Prosperity
Paradox

How Innovation Can Lift
Nations Out of Poverty

Clayton M. Christensen,
Efosa Ojomo, and Karen Dillon

HARPER
BUSINESS

An Imprint of HarperCollinsPublishers

HarperCollins books may be purchased for educational, business, or sales promotional use. For information, please email the Special Markets Department at SPsales@harpercollins.com.

FIRST EDITION

Library of Congress Cataloging-in-Publication Data

Names: Christensen, Clayton M., author. | Ojomo, Efosa, author. | Dillon, Karen (Editor), author.
Title: The prosperity paradox / Clayton M. Christensen, Efosa Ojomo, and Karen Dillon.
Description: First edition. | New York, NY : HarperBusiness, [2019] | Includes bibliographical references and index.
Identifiers: LCCN 2018028690 | ISBN 9780062851826 (hardcover)
Subjects: LCSH: Economic development. | Wealth. | Poverty.
Classification: LCC HD82 .C5224 2019 | DDC 339.2—dc23 LC record available at https://lccn.loc.gov/2018028690

19 20 21 22 23   LSC   10 9 8 7 6 5 4 3 2 1

Contents

Contents

Preface

I spent two years in the early 1970s serving as a Mormon missionary in South Korea, one of the poorest nations in Asia at the time. In South Korea, I witnessed firsthand the devastating effects of poverty: I lost friends to preventable illnesses and saw families routinely having to make impossible choices among putting food on the table, educating their children, or supporting the older generation. Suffering was part of daily life. I was so moved by that experience that when I received a Rhodes Scholarship to attend Oxford, I decided to study economic development, with a focus on South Korea. I hoped that might lead to a position at the World Bank, where I could try to help solve the problems I had seen in my time in South Korea. The particular year I wanted to join, however, the World Bank wasn't hiring any more Americans. That option was closed to me. So in the twists and turns of fate, I ended up at Harvard studying business instead. But the haunting images of the impoverished country stayed with me.

I am happy to say that when I visit South Korea today, it bears no resemblance to the South Korea I remember. In the decades since I lived there, South Korea has not only become one of the world's richest countries but has also joined the respected ranks of the Organization for Economic Cooperation and Development (OECD) countries, and has gone from a foreign aid recipient to a foreign aid donor.[1] American journalist Fareed Zakaria has gone so far as to call South Korea "the most successful country in the world."[2] I could not agree more. South Korea's transformation in just a few decades is nothing short of miraculous.

Unfortunately, such a dramatic transformation has not been possible for many other nations that resembled South Korea a few decades ago. By contrast, Burundi, Haiti, Niger, Guatemala, and many other countries that were desperately poor in the 1970s are still desperately poor. The questions that originally spurred my interest in helping South Korea years ago have continued to nag at me for decades. Why do some countries find their way to prosperity, while others languish in profound poverty?

Prosperity, it turns out, is a relatively recent phenomenon for most countries. Most wealthy nations have not always been prosperous. Consider, for example, the United States. We may forget just how far America has come. Not too long ago, America, too, was desperately poor, rife with corruption, and chaotically governed. By almost any measure, America in the 1850s was more impoverished than present-day Angola, Mongolia, or Sri Lanka.[3] Infant mortality at the time was roughly 150 deaths per 1,000 childbirths—three times worse than sub-Saharan Africa's infant mortality rate in 2016.[4] American society then—with a lack of stable institutions and infrastructures—looked nothing like it does today. But that is exactly why the story of America offers hope to poor nations everywhere. Finding a path out of poverty is possible. The question is *how*.[5]

For decades, we have studied how to stem poverty and create economic growth in poor countries, and we have seen some real progress. For example, the rate of extreme poverty globally decreased from 35.3 percent in 1990 to an estimated 9.6 percent in 2015.[6] That represents more than one billion people being lifted out of poverty since 1990. But as dramatic as that statistic may be, it might be presenting a false sense of progress. Of the approximately one billion people who have been lifted out of poverty, the majority— approximately 730 million—are from one country: China. China was able to reduce its rate of extreme poverty from 66.6 percent in 1990 to less than 2 percent today.[7] That is indeed impressive. But in some regions, such as sub-Saharan Africa, the number of people living in extreme poverty has actually *increased* significantly.[8] Even for those who are not technically living in extreme poverty, survival is still very precarious.

Although it is true that we have certainly made some progress, there seems to be no consensus on how to eradicate poverty. The suggestions range from fixing dismal societal infrastructure (including education, health care, transportation, and so on) to improving institutions, to increasing foreign aid, to boosting foreign trade, and many others.[9] But even those who disagree on the right solution would surely agree with the assessment that progress has been too slow.

	Country	1960s	2015	% change
1	Burundi	$470	$315	-33%
2	Central African Republic	$677	$339	-50%
3	Malawi	$412	$363	-14%
4	Gambia	$773	$384	-50%
5	Madagascar	$1,108	$393	-65%
6	Niger	$1,196	$403	-66%
7	Liberia	$1,447	$469	-68%
8	Democratic Republic of Congo	$1,742	$478	-73%
9	Togo	$783	$578	-26%
10	Afghanistan	$698	$615	-12%
11	Uganda	$686	$625	-9%
12	Sierra Leone	$1,128	$675	-40%
13	Benin	$802	$709	-12%
14	Senegal	$2,003	$935	-53%
15	Zimbabwe	$2,207	$1,037	-53%
16	Ivory Coast	$1,545	$1,319	-15%
17	Ghana	$1,632	$1,401	-14%
18	Zambia	$2,252	$1,576	-30%
19	Venezuela	$8,507	$4,263	-50%
20	Kuwait	$34,087	$29,983	-12%

Figure 1: Per capita income from 1960–1969 was averaged to get a 1960s per capita income value. Values were adjusted for inflation.
Source: IMF World Economic Outlook Database

Consider this. Since 1960, we have spent more than $4.3 *trillion* in official development assistance trying to help poorer countries.[10] Unfortunately, many of our interventions have not had the impact in poor countries that we'd hoped they would. In fact, many of the world's poorest countries in 1960 are still poor today. And even worse, at least twenty countries were poorer in 2015 than they were in 1960 (see Figure 1), in most cases, even after billions of dollars' worth of aid.[11]

Efosa Ojomo, my coauthor on this book and one of my former students at Harvard, knows firsthand the pain of failing despite well-intended efforts. His experience offers insight into the frustration surrounding so many once-hopeful projects designed to bring better living and working conditions to impoverished economies. Efosa is originally from Nigeria, but he has spent the bulk of his adult life living and working in the United States. So while he recognized the poverty that plagued poor countries, it was somewhat of a distant concern for him, until he found himself reading the dedication in the book *The White Man's Burden*, New York University professor William Easterly's attack on Western efforts to aid impoverished countries. In this book, Easterly told the story of Amaretch, a ten-year-old Ethiopian girl who rose at three each morning to fetch firewood. She then had to walk miles to sell the firewood in the market to help provide for her family.

Efosa couldn't sleep that night after he read her story. No child deserved to live such a difficult life. So Efosa, together with some of his friends, set up a nonprofit organization, Poverty Stops Here, to raise money to build wells in various parts of his native Nigeria. "The lack of water is the first thing that hits you when you visit a poor community," Efosa later shared with me. "Water is life. It's why there are so many water projects throughout the world. We just need to get people water. Everything starts there." In a similar vein, when you visit a poor country, the lack of quality education, unpaved roads, bad governance, and other poverty indicators are painfully obvious. Isn't it reasonable to assume that the answer to solving poverty lies in providing one or all of those things?

Efosa managed to raise more than $300,000 and identified five communities in which to help build wells. The day Efosa and his supporters visited those communities to turn on the wells for the first time was one of unmitigated joy, for both Efosa and the local residents. I can imagine there are few more moving sights than seeing plentiful, clean water coming from a well in a village that previously had none.

But as it turned out, wells break down. About six months after building a new well, Efosa would get a call in his Wisconsin home that the water wasn't coming out anymore, and he would have to figure out from thousands of miles away how to get someone in Nigeria to go and fix it. Since all the wells his organization built were in rural areas, finding a skilled technician to source parts and go to the village was always challenging. One problem would be fixed and another would spring up. Today, only one of the five wells that Poverty Stops Here installed is still functional. Efosa and his friends, who had so earnestly set out to help these villages, reluctantly gave up on building additional wells.

Poverty Stops Here, however, is not a unique story. There are more than fifty thousand broken wells across Africa alone, according to a study by the International Institute for Environment and Development. In some communities, as many as 80 percent of the wells were broken.[12] In one of the villages that Efosa targeted for a well, he noticed that there was already a broken-down well just a few hundred feet from the one Poverty Stops Here built, having previously been installed by an international aid organization but then abandoned.

The experience was profoundly disheartening for Efosa, who was so eager to help alleviate suffering. His failure raised some difficult questions for him. If these vexing problems couldn't be solved by an injection of resources and goodwill, then what would help instead? Why do some efforts succeed and not others? Why do some countries fare better than others? Perhaps most profoundly, Efosa recognized that easing poverty—or the most obvious signs of poverty—may not solve the problem long term. Alleviating poverty is not the same as creating prosperity. We need to start thinking differently. We hope that this book will change the way you think about the problem of economic development, the questions that you ask, and the solutions you develop for helping communities that desperately need it.

———

What do we mean by "prosperity"? There are some obvious and commonly used proxies for prosperity, such as access to education, health care, safety and security, good governance, and so on. The Legatum Prosperity Index, which ranks 148 nations in these categories, also includes several other metrics, such as environmental efforts. Not surprisingly, countries such as Norway, New Zealand, and Finland are top performers while Sudan, Yemen, and Central African Republic are at the bottom of the index.

While these measures are important in assessing the well-being of members of a society, we believe that an even more important proxy is access to gainful employment and upward social mobility. So for the purposes of this book, we define "prosperity" as the process by which more and more people in a region improve their economic, social, and political well-being.

This is an important distinction because we might classify some countries as "rich" but not particularly prosperous, such as nations that are endowed with valuable natural resources. Prosperity breeds increasing freedoms—economic, social, and political—and is less dependent on access to one or two singular resources, like oil. And so, while some countries are rich and have figured out ways to distribute their riches to some of their citizens, we would not consider them prosperous because their riches have not bred a culture of inquiry, innovation, and a diversity of markets. They have not led to socioeconomic mobility for all. And those resources have not led to an environment in which prosperity will become sustainable after those natural resources run dry or lose their value in the future. This illustrates the importance of understanding what creates poverty.

And so my coauthors, Efosa Ojomo and former *Harvard Business Review* editor Karen Dillon, and I have set out to investigate how poor nations can become prosperous.

To make this book easier to read, we've written in the first person (my voice), but the thinking captured here is very much the product of our joint collaboration. Efosa and Karen have been coauthors in every sense of that word, and I'm grateful for their partnership and passion for trying to make the world a better place. We know many of you share our goals.

We have written this book with four stakeholders in mind.

First, we wrote this book for those in the development industry who are working diligently to rid the world of poverty. We applaud your efforts and hope that the approach we present in this book will help you think differently, perhaps even counterintuitively, about the problems you are trying to solve.

Second, we wrote this for investors, innovators, and entrepreneurs looking to build successful enterprises in emerging markets. Your work plays a critical role in creating prosperity in low- and middle-income countries. The world needs you now more than ever. But our ideas here aren't built to drive you to invest in these countries purely out of a sense of civic responsibility—they're built on seeing potential opportunities that others might miss.

Third, we wrote this book for the policy makers seeking to institute policies that spur development in their countries. There are few jobs in the world more difficult than that of a public servant in an under-resourced country. We hope that, by providing a model for development grounded in theory, we will enable you to translate these ideas into development policies that are appropriate for your country's unique circumstances.

Last and most important, we wrote this book for the ten-year-old children all over the world, like Amaretch, who deserve a better life. This book is for residents of the villages in Nigeria that celebrated the gushing water from Efosa's wells, only to watch them break down months later. This book is for the fathers and mothers who work tirelessly to provide for their families, but are unable to rise above a life of subsistence. And finally, we wrote *The Prosperity Paradox* for the increasing number of youth who, with each passing day, feel their hopes extinguishing because their world seems devoid of opportunity. We hope that this book reignites their confidence and optimism; a better future awaits them. A better future awaits us all.

NOTES

1. OECD stands for Organization for Economic Cooperation and Development, and is a group of thirty-five member nations, including the United States, France, Germany, and several of the world's most developed countries. "About the OECD: Members and Partners," OECD, accessed January 16, 2018, http://www.oecd.org/about/membersandpartners/#d.en.194378.

2. Fareed Zakaria, "Give South Korea a Gold Medal," *Washington Post*, February 8, 2018, https://www.washingtonpost.com/opinions/give-south-korea-a-gold-medal/2018/02/08/76be5e7e-0d1a-11e8-8890-372e2047c935_story.html?utm_term=.ac6f9aa492cf.

3. For example, in today's dollars, America's annual income per capita in that era was approximately $3,363, Angola's today is $3,695, Mongolia's is $3,694, and Sri Lanka's is $3,844. Unless otherwise stated, GDP per capita numbers are based on 2016 figures and are retrieved from the World Bank. "GDP per capita (current US $)," Data, The World Bank, accessed February 5, 2018, https://data.worldbank.org/indicator/NY.GDP.PCAP.CD?locations=AO-MN-LK.

4. Michael Haines, "Fertility and Mortality in the United States," Economic History Association, accessed January 16, 2018, https://eh.net/encyclopedia/fertility-and-mortality-in-the-united-states/.
    "Mortality rate, infants (per 1,000 live births)," The World Bank, accessed February 21, 2018, https://data.worldbank.org/indicator/SP.DYN.IMRT.IN.

5. Much has been written about the question of how the West became prosperous and, more generally, how poor countries can become prosperous. We recognize that there is a large body of important work in this field. Several books and papers provide very important insight to these questions. The fundamental work is Joseph Schumpeter's *The Theory of Economic Development: An Inquiry into Profits, Capital, Credit, Interest, and the Business Cycle* (1934, translated from the original 1911 German transcript). In this book, Schumpeter helps us see clearly the role of innovation and the entrepreneur in economic development. As entrepreneurs innovate, or create new products or new methods of production, they disturb the "circular flow" in an economy, a process which describes a state of equilibrium in society. Although this perpetual "disturbance"—a process marked by new innovations—does come with some measure of instability and uncertainty, the end result is often a more prosperous society. For example, the car destabilized the horse and carriage and electric railcars, but has made us more prosperous. For Schumpeter, entrepreneurs—the Henry Fords of the world—are the stars in the economic development story. As you'll read throughout this book, we certainly agree.

    In the last half century, must-reads for those interested in the ascendency of the West include Douglass North and Robert Thomas's *The Rise of the Western World:*

A New Economic History (1973), Nathan Rosenberg's and Luther E. Birdzell's *How the West Grew Rich: The Economic Transformation of the Industrial World* (1986), and David Landes's *The Wealth and Poverty of Nations: Why Some Are So Rich and Some So Poor* (1999). David Landes provides rich economic history and stresses several factors, including geography and culture, that helped Europe prosper. North and Thomas summarize their argument as follows, "Efficient economic organization is the key to growth; the development of an economic organization in Western Europe accounts for the rise of the West." In essence, they helped bring to light the importance of institutions and property rights.

In addition, several seminal papers have shed light on this topic. For instance, we have learned from Robert Lucas's *Making a Miracle* (1993), Ricardo Hausmann and Dani Rodrik's *Economic Development as Self-Discovery* (2002), and Richard Nelson and Edmund Phelps's *Investment in Humans, Technological Diffusion, and Economic Growth.* In their own way, each of these economists have helped simplify, in varying degrees, the complexity inherent in the topic of economic growth and development. This has helped us better understand some of the ingredients necessary for sustained economic growth. Robert Lucas helps us understand the importance of on-the-job "learning by doing" in increasing the productivity of economies. Lucas additionally explains that the main features of the East Asian miracles have all "involved sustained movement of the workforce from less to more sophisticated products," beyond increased efficiencies in the production of existing products. Hausmann and Rodrik explain that, while it is important for entrepreneurs within a country to learn what they're good at making, the social returns often outweigh the private returns. This is because, on paper, firms that learn how to develop innovations that can solve a societal problem can be easily copied by "second-entrants," which has the effect of strongly diluting *a priori* incentives to take on the arduous work of developing the innovation in the first place. As such, this makes investments in the kind of learning that leads to structural economic change difficult. In these circumstances, development professionals and policy makers can play a significant role. Nelson and Phelps focus on human capital and technology diffusion. In effect, they hypothesize that "in a technologically progressive or dynamic economy, production management is a function requiring adaption to change and that the more educated a manager is, the quicker he will be to introduce new techniques of production."

In this book we focus on the impact that market-creating innovations have on creating and sustaining economic prosperity. In Chapter 2, we provide both a definition and a categorization for the word innovation, and explain how different types of innovation impact economies.

6. Press Release, "World Bank Forecasts Global Poverty to Fall Below 10% for First Time; Major Hurdles Remain in Goal to End Poverty by 2030," The World Bank, October 4, 2015, http://www.worldbank.org/en/news/press-release /2015/10/04/world-bank-forecasts-global-poverty-to-fall-below-10-for-first-time -major-hurdles-remain-in-goal-to-end-poverty-by-2030.

7. In some ways, China's meteoric development over the past fifty years won't

come as a surprise to students of history. The wheelbarrow, soil science, cardboard, the magnetic compass, deep drilling for natural gas, knowledge of circulation of blood, paper and printing, gun powder, and hundreds of other inventions are attributed to the Chinese. It was the Europeans who were playing catch up in the Middle Ages. In the 1500s for instance, China's economy accounted for 25% of global GDP. But by 1950, it was only 5%. Today, however, as China is making a comeback, its share of global GDP hovers around 19%.

Still, China's recent economic growth is spectacular, especially considering the hundreds of millions of people who have been lifted out of poverty. The conventional story of China's growth is that discontinuities in policy initiated by Deng Xiaoping in the late 1970s unleashed the previously dormant economic giant. This is certainly true to a point. However, it is not possible to tell the story of China's rise without emphasizing the initiative of entrepreneurs and other citizens. MIT's Yasheng Huang explains that China's economic policy in the 1980s actually favored entrepreneurship and market-driven solutions as we saw a significant rise in Town and Village Enterprises in the country. He calls the 1980s "the Entrepreneurial Decade." However, by the 1990s, the country's economic policy shifted more toward a state-led, top-down approach with the rise of many state-owned enterprises. While the economy still grew, Huang explains that this type of growth was not as robust and inclusive as China's growth in the 1980s.

Even then, we still see China on the ascent. Just recently, the *Washington Post* published a piece titled "China increasingly challenges American dominance of science." The authors note that an increasing number of scientists in some of the most prestigious institutions in the United States are leaving to set up labs in China. Although the United States still spends roughly half a trillion dollars on scientific research annually, China is close behind and is on track to surpass the US by the end of 2018. And for the first time, in 2016, annual scientific publications from China outnumbered those from the United States. China's economy is a far cry from where it was in the 1960s and 1970s, and seems to be returning to its dominance in the yesteryears.

Yasheng Huang, *Capitalism with Chinese Characteristics: Entrepreneurship and the State* (New York: Cambridge University Press, 2008).

Ben Guarino, Emily Rauhala, and William Wan, "China increasingly challenges American dominance of science," *Washington Post*, June 3, 2018, https://www.washingtonpost.com/national/health-science/china-challenges-american-dominance-of-science/2018/06/03/c1e0cfe4-48d5-11e8-827e-190efaf1f1ee_story.html?noredirect=on&utm_term=.99a54422d595.

Philip Auerswald, "China's sudden fall and slow recovery," *New York Times*, August 11, 2008, https://www.nytimes.com/2008/08/11/opinion/11iht-edauerswald.1.15175911.html.

8. In 1990, there were approximately 282 million people living in poverty, representing about 55 percent of sub-Saharan Africa's population. In 2013, that number was 401 million, roughly 42 percent of the population. "Poverty headcount ratio at $1.90 a day (2011 PPP)," Data, The World Bank, accessed March 13, 2018, http://povertydata.worldbank.org/poverty/region/SSF.

9. Deirdre McCloskey's Bourgeois series provides a detailed overview of economic history and an analysis of the many suggested causes of economic growth. In the second of the three, *Bourgeois Dignity: Why Economics Can't Explain the Modern World*, McCloskey details many of the widely held theories—institutions, transportation infrastructure, foreign trade, slavery, thrift, capital accumulation, the Protestant work ethic, expropriation, human capital (education), geography or natural resources, science, and a few others—on what might have caused the economic transformation brought about by the Industrial Revolution and suggests that they all miss the mark. This particular 592-page volume explains why, as interesting and plausible as all these explanations seem, they are not responsible for bringing us toilets, air conditioners, automobiles, and mobile phones. Deirdre McCloskey, *Bourgeois Dignity: Why Economics Can't Explain the Modern World* (Chicago: University of Chicago Press, 2010), 34–35.

10. This amount does not include private funds spent by some of the world's heavily endowed foundations and organizations, such as the Bill and Melinda Gates Foundation, the Skoll Foundation, the Omidyar Network, and many others.
    "ODA 1960-16 Trends," Official Development Assistance 2016, Compare Your Country, accessed February 1, 2018, http://www2.compareyourcountry.org/oda?cr=20001&lg=en&page=1#.

11. Many of the countries in the above table have received official development assistance for poverty eradication programs from the World Bank and several other development institutions. Niger, for instance, has received $2.9 billion worth of World Bank aid since 1964, but in 2015 its per capita income was less than half what it was in the 1960s. "Urban Water and Sanitation Project," The World Bank, http://www.worldbank.org/projects/P117365/urban-water-sanitation-project?lang=en.

12. Jamie Skinner, "Why every drop counts: tackling rural Africa's water crisis," IIED briefing, accessed February 1, 2018, http://pubs.iied.org/pdfs/17055IIED.pdf.

The

Prosperity
Paradox

The Power of Market-Creating Innovations

Chapter 1

An Introduction to the Prosperity Paradox

It's not an easy thing to be laughed at by serious people. And serious people laughed at me when I told them I wanted to build a telecommunications network in Africa twenty years ago. They told me all the reasons the project would never succeed. Somehow I just kept thinking, I know there are challenges but why can't they see the opportunity?

—MO IBRAHIM

The Idea in Brief

Starving children on street corners. Slums without adequate clean water and sanitation. Hopeless prospects for employment amid a growing youth population. Most of us are moved by the painful signs of poverty we see in poor countries all around the world. According to the World Bank, more than 750 million people still live in extreme poverty, surviving on less than $1.90 a day. We all want to help. But what might seem to be the most obvious solution to these problems—directly assisting poor countries by investing to fix these visible signs of poverty—has not been as successful as many of us would like. You only have to look at the billions of dollars that have been channeled to these problems over the years with relatively slow progress to conclude that something is not quite right. With these efforts, we may be temporarily easing poverty for some—but we're not moving the needle enough.

What if we considered this problem through a different lens?

What if, instead of trying to fix the visible signs of poverty, we focused on creating lasting prosperity? This may require a counterintuitive approach, but one that will cause you to see opportunities where you might least expect them.

———

In the late 1990s, when Mo Ibrahim first conceived of setting up a mobile phone company in Africa, people said he was, well, nuts. "Everybody said Africa is a basket case," he recalls now. "It's a dangerous place, it's full of dictators, it's full of crazy people . . . who are all corrupt." In fact, people laughed when he shared his idea.

Ibrahim, the former technical director for British Telecom, who was running his own successful consulting firm, planned to develop, from scratch, a mobile communications network in sub-Saharan Africa—where most people had never *used* a phone, let alone owned one. The African continent, which ranges from the bazaars of Morocco to the big business complexes of Johannesburg, is home to fifty-four countries. The total population of more than one billion is spread over 11.7 million square miles—more than three times the size of the United States. The vast majority of this territory had no existing infrastructure for old landline telephones, let alone the cell towers necessary for a mobile phone company to function. At the time, mobile phones were seen as an expensive toy for the rich, a luxury that the poor could not afford, and, more important, did not need. When many, including Ibrahim's clients and former colleagues at the major telecommunication companies, assessed the opportunity in Africa, they noted the level of poverty, lack of infrastructure, fragility of governments, and even lack of access to water, health care, and education. They saw pervasive and palpable poverty permeating every aspect of society, not fertile territory for new business.

But Ibrahim, to his credit, saw things differently. Instead of seeing just poverty, he saw *opportunity*. "If you live far away from the village where your mother lives and you want to talk to her, you might have to make a seven-day journey," Ibrahim recalls now. "If you could just pick up a device and speak to her instantly, what would be the value of that? How much money would you save? How much time?" Notice that Ibrahim did not say *How will millions of Africans, for whom three meals a day is often a luxury, afford a mobile phone?* or *How can you justify the investments in infrastructure for a market that does not exist?* He focused on the struggle to accomplish something important for which there were few good solutions. For Ibrahim, struggle represented enormous potential.

This struggle often presents itself as "nonconsumption"—where would-be consumers are desperate to make progress in a particular aspect of their lives, but there's no affordable and accessible solution to their problem. So they simply go without, or develop workarounds, but their suffering continues—usually under the radar of conventional metrics used to evaluate business opportunities. But in that nonconsumption, Ibrahim saw the chance to *create* a market. So with very little financial backing and just five employees, Ibrahim founded Celtel[1] with the goal of creating a pan-African mobile telecommunications company.

The obstacles were enormous. Creating the necessary cellular network infrastructure was a mind-boggling undertaking—done without relying on support from local governments or from major banks. Raising capital was so difficult that even after he'd proved his business model and reached predictable cash flow in the millions of dollars, banks still refused to lend him money. Ibrahim had to fund Celtel entirely with equity financing, "a first in the telecommunications industry for a company of our size and scale," he explains. But that, and the many other challenges he faced, didn't deter him. Where there was no power, he provided his own power; where there were no logistics, he developed his own; where there was no education or health care, he provided training and health care for his staff; and where there were no roads, he either built makeshift roads or used helicopters to move equipment around.

Ibrahim was fueled by the vision he had of the immense value of millions of Africans no longer having to struggle to keep in touch with one another. Eventually, he succeeded.

In just six years, Celtel built operations in thirteen African countries—including Uganda, Malawi, the two Congos, Gabon, and Sierra Leone—and gained 5.2 million customers. At the openings of many of Ibrahim's stores, it wasn't uncommon to see eager customers line up by the hundreds. Ibrahim's Celtel was so successful that by 2004, revenues had reached $614 million and net profits were $147 million. In 2005, when Ibrahim decided to sell the company, he did so for a handsome $3.4 billion. In such a short time, Ibrahim's Celtel unlocked billions of dollars' worth of value from some of the poorest countries in the world.

But Celtel was just the tip of the iceberg. Today, Africa is home to a sophisticated mobile telecommunications industry, with numerous mobile phone companies (including Globacom, Maroc Telecom, Safaricom, MTN, Vodacom, Telkom, and others) providing more than 965 million mobile phone lines. These companies have not only raised billions of dollars in debt and equity financing, but by 2020, the industry is forecast to support 4.5 million jobs, provide $20.5 billion in taxes, and add more than $214 billion of value to African economies.[2] Mobile phones have also unlocked value in other industries, such as financial technology, where companies now use phone usage records as a proxy for credit-worthiness, extending credit to millions of credit-worthy people who historically could not receive it.

It may seem obvious now that mobile phones are ubiquitous all over the world—and all over Africa—but remember that twenty years ago, Ibrahim saw what others did not.

The market Mo Ibrahim built, and the difficult and seemingly unlikely circumstances in which he built it, represents a solution to what we call the Prosperity Paradox. It may sound counterintuitive, but our research suggests that enduring prosperity for many countries will not come from fixing poverty. It will come from investing in innovations that create new markets within these countries.[3] True and lasting prosperity, we have found, is not reliably generated through the flood of resources we are directly pouring into poor countries to improve poverty indicators such as low-quality education, subpar health care, bad governance, nonexistent infrastructure, and many other indicators in which an improvement would suggest prosperity. Instead, we believe that for many countries prosperity typically begins to take root in an economy when we invest in a particular type of innovation—market-creating innovation—which often serves as a catalyst and foundation for creating sustained economic development.

Contrast Mo Ibrahim's approach to building Celtel with Efosa's efforts to build wells through his nonprofit organization, Poverty Stops Here. Poverty Stops Here is significantly smaller in size, but it is emblematic of the thinking behind many of the efforts undertaken to help poor countries today. For example, just 18.2 percent of Official Development Assistance goes toward "economic infrastructure" projects, while the bulk funds education, health, social infrastructure, and other conventional development projects.[4] In addition to aid from OECD countries representing a vast majority of foreign aid expenditures, the pattern of expenditure also has a signaling effect to many others who donate and fund projects in poor countries. In a sense, it's what inspired Efosa's projects, the belief that if we just channel resources into an impoverished area, we can fix poverty.

But what might happen if we flipped the emphasis to innovation and market-based solutions rather than conventional development-based solutions? Or to put it another way, what if we focused less on Efosa-type projects and more on Mo Ibrahim–type ones? Efosa wanted to fund and build more wells as a way of solving a problem. Ibrahim figured out how to solve problems by creating a market that targeted people who were willing to pay for a product. They're not the same thing. And as our research has demonstrated, they have very different long-term effects.

Understanding the Prosperity Paradox

I'm not an expert on every low- and middle-income economy, but my personal toolbox for solving difficult challenges relies on theory, which helps us get to the core of a problem. Good theory helps us understand the underlying mechanism driving things.

Consider, for example, the history of mankind's attempts to fly. Early researchers observed strong correlations between being able to fly and having feathers and wings. Stories of men attempting to fly by strapping on wings date back hundreds of years. They were replicating what they believed allowed birds to soar: wings and feathers.

Possessing these attributes had a high *correlation*—a connection between two things—with the ability to fly, but when humans attempted to follow what they believed were "best practices" of the most successful fliers by strapping on wings, then jumping off cathedrals and flapping hard . . . they failed. The mistake was that, although feathers and wings were correlated with flying, the would-be aviators did not understand the fundamental *causal mechanism*—what actually causes something to happen—that enabled certain creatures to fly.

The real breakthrough in human flight didn't come from crafting better wings or using more feathers, even though those are good things. It was brought about by Dutch-Swiss mathematician Daniel Bernoulli and his book *Hydrodynamica*, a study of fluid mechanics. In 1738, he outlined what was to become known as Bernoulli's principle, a theory that, when applied to flight, explained the concept of lift. We had gone from correlation (wings and feathers) to causality (lift). Modern flight can be traced directly back to the development and adoption of this theory.

But even the breakthrough understanding of the cause of flight still wasn't enough to make flight perfectly *reliable*. When an airplane crashed, researchers then had to ask, "What was it about the circumstances of that given attempt to fly that led to failure? Wind?

Fog? The angle of the aircraft?" Researchers could then define what rules pilots needed to follow in order to succeed in each different circumstance. That's a hallmark of good theory. It dispenses its advice in "if/then" statements.

As a business school professor, I'm asked hundreds of times a year to offer opinions on specific business challenges in industries or organizations in which I have no special knowledge. Yet I'm able to provide insight because there is a toolbox of *theories* that teach me not *what* to think, but *how* to think about a problem. Good theory is the best way I know to frame problems so that we ask the right questions to get us to the most useful answers. Embracing theory is not to mire ourselves in academic minutiae but, quite the opposite, to focus on the supremely practical question of *what causes what*—and why? This approach is at the core of this book.

So how, then, does theory relate to our quest to create prosperity in many poor countries and ultimately make the world a better place? The appeal of many things that correlate with prosperity—of strapping on wings and feathers—is incredibly alluring. Who isn't moved by the sight of a newly dug well providing clean water to a deprived community? But in reality, no matter how many good efforts we invest in, if we aren't improving our understanding about what creates and sustains economic prosperity, we will be slow to make progress.

In our study of the path to prosperity, examining progress (or the lack thereof) in a variety of economies around the world—including Japan, Mexico, Nigeria, Russia, Singapore, South Korea, the United States, and several others—we have found that different types of innovations have vastly different impacts on the long-term growth and prosperity of a nation.

We must be clear, however, that the process we will describe here, and throughout this book, does not explain how every prosperous country has emerged from poverty. For example, some countries, such as Singapore, started out with a government that prioritized economic development and wealth creation, while others, like the

United States, began their march toward prosperity a long time ago, and more gradually. All good theories must be used in context— they are only useful in certain circumstances. Every country in the world is different in size, population, culture, leadership, and capabilities. Those circumstances play a role in their destiny.

But overall, we have found that investing in innovations, and more specifically market-creating innovations, has proven a reliable path to prosperity for countries around the world. This book draws on the histories of now-prosperous economies in order to illustrate the key elements of our theory, which describes the process by which the creation of new markets impacts a society. It is through this process that some of the poorest countries in the world were able to create billions of dollars' worth of value and millions of jobs for their citizens.

An Overlooked Path to Prosperity

Our thinking focuses on what we have identified as critical drivers for creating and sustaining prosperity for many countries: finding opportunity in struggle, investing in market-creating innovations (which, among other things, creates the jobs that help grow a local economy), and executing a "pull" strategy of development (in which the necessary institutions and infrastructures are pulled into a society when new markets demand them)—which we will discuss in more detail throughout this book. All of these ideas and themes are essential to solving the Prosperity Paradox, and you will see them repeated and examined from different perspectives through the innovations and the stories we share here.

When we talk about innovation, we don't just mean high-tech or feature-rich products. Our definition of innovation refers to something rather specific: *a change in the processes by which an organization transforms labor, capital, materials, and information into products and services of greater value.*[5] "Market-creating innovations" transform complex and expensive products and services into simple and more affordable products, making them accessible to a whole new segment of people in a society whom we call "nonconsumers."

Every economy is made up of consumers and nonconsumers. In prosperous economies, the proportion of consumers for many products often surpasses that of nonconsumers. Nonconsumers are people who are struggling to make progress in some way, but have been unable to do so because historically a good solution has been beyond reach. This does not mean there isn't a solution on the market, but often nonconsumers are unable to afford existing solutions or lack the time or expertise required to successfully use the product.

Market-creating innovations can ignite the economic engine of a country. Successful market-creating innovations have three distinct outcomes. First, by their very nature, they create **jobs** as more and more people are required to make, market, distribute, and sell the new innovations. Jobs are a critical factor in assessing the prosperity of a country.

Second, they create **profits** from a wide swathe of the population, which are then often used to fund most public services in society, including education, infrastructure, health care, and so on.

And third, they have the potential to change the **culture** of entire societies. As we will show, many prosperous countries today were once poor, corrupt, and badly governed. But the proliferation of innovations began a process that helped transform these economies. In the United States, for instance, market-creating innovations like the Singer sewing machine, Eastman Kodak's film cameras, and Ford's Model T (innovations we discuss in detail later) helped cultivate a culture of innovation that drastically changed American society. Once new markets that serve nonconsumers are created, these markets "pull" in other necessary components—infrastructure, education, institutions, and even a change in culture—to ensure the market's survival, as we'll explain in detail throughout this book. This is how a society's trajectory can begin to change.

Elements of our model can be seen in what Ibrahim did when he built Celtel. First, in the most unlikely of circumstances, he developed an innovation that made a historically complex and expensive product more affordable so that millions of people could more easily have access. And in so doing, he created a vibrant market that not only directly created thousands of jobs for people, but also enabled the creation of other industries, such as financial services and mobile health. Second, Ibrahim pulled in the resources he needed to build his company. Because he pulled only the resources he needed into a new, large, and profitable market he was creating, the things he built were able to be sustained. This is a theme we will keep coming back to because of its importance in helping us make smart investments. Third, Ibrahim's Celtel was also developed with a focus on local citizens. For example, instead of developing a business model where customers had to pay monthly cell phone bills, as is the case in wealthier countries with citizens with higher earning power, Ibrahim introduced prepaid cards. New customers could purchase these cards for as little as 25 US cents, resulting in many more purchases. In addition to that, 99 percent of the jobs he created were held by native Africans.

While Ibrahim's efforts may seem anomalous, especially today, when we expect poor-country governments to take care of many of the things Ibrahim took care of as is the case in many prosperous countries, we will show that his efforts are little different from those of many innovators responsible for igniting the flames of prosperity in their countries.

Certainly, for nations to sustain long-term prosperity, they ultimately need good governments that foster and support a culture of innovation. Market-creating innovators can, however, light the fire, and governments can fan the flame. We believe that by understanding how market-creating innovation can ignite and catalyze good governance—a pattern we observed in many of today's prosperous countries—we can help create long-term, sustainable prosperity.[6]

A Guide to This Book

What might seem hopeless on the surface is often actually an opportunity to create new and thriving markets. This insight is not only important for the stakeholders actively trying to make things better, such as governments and NGOs (non-governmental organizations) and others in the development industry, but for innovators and entrepreneurs who might not have seen opportunity before now. For instance, instead of seeing the roughly six hundred million people in Africa who don't have electricity as only a sign of their immense poverty, we should see them as a vast market-creation opportunity waiting to be captured. It should be a call to innovate, not a flag of caution. It is in that spirit that we offer you the ideas in this book.

We understand we are wading into complicated territory in writing about economic development, but we hope that the models, stories, and cases we share here provide you with fresh perspective. We have written this book in four sections, detailed below, to help you follow our thinking and its practical applications in the world.

In **Section 1**, we explain **the importance of innovation in creating prosperity in an economy.** We detail how a particular type of innovation—market-creating—serves as a strong foundation for generating and sustaining lasting prosperity.

In **Section 2**, we illustrate our model by providing examples of **how innovation, and the culture it creates, have impacted the United States, Japan, South Korea, and Mexico.**

In **Section 3**, we focus on the perceived **barriers to development.** We discuss the relationship between market-creating innovations and the development of good institutions, the reduction of corruption, and the construction and maintenance of a nation's infrastructures.

In our **Conclusion**, we discuss the importance of turning the prosperity paradox into a **prosperity process** and review some **key principles of this book.**

In the **Appendix**, we profile several new-market opportunities and development efforts by entrepreneurs, governments, and NGOs to change the game in different parts of the globe. We hope this helps those of you seeking opportunity to think differently about where and how you might spend your precious resources to create wealth and generate prosperity.

We know that there are few issues more complex than creating prosperity in poor countries, and we wade into this debate with the hope that our thinking will spur new ways of tackling these entrenched and heartbreaking problems. At the core, this book is about celebrating the power and potential of innovation to change the world. But it is, we hope, just the start of a worthwhile conversation.

NOTES

1. Now part of Bharti Airtel Limited.

2. "Number of unique mobile subscribers in Africa surpasses half a billion, finds new GSM study," GSMA, accessed February 1, 2018, https://www.gsma.com/newsroom/press-release/number-of-unique-mobile-subscribers-in-africa-surpasses-half-a-billion-finds-new-gsma-study/.

3. By "market," we mean *a system that enables the making, buying, and selling of a product or service.*

4. "Aid at a glance charts," Development Finance Statistics, OECD, accessed April 23, 2018, http://www.oecd.org/dac/stats/aid-at-a-glance.htm.

5. Clayton Christensen, *The Innovator's Dilemma: When New Technologies Cause Great Firms to Fail* (New York: HarperCollins Publishers, 2000).
This definition is consistent with Schumpeter's writing in *The Theory of Economic Development* defining innovation as taking an invention and placing it firmly into a market, a process which leads to *development* or *the production of new combinations.* In Chapter 2, Schumpeter writes, that "to produce means to combine materials and forces within our reach. To produce other things, or the same things by a different method, means to combine these materials and forces differently" (65). This is important because innovation is often mistaken for invention, or something entirely new. For the purpose of economic development, this isn't the case. According to Schumpeter, one of the illustrations of this process of combination is "the opening of a new market, that is a market into which the particular branch of manufacture of the country in question has not previously entered, whether or not this market has existed before." In essence, it does not matter that something existed in another country in so far as it is new to the country where it is being introduced, it is bound to have development impact.
Ricardo Hausmann at Harvard and César Hidalgo at MIT provide data showing that the prosperity of an economy is directly correlated with the amount of know-how in the nation. In their research, they refer to this concept as "economic complexity," which is a "measure of the amount of capabilities and know-how that goes into the production of any given product. Products are vehicles for knowledge. [Their] theory and supporting empirical evidence explain why the accumulation of productive knowledge is the key to sustained economic growth." But

accumulating productive knowledge is not easy, and is often quite expensive. In addition, knowledge accumulation is not enough, it must be dynamic accumulation. Sidney Winter at the Wharton School of Business at the University of Pennsylvania has written extensively about the evolution of organizational capabilities. His research helps explain that one of the reasons for business success is an organization's ability to develop dynamic capabilities. But he also explains that developing those capabilities is no easy feat. See *Toward a Neo-Schumpeterian Theory of the Firm* (1968), *Understanding Dynamic Capabilities* (2003), and *Deliberate Learning and the Evolution of Dynamic Capabilities* (2002).

Joseph A. Schumpeter, *The Theory of Economic Development: An Inquiry into Profits, Capital, Credit, Interest, and the Business Cycle* (Cambridge: Harvard University Press, 1934), 65.

Ricardo Hausmann et al., *The Atlas of Economic Complexity: Mapping Paths to Prosperity*, 2nd ed. (Cambridge: MIT Press, 2013).

6.   We delve into more detail about this in Chapters 8 and 9, which tackle *institutions* and *corruption* respectively, but consider how Mancur Olson put it in his book, *Power and Prosperity*: "When we shift from what is best for prosperity to what is worst, the consensus would probably be that when there is a stronger incentive to take than to make—more gain from predation than from productive and mutually advantageous activities—societies fall to the bottom." Olson then goes on to highlight the virtues and importance of entrepreneurship, due to the unpredictable nature of society. He writes, "Because uncertainties are so pervasive and unfathomable, the most dynamic and prosperous societies are those that try many, many different things. They are societies with countless thousands of entrepreneurs who have relatively good access to credit and venture capital. There is no way a society can predict the future, but if it has a wide enough span of entrepreneurs able to make a broad enough array of mutually advantageous transactions, including those for credit and venture capital, it can cover a lot of the options—more than any single person or agency [or government] could ever think of." In effect, if we harness the power of entrepreneurs to develop more and more market-creating innovations, this can—and indeed does—lead to better and better governance.

Mancur Olson, *Power and Prosperity: Outgrowing Communist and Capitalist Dictatorships* (New York: Basic Books, 2000), 1, 188-189.

Iqbal Quadir, who founded the Legatum Center for Development and Entrepreneurship at MIT, puts it this way in his article in the *Innovations* journal, "Western intellectuals from Adam Smith to Georg Simmel to Max Weber have recognized that commerce has positively transformed governments, cultures, and behavior by making people more rational and mutually accountable."

Chapter 2

Not All Innovations
Are Created Equal

One of the things that people don't understand is that markets are creations. They are not something which we can [just] find. A market has to be created.[1]

—RONALD COASE, 1991 NOBEL LAUREATE IN ECONOMICS

The Idea in Brief

Many of us understand the value of building strong institutions and developing a nation's infrastructure. However, the role of innovation isn't quite as clear. We know it's important, but because innovation means different things to different people, what's not widely recognized is how different types of innovations can impact an economy. In this chapter, we will describe how we categorize innovation into three types—sustaining, efficiency, and market-creating—and explain the different impact each has on an organization and an economy. While all innovations are important to keeping an economy vibrant, one type in particular—market-creating innovation—plays a significant role, providing a strong foundation for sustained economic prosperity. When a country's prosperity is not improving, in spite of what might seem to be a lot of activity within its borders, the country might not have a *growth* problem. Instead, we believe it might have an *innovation* problem.

Ever since I published *The Innovator's Dilemma,* in which I explained how great companies are sometimes blind to the threat posed by upstarts, I have worked with hundreds of corporations to help them tackle their own dilemmas. At the core of that work is my theory of disruptive innovation,[2] which describes how a company with fewer resources is able to challenge more established businesses by introducing simpler, more convenient, and more affordable innovations to an overserved or overlooked segment of customers, ultimately redefining the industry.

In the decades since I published my thinking, the theory has taken root in the business community and others, including education and health care. As such, I'm regularly peppered with questions about my theory and how it applies to one specific industry or another. While I know that I will never be an expert on every industry, I have found that I can consistently turn to my toolbox of theories to help people see through a different set of lenses, to view problems in a new way.

A few years ago, after I gave a talk at a CEO summit at Innosight, the consulting firm I cofounded, an executive made an observation that reminded me of the importance of putting on the right set of lenses to begin to solve a problem. "At our company, we categorize everything in the research and development group as 'innovation,'" she said. "But based on your presentation, I can see that there are different types of innovation. And they seem to achieve different goals. We need to restructure R&D at my organization to reflect what we're really trying to accomplish. If we're ever going to truly grow through our innovation, we can't think of it as just one uniform thing."

The executive was right. Not all innovations are created equal. Over the years our research has found that there are three types of innovation: sustaining innovation, efficiency innovation, and market-creating innovation. None of the types of innovation is inherently bad or good, but each type plays a unique role for organizations trying to sustain their growth.[3]

As I thought about the executive's observation about choosing the right type of innovation to secure her company's future, I realized that the insight applied much more broadly. We tend to do the same thing when we talk about all the innovation activities happening within an economy. We often categorize all innovation activities in the same way. We use proxies, such as patent applications, investment in research and development, and quality of scientific research institutions, to assess the innovation prowess of a country.[4] But if different types of innovation affect organizations differently, doesn't it stand to reason that different types of innovations will impact economies differently as well?[5]

Economies, after all, are largely defined by the firms (public and private) within them.[6] And innovation—as we defined in the last chapter as a change in the processes by which an organization transforms labor, capital, materials, and information into products and services of greater value—is what most firms do. Note that *innovation* is not the same thing as *invention*, which describes the process of creating something entirely new that has never existed before. Innovations are often borrowed, from one country to another and from one firm to another, and then improved upon. Thus, we take as our unit of analysis, innovation, and seek to understand how the type, scale, and impact on a company influences the broader economy.[7]

Is this just an academic distinction that doesn't matter in the real world? Not at all. In my classroom, my focus is always on the importance of understanding what causes what to happen—and why.

To make that point to my students, every semester I stand in front of my class with a pen or a piece of chalk in my hand, and then I drop it and just watch it fall to the floor. As I stoop over to pick it up, I grouse, "You know what, I just hate gravity. But gravity doesn't care. It always pulls you down." The point is, whether we consciously think about it or not, gravity is always at work. But if we do consciously think about it and learn how gravity works, we can harness gravity for our own goals. The same thinking holds true for innovation. If we understand what type of innovation causes what to happen, we can harness it for our own goals. Knowing these differences is a crucial first step in understanding what leads to sustainable economic development.[8]

Sustaining Innovations

Sustaining innovations are improvements to existing solutions on the market and are typically targeted at customers who require better performance from a product or service. My friends who work in the consumer-packaged goods industries call this "SKUS for news"—when they create new flavors or colors or features of an existing product so they can generate some excitement in consumers who are already purchasing their product. Think about Unilever's Lipton tea brand. Today, there are almost as many Lipton tea flavors as there are people on the planet. Or at least it feels that way. From flavors such as Matcha Green Tea and Mint to others like Green Iced Tea, the brand is developing new and exciting products to capture more and more of an *existing* tea-drinking market—or at least retain its market share. These are sustaining innovations. They are not designed to pull in new tea-drinking customers per se; they are *substitutive* in character. They are important for the Lipton brand and for customers to know the company is not stale, but the new Berry Hibiscus flavor will not necessarily create a market of entirely new tea drinkers.[9]

Sustaining innovations are often sold for more money and at a higher margin. Heated seats in our cars are a good idea, especially if the automakers can sell us the cars for more money, but they are usually targeted at existing car-buying customers. They aren't what made people stop using horses for transportation.

Sustaining innovations are all around us and, in effect, are a critical component of our economies. They are important for companies and countries to remain competitive. But they have a very different impact on an economy than the other two types of innovations—market-creating and efficiency. Companies rarely need to build new sales, distribution, marketing, and manufacturing engines when they develop sustaining innovations in a mature market, because they are selling to a relatively known segment of the population in a largely established way. As a result, when compared with market-creating innovations, sustaining innovations have a very different effect on job creation, on profit generation, and on changing the culture in a region.

Consider the three concentric circles, with each circle representing a different market composed of different members of a society. It's a simple illustration, but we hope it makes our point

A SIMPLE ILLUSTRATION OF MARKETS

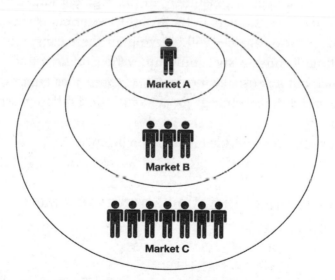

Market A

Market B

Market C

Figure 2: Sustaining innovations improve existing products and target people who can already afford the product in a particular segment of the economy. When that segment gets saturated, sustaining innovations often have a substitutive effect on consumption.

easy to follow. Market A represents the smallest, wealthiest, and most skilled consumers. Market B represents a larger but less wealthy and less skilled set of consumers. And similarly, Market C represents the largest segment but also the least wealthy and least skilled. Sustaining innovations in any of the concentric circles—no matter the size of the market—are typically concerned with selling more products to the same customers in that particular market.

Understandably, many companies are drawn to selling to the wealthier segments of the economy because they hope that by adding new features and benefits to an existing product (or service), they will be able to continue to sell more, and more profitably. Sustaining innovations do lead to some growth and they do enable development, but as you can see, the impact of this growth is limited by the number of consumers in the segment targeted. Also, competition for customers in the wealthier segment is very fierce, as many other companies will be vying for these consumers, too. From time to time, a sustaining innovation might attract a new customer, but it is usually incidental, as companies typically need to develop a different strategy for customers in a different segment or circle.[10]

Let us consider a detailed illustration below.

The Sustaining Innovation Strategy of America's Bestselling Car

Few cars have sold better in America than the Toyota Camry. At the time of this writing, the Camry had been America's bestselling car for nineteen of the past twenty years.[11] But even with the Camry's remarkable success, sales of the Camry have remained relatively flat since 2000. While the innovations Toyota has made in its Camry over the past twenty years have kept the company competitive, relevant, and profitable, these innovations have not had a grand impact on the Camry's growth. In 1997, Toyota sold 394,397 Camrys. Twenty years later, in 2017, Toyota sold 387,081 Camrys. (2007 was the best year for the Camry, when Toyota sold 473,108 units.[12])

Sustaining innovations for the Camry are very important to Toyota; that's what helped keep the Camry as the bestselling car in America for nineteen of the past twenty years. But steady Camry sales do not represent a new growth engine for Toyota. Nor do they represent major growth for the economy. Camry sales are targeted at "the consumption economy"—customers Toyota, and other carmakers, can already see, count, and reach with existing distribution channels. Camry sales generate steady revenue year after year, often by retaining an existing customer who simply traded up to a better model of a car he or she already owned.

But even as a reliable bestseller, Toyota does not necessarily need to build a new manufacturing plant and hire entirely new staff every time it decides to release a new version of the Camry. It also does not hire a new sales force, build a new distribution channel, or invest in an entirely new design team when working on a new model. The company, as do most companies, simply repurposes its existing resources. As a result of this repurposing, Toyota does not need as much capital or as many people to develop new models of the Camry. No new factories are built; few new workforces are employed.

Sustaining Growth in a Mature and Established Market

The Camry's innovation trajectory is not an unusual story. Most innovations are sustaining in nature. And that's actually a good thing for a company—and its customers, who might want a better product or service. Examples of sustaining innovations range from faster processors in our computers to more memory in our phones.

The original iPhone was a market-creating innovation, catalyzing a new market for smartphones and corresponding apps, but the iPhone X is a sustaining innovation. The vast majority of iPhone X customers, people who were able to shell out $1,000, were simply trading up, and now have access to facial recognition, a super Retina display, and an OLED screen. Or consider TaylorMade's new P790 golf club, which the company promises will help golfers experience "feel, forgiveness, and workability unlike any other iron of this caliber." It retails for $1,299.99. Surely TaylorMade's P790 golf clubs are not bringing vastly more consumers into the sport, and as such, not creating many new jobs relative to its existing job numbers. But just like the iPhone X, they are certainly making TaylorMade more money, making the company more vibrant, and stamping their place as a relevant player in their industry. We cannot overstate the importance of sustaining innovations.

Sustaining innovations don't refer only to product innovations; they often come in the form of services as well. For instance, at least once a month my bank sends me a new offer for a credit card, an innovation that has existed since 1950. It's already an enormous market: America's credit card debt currently stands at just over one trillion dollars—an amount larger than the GDPs of Mexico, Turkey, and Switzerland. My bank isn't necessarily trying to create a new market for credit cards; instead it is trying to make more money by selling me extra services, such as travel insurance, warranty extensions, and cash back on whatever I spend. The same thing happens when my mobile phone provider tries to sell me larger and larger data plans. Those are sustaining innovations, designed to sell more services and get more money from customers like me.

Efficiency Innovations

Efficiency innovations, as the name implies, enable companies to do more with fewer resources. In other words, as companies squeeze as much as possible from existing and newly acquired resources, their underlying business model and the customers they are targeting with their products remain the same. Efficiency innovations are crucial for the viability of companies as industries become more crowded and competitive. Typically, efficiency innovations are *process* innovations—they focus on *how* the product is made. With efficiency innovations, companies can become more profitable and, critically, free up cash flow.

Efficiency innovations exist in every industry and are a critical part of managing the levers of improving profitability and retaining customers in any organization. But efficiency innovations, while good for the productivity of an organization, are not always good for existing employees. Think of the plants that have shut down or been relocated as a result of outsourcing, one of the markers of efficiency innovations at play. By themselves, efficiency innovations tend not to create jobs. (That is, unless the capital these innovations free up is funneled back into developing market-creating innovations. More on this later.)

Consider the resource extraction industry, a sector that thrives on investments in efficiency innovations.[13] Due to the fact that oil, gas, gold, diamonds, and many of the other resources we extract and process are commodities, the typical manager in this industry is always looking for ways to improve efficiency and decrease cost, a process that frees up cash flow and improves margins. All you need to do is look at any nation with a vast resource extraction sector and assess whether those sectors are consistently adding more and more jobs to the economy even as they extract more resources. Take the United States for example.

In 1980, there were approximately 220,000 employees in the oil and gas extraction industry responsible for producing roughly 8.6 million barrels of oil.[14] By 2017, the number of employees in the sector had fallen by more than a third to about 146,000, but production had increased to over 9.3 million barrels a day.[15] The figures are not much better for Nigeria, one of the world's largest oil producers. According to data from Nigeria's National Bureau of Statistics, the oil and gas sector employs only about 0.01 percent of the Nigerian workforce even though the oil and gas sector accounts for more than 90 percent of Nigeria's export revenue and more than 70 percent of government revenues.[16] Efficiency innovations free up cash flows, but they rarely add new jobs to an economy. In most cases, they eliminate more than they create. Because the very nature of resource extraction is efficiency driven, countries such as Nigeria, Venezuela, Saudi Arabia, South Africa, Qatar, and others that rely heavily on resource extraction cannot depend on that sector for job creation for their citizens.

We can't stress this enough. Neither efficiency nor sustaining innovations are inherently bad for a country. In fact, they are good for our economies, but they play very different roles in fostering sustainable economic growth and job creation. While they keep our economies competitive and vibrant, freeing up much-needed cash for future investments, neither efficiency nor sustaining innovations in mature markets seed new growth engines. That is the result of something completely different, what we call market-creating innovations.

Market-Creating Innovations

Market-creating innovations do exactly what the name implies—they create new markets. But not just any new markets, new markets that serve people for whom either no products existed or existing products were neither affordable nor accessible for a variety of reasons. These innovations transform complicated and expensive products into ones that are so much more affordable and accessible that many more people are able to buy and use them. In some cases, they even create entirely new product categories. Mo Ibrahim's Celtel made a previously expensive solution—mobile telecommunications—simple and affordable to millions and millions of new customers. In a sense, market-creating innovations democratize previously exclusive products and services.

Although the scale of the impact of a new market depends on the characteristics of the innovation being democratized—for example, not all innovations will have the impact that democratizing a car has—the impact of market-creating innovations is significant when compared to that of other types of innovations. Market-creating innovations collectively serve as a foundation for many of today's wealthy economies, and have helped lift millions of people out of poverty in the process.[17]

This type of innovation not only creates markets, but jobs, too. This is because as new markets with new consumers are born, companies must hire more people to make, market, distribute, sell, and service the product. Market-creating innovations have the potential to create what we call *local* and *global* jobs.

Local and Global Jobs

Local jobs are jobs that must be created in order to serve the local market. They are also jobs that are not as easily transferable or outsourced to other countries. For example, jobs in design, advertising, marketing, sales, and after-sale service typically fall into this category. They are often higher-paying jobs when compared with global jobs. *Global jobs*, while also important, are more easily moved to other countries to take advantage of lower wages. Manufacturing and sourcing of raw materials are perhaps the biggest culprits. With the advances in global supply chain management, global jobs are often at risk of moving across national boundaries to the next most "efficient"—or low-cost—labor market. By contrast, local jobs are essential to support market-creating innovations; they are less vulnerable to the allure of lower wages elsewhere.[18]

When innovators create a new market, targeted at a large population that has historically been unable to afford the product—

THE DEMOCRATIZING EFFECT OF MARKET-CREATING INNOVATION

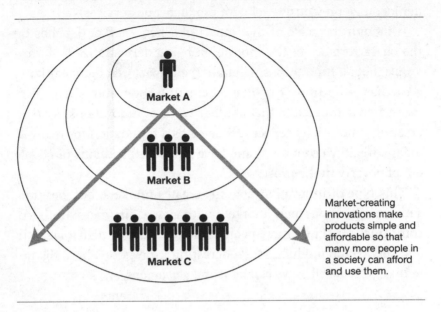

Figure 3: Market-creating innovations make products available to customers in a new concentric circle.

nonconsumers—the innovator must hire many more people not only to make the product or service, but also to get it to the new customers. The bigger the nonconsumption, the bigger the potential market. And the bigger the market, the bigger the impact. This dedication to market-creating innovations often establishes the underlying infrastructure, including education, transportation, communications, and institutions such as government policies and regulations, and other components of many of today's thriving societies. This activity creates a virtuous cycle in economies that further fosters the development of more new markets.

Another virtue of investing in market-creating innovations is that when local entrepreneurs develop innovations and reap the rewards from the innovation's success, the returns are more likely to fund future innovations locally. Consider this: of the more than

HOW A PRODUCT CREATES JOBS

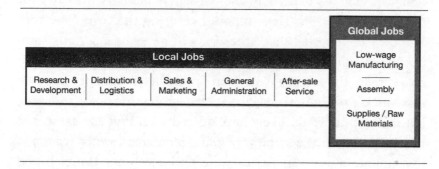

Figure 4: Market-creating innovations generate local jobs that are more sustainable.

$70 trillion worth of global assets under management, less than $2 trillion are targeted at foreign direct investments (FDI).[19] Most money stays home.

In Chapter 1, we explained that investing in market-creating innovations does not describe how every prosperous country today developed. Countries are too different in size, capabilities, and other parameters and we don't assert that there is only one strategy for development. Market-creating innovations, however, do provide us with one of the most viable strategies for creating prosperity in today's poor countries.

5 Keys to Targeting Market-Creating Innovations

Because market-creating innovations rely on having the foresight to see what others cannot, it's always easier to identify market-creating innovations in hindsight than to have the foresight to develop them. Before cars, computers, and bank accounts became the norm for most of us, entrepreneurs first had to create a new market for these products and services. What I have found is that

most new markets do not make sense at the onset of their forma-
tion, especially to experts in the particular industry. In 1939, for
instance, a *New York Times* reporter covering the 1939 New York
World's Fair reported that "[the] TV will never be a serious competitor for radio because people must sit and keep their eyes glued
on a screen; the average American family hasn't time for it."[20] We
may snicker (or sigh in despair) at how wrong that prediction was,
but most of us would likely have agreed with that assessment at
the time—much the same way many predicted twenty years ago
that mobile phones in Africa were exclusively for the rich and
would never take root.

So how do you go about targeting market-creating innovations?
They have to be evaluated through the right lens, both for entrepreneurs who see potential to build something from scratch, and for
existing organizations who want to drive market-creating innovations into their innovation portfolio mix. Here is a helpful frame
of reference for five attributes that entrepreneurs and managers
should look for as they consider creating new markets.

1. BUSINESS MODELS THAT TARGET NONCONSUMPTION—A
majority of the innovations and business models that exist today
are targeted at existing consumers—those who can already afford
products on the market. When analysis and consumer reports use
terms like *rising middle class*, *increasing disposable income*, and *demographic dividend*, oftentimes they are referring to existing consumption patterns. Nonconsumption is different. It's the inability
of a would-be consumer to purchase and use (consume) a product
or service. From inception, Mo Ibrahim's Celtel focused its business model on nonconsumption of mobile phones in Africa, as opposed to targeting the more affluent population.

2. AN ENABLING TECHNOLOGY—An enabling technology is
one that provides improving levels of performance at progressively
lower cost. A technology is any process within an organization that

converts inputs of lower value into outputs of greater value. Enabling technologies such as the Internet, smartphones, the Toyota Production System, or even an efficient distribution and logistics operation can provide a competitive edge to companies as they build new markets. Celtel leveraged the rapidly changing wireless cellular technology network in order to provide a service to many that had historically relied on wired connections.

3.   A NEW VALUE NETWORK—A value network is what defines a company's cost structure. For example, before a product goes from farm to grocery store, it must first be harvested, processed, stored, transported, packaged, marketed, and so on. This network of activities constitutes what's called the product's value network, with each adding a little bit of cost to the price of the final product. Because most businesses are targeted at existing consumers, their cost structures prevent them from targeting nonconsumers. Creating a new value network enables companies to redefine their cost structure so that their solutions can be afforded by nonconsumers and profitable at the same time. One of the ways Celtel did this was by changing how people purchased cell phone minutes. The company not only developed "scratch cards" (cards that enabled people to purchase minutes of talk time), but it also leveraged the informal retail network all across the continent. This helped Celtel redefine its cost structure.

4.   AN EMERGENT STRATEGY—When creating a new market, innovators typically use an emergent (or flexible) strategy because they are going after markets that are not yet defined, and so must learn much from their soon-to-be-customers. Deliberate (or fixed) strategies are typically used when companies know the needs of the market. Managers and entrepreneurs must be willing to learn and modify their intended strategies based on the feedback they get from the new customers they are trying to serve, as Celtel did in different countries.

5. EXECUTIVE SUPPORT—Businesses that attempt to create a new market are often unpopular because not only do they target a market that technically does not yet exist, but also they often require more resources than sustaining and efficiency innovations. This is why no banks lent to Mo Ibrahim at the onset. So, in order to survive in existing organizations, market-creating innovations require support from the CEO or someone high up in the executive team.

The Model T Effect

Perhaps the clearest example of the potential power of market-creating innovations can be found in the innovation of the Model T. About a century ago, cars in America were toys and status symbols for the rich. Fewer than ten thousand cars were registered in America in 1900, and these were custom-made cars that were bought as much for status as for their practical utility (not unlike the market for private jets today). There were few paved roads on which cars could be driven, few gas stations where they could be refueled, and few Americans rich enough to afford a car. Henry Ford would change all that.

In fact, so many Americans purchased cars—annual production went from twenty thousand in 1909 to more than two million by 1922—that the automobile boom led to a major cultural revolution in the country. Americans changed where and how they lived, worked, and played; schools and suburbs began to develop. The transportation of agricultural products became more efficient, and new businesses and industries—tourism, hotels, fast food, auto repair shops, auto insurance, gas stations, and so on—emerged. Many other industries were created to provide supplies directly to automakers, such as steel, oil, paint, lumber, cement, glass, and rubber. Schools began to offer programs that taught people how to make and service cars. And our public institutions began to respond by building new roads and creating new laws that made driving safer for America. The car, and the market Ford helped create, however, came first.

In addition to the Model T creating a new market that generated significant employment and tax revenue, the innovation had major downstream effects on the American economy. As more people continued to purchase Model T cars, competitors arose, making the industry even more efficient, vibrant, and mainstream. Americans loved their cars, and the government had to keep responding by building more roads. All this continued the virtuous cycle that Ford started—from 1909 to 1927, the company built fifteen million Model T cars. Cars led to more roads, which led to more suburbs, which led to more jobs, which—research tells us—lead to less crime.[21]

THE MODEL T EFFECT

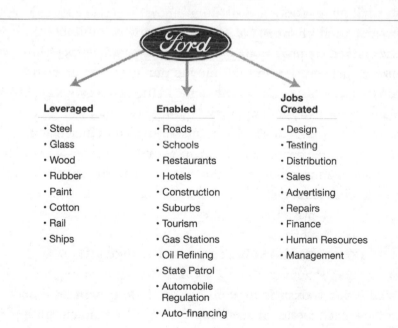

Leveraged	Enabled	Jobs Created
• Steel	• Roads	• Design
• Glass	• Schools	• Testing
• Wood	• Restaurants	• Distribution
• Rubber	• Hotels	• Sales
• Paint	• Construction	• Advertising
• Cotton	• Suburbs	• Repairs
• Rail	• Tourism	• Finance
• Ships	• Gas Stations	• Human Resources
	• Oil Refining	• Management
	• State Patrol	
	• Automobile Regulation	
	• Auto-financing	

Figure 5: Impact of Ford Model T

Ford's innovation, however, was not simply a car. It was an entire business model born out of his vision to create an entirely new market for the automobile. As was true for the Model T, market-creating innovations are less about the actual product being sold and more about the value network and business model an innovator develops. For Ford to sell his car to millions of Americans, he not only had to make a product that was simple to drive and affordable to purchase, but he also had to invest in many other things, such as gas and service stations, railroads to help him transport his product, and an aggressive advertising campaign targeted at average Americans who had never owned a car.

But as successful as the Model T and the new market it created were, Ford was slow to invest in sustaining innovations. To illustrate the importance of sustaining innovations, consider the following. In 1921, Ford Motor Company commanded a dominant 60 percent of the auto market in the United States. But the company's failure to invest in sustaining innovations caused it to lose its position, and by 1936 Ford Motor Company was number three in the market. General Motors, which gave customers such things as new models every year, the ability to purchase cars on credit, and different colors, became number one in the market with 43 percent share, while Chrysler leapt to the number two spot with 25 percent share. As we described earlier, sustaining and efficiency innovations are important to keep companies and economies vibrant, but market-creating innovations provide the platform upon which future growth is created.

The Force of Market-Creating Innovations

While each type of innovation has a role to play in an economy, because each creates or keeps markets vibrant, market-creating innovations are especially powerful because they often target large swathes of the population with a solution that helps them make progress with a struggle. And since each market is a function of both the value of the product being sold and the quantity of that product, a market that targets nonconsumption has the potential to create significant gains for investors, for innovators, and for society. Think of it like this: every successful new market that is created, regardless of the product or service being sold, has three distinct outcomes: *profits*, *jobs*, and the most difficult to track, but perhaps most powerful of the three, *cultural change*. Together, these create a solid foundation for future growth.

For a market to be created and then sustained, it must create **profits** or at least have the prospect of profit generation in the future. Profits provide the fuel for further growth.

Jobs, the second output of markets, are created in order for the market to deliver on its promise of making, distributing, selling, improving, and providing solutions to its new customers. I have always felt that the creation of a job is far more important for a society than the simple calculation of economic value. Jobs give people dignity and build self-esteem. Jobs enable people to provide for themselves and their families. Research has repeatedly told us that people who are employed have less time (or inclination) to engage in crime.[22]

The third and perhaps most important output of a market is the **cultural change** the new market triggers and reinforces. In addition to democratizing products and services so that many more people in society have access, market-creating innovations also democratize the benefits of successful new markets that are created. These benefits aren't limited to just jobs, but also ownership opportunities that are often offered to investors and employees. When many people in a region understand that they can begin to solve many of their problems (fend for themselves and their families and gain status and dignity in society) in a productive manner— that is, by participating in the new market as investors, producers, or consumers—they are more likely to change the way they think about their society. This is one of the ways new markets begin to change a society's culture, which can make all the difference for a country looking to prosper.

When All Is Said and Done

The late Nobel laureate Milton Friedman once stated, "The great virtue of the free market, of the private market, [is that] it enables people . . . to cooperate together economically."[23] We have found markets to be a powerful force that has the ability to pull into societies many of the components that make societies safer, more secure, and more prosperous. This is why understanding the critical role different types of innovations play is vital to economic development.

By investing in market-creating innovations, investors and entrepreneurs inadvertently engage in nation-building. These innovations create a viable market that serves nonconsumption—typically the majority of people in a poor economy—thereby creating jobs and profits that can fund other important elements of a developed society, which, in a nice virtuous circle, are pulled in by the innovation for it to succeed.

While market-creating innovations are about developing simpler and more affordable products so that many more people than before can afford them, they also begin to lay the foundations necessary to build an economy. Once these new markets are created, the economy becomes more resilient, as it generates more income to fund schools, roads, hospitals, and even better governance—a process we will explore later in this book. Obviously not all market-creating innovations will have the same impact that Ford's Model T had, but our research shows that even small innovations can begin to transform countries economically and culturally.

NOTES

1.   Ronald Coase, "Address at Markets, Firms and Property Rights: A Celebration of the Research of Ronald Coase Conference," published on April 20, 2012, video, 25:40, https://www.youtube.com/watch?v=ZAqo6n79QIs.

2.   Christensen, Raynor, and McDonald (2015) offer a concise summary: "Disruption describes a process whereby a company with fewer resources is able to successfully challenge established incumbent businesses. Specifically, as incumbents focus on improving their products and services for their most demanding (and usually most profitable) customers, they exceed the needs of some segments and ignore the needs of others. Entrants that prove disruptive begin by successfully targeting those overlooked segments, gaining a foothold by delivering more-suitable functionality—frequently at a lower price. Incumbents, chasing higher profitability in more-demanding segments, tend not to respond vigorously. Entrants then move upmarket, delivering the performance that incumbents' mainstream customers require, while preserving the advantages that drove their early success. When mainstream customers start adopting the entrants' offerings in volume, disruption has occurred." The type of innovation most likely to be disruptive is market-creating innovation (as we'll see in examples throughout this book).

See also Clayton M. Christensen, *The Innovator's Dilemma: When New Technologies Cause Great Firms to Fail* (Boston: Harvard Business School Press, 1997).

3.   In a 2017 World Bank publication titled *The Innovation Paradox: Developing-Country Capabilities and the Unrealized Promise of Technological Catch-Up*, authors Xavier Cirera and William F. Maloney suggest that "innovation capacity appears to be the more critical policy priority for economic development." The report goes on to suggest that "equating innovation policy to frontier science and technology policy will lead to frustration and waste if the firm dimension is neglected . . . without a corps of capable firms to take these ideas to market, these investments will yield little in terms of growth." Our hope is that the categorization we offer here helps further the Bank's work and helps us better understand how important firms are to economic development.

Xavier Cirera and William F. Maloney, *The Innovation Paradox: Developing-Country Capabilities and the Unrealized Promise of Technological Catch-Up* (Washington, DC: World Bank), doi:10.1596/978-1-4648 -1160-9. License: Creative Commons Attribution CC BY 3.0 IGO.

4.   The World Economic Forum publishes an annual report titled "Global Competitiveness Report," where the organization ranks countries based on their competitiveness. One of the metrics used to measure a country's competitiveness is its "innovation." Institutions, infrastructure, health, and education are others. For assessing a country's innovation, the report measures things such as investment in research and development, patent applications, and a country's ability to provide new or unique products.

Alex Gray, "These are the ten most innovative countries in the world," *World Economic Forum*, October 11, 2017, http://www.weforum.org /agenda/2017/10/these-are-the-10-most-innovative-countries-in-the-world/.

5.   Understanding how different types of innovations impact an economy is critical because there are several distinct actors in an economy. My friend Lant Pritchett, a highly respected former World Bank economist and professor of International Development at Harvard's Kennedy School of Government, provided me with a helpful conceptual framework for thinking about why poor economies have such a difficult time breaking out of their economic rut—and where innovation might make a profound difference. Pritchett identifies four primary entities in an economy: what he calls "rentiers," "magicians," "power brokers," and "workhorses."

Rentiers are resource extraction or agricultural firms that mainly export to world markets. They are often subject to regulatory rents. Think oil companies and diamond miners. *Magicians* are exporters that operate in highly competitive global industries. Think of the factory owners that make commoditized T-shirts and jeans. *Power brokers* are those firms that work in the domestic sector, but are also subject to "regulatory rents." These are the big construction companies, the hoteliers who own or manage expensive hotels, the port operators, and the electricity providers. And finally, the *workhorses*. These are the less-than-glamorous firms that operate in the highly competitive domestic environments. From the petty trader on the side of the road to the hairdresser in her home, these make up a majority of the world's poor. They are workhorses.

"Regulatory rents are defined as those derived from some discretionary action of government, such as: offering licenses for commercial use of a resource (e.g. mining); bestowing firm-specific (rather than industry-specific) tax advantages; market exclusivity; or application of applicable regulations. It could also be derived from deliberate government inaction, such as permitting monopolies to charge prices significantly above marginal cost, or not enforcing anti-trust law or pursuing competitive markets when it would be appropriate for consumer welfare."

Lant Pritchett, Kunal Sen, and Eric Werker, *Deals and Development: The Political Dynamics of Growth Episodes* (Oxford: Oxford University Press, 2018).

6.   We view economics as a nested system. The global economy contains national economies, which are composed of industries, which in turn contain corporations. Corporations are composed of business units, which are organized around teams, which define how employees coordinate their work. Employees, in turn, make and sell products and services to consumers, who have preferences that define what they will and will not do. Scholars in the two traditional branches of economics—macro and micro—build models of how the global and national systems work on the one end, and at the other end how individuals prioritize and make decisions. However, most economic activity actually occurs somewhere between these two ends of the nested system: namely, in companies. Aside from welfare payments and people employed in government entities, companies essentially *are* the economy. Companies create and eliminate jobs, and pay wages and taxes. They implement government policy. They choose to invest or not invest. They respond to changes in interest rates. Companies build economies' infrastructure, and in many ways companies *are* our infrastructure.

7.   Economists have long understood the importance of innovation, or what they often refer to as *technical change*, in spurring economic growth. For example, in 1956, Stanford economist Moses Abramovitz published a landmark paper, "Resource and Output Trends in the United States Since 1870," that highlighted the link between innovative activity and long-term economic development. In his paper, Abramovitz analyzed the United States' growth from 1870 to 1950 and found that capital and labor accounted for roughly 15 percent of the growth. Productivity or what is now called technology, innovation, or technical innovation, he asserted, accounted for the remaining 85 percent. Abramovitz wrote that "since we know little about the causes of productivity increase, the indicated importance of this element may be taken to be some sort of measure of our ignorance about the causes of economic growth in the United States and some sort of indication of where we need to concentrate our attention."

Moses Abramovitz, "Resource and Output Trends in the United States Since 1870," *National Bureau of Economic Research* (1956), http://www.nber.org/chapters/c5650.pdf.

In parallel, Massachusetts Institute of Technology's Robert Solow also reached a similar conclusion as Abramovitz while using different methods and analyzing different time periods. Among Solow's works is a 1957 article, "Technical Change and the Aggregate Production Function," that sheds light on the impact that technological innovation can have on economic growth. Solow was awarded the Nobel Prize in Economics in 1987 for his contributions to the world's understanding of economic growth. After this insight, the quest to further understand how technological innovation impacted economic growth, and the belief that it did, took off.

Robert Solow, "Technical Change and the Aggregate Production Function," *The Review of Economics and Statistics* 39, no. 3 (August 1957), 312–320, https://faculty.georgetown.edu/mh5/class/econ489/Solow-Growth-Accounting.pdf.

Economists have traditionally looked at growth through the lens of productivity: aggregating all the assets in an economy and multiplying that by a production (or an innovation) function. While mathematically valid, thinking about growth through the benchmark of productivity is less helpful when thinking about policies and programs for economies that are made of people with varying capabilities and cultures, and living in different contexts.

8. In most poor countries, the distribution of money, power, and influence tips disproportionately to the rentiers and power brokers. They run the economies and have little to no incentive to change the system. The majority of the poor—the workhorses, in Pritchett's language—in our world toil and labor incessantly only to find themselves perpetually living a life of struggle and suffering. The question then becomes, how do we give more power and influence to the workhorses?

Or maybe a better question to ask is how do we find and nurture, to borrow Pritchett's metaphor, a few "thoroughbreds" among the workhorses—companies that have the potential to create a new market through innovation and scale? We call them "thoroughbreds" because they are the individuals or organizations that can develop market-creating innovations with the potential to change the dynamics of an economy.

9. This is unlike what Sir Thomas Lipton did in 1890 when he purchased a tea garden in modern-day Sri Lanka and began producing tea. Sir Lipton thought the price of tea was too high and that he could offer it for less money to many more tea drinkers.

10. There are instances when companies include features in a new product, charge more, but find many new consumers ready to pull said product into their lives. This tends to happen when the new feature has the potential to upend or displace an existing product on the market. For example, when Apple added the global positioning satellite (GPS) feature to its phones, the company effectively rendered the use of stand-alone GPS devices obsolete.

11. "Toyota Camry Awards," 2018 Camry Overview, Toyota, accessed February 16, 2018, https://www.toyota.com/camry/awards.

12. It is important to note that, at one point, models of the Toyota Camry were growing exponentially in the United States, but over time the market saturated and sales began to level out. In other words, the Camry filled out the concentric circle where it was targeting new customers who could afford its product, and now it struggles for market share with other brands such as Honda's Accord or Hyundai's Sonata.

"Monthly and annual sales figures for the Toyota Camry in the US," Toyota Camry, Carsalesbase.com, accessed February 16, 2018, http://car salesbase.com/us-car-sales-data/toyota/toyota-camry/.

13. The "resource curse"—a phenomenon that explains how many nations endowed with natural resources such as oil, gas, gold, diamonds, and many others often end up with less democracy, less economic growth, and effectively less prosperity than nations without these natural resources—has been widely studied in economics. It is sometimes referred to as the "paradox of plenty." In using resource extraction as an example here, we don't focus on the already widely studied macroeconomic effects of natural resources endowments. Instead, we focus on the profit-maximization and cost-reduction incentives of a typical manager in this industry who finds herself selling commodities for which the global market sets a price. For more on the resource curse, see Jeffrey Frankel's paper, *The Natural Resource Curse: A Survey* (2010).

14. "U.S. Field Production of Crude Oil," Petroleum and Other Liquids, U.S. Energy Information Administration, accessed April 6, 2018, https://www.eia.gov/dnav/pet/hist/LeafHandler.ashx?n=PET&s=MCR FPUS2&f=A.

15. "Employment, Hours, and Earnings from the Current Employment Statistics Survey (National)," Databases, Tables & Calculators by Subject, Bureau of Labor Statistics, accessed April 6, 2018, https://data.bls.gov /pdq/SurveyOutputServlet.

16. Micheal Eboh, "Unemployment: Oil sector employs 0.01% of Nigerian workforce," *Vanguard*, June 3, 2014, http://www.vanguardngr.com/2014/06 /unemployment-oil-sector-employs-0-01-nigerian-workforce/.

17. Iqbal Quadir of MIT explains it this way: "Every innovation spurs a complex chain of reactions, but entrepreneurs push consistently toward lower costs and larger markets. This saves known resources or creates new ones, puts price pressures on existing products, and engages more people in the economy." He later goes on to write that "today's innovations may show up in unexpected ways and places, but they follow the same pattern and are no less spectacular than they were in Henry Ford's

day." In effect, as entrepreneurs make products simpler and more affordable, more and more people in society not only buy and use them, but also
are employed in their creation. This process leads to a more vibrant and
prosperous economy.

Iqbal Quadir, "Inclusive Prosperity in Low-Income Countries," *Innovations* 9, no. 1/2 (2014): 65-66.

18. Apple's iPhone is often pointed to as an example of the vulnerability
of global jobs—there's even an inscription on the back of every iPhone:
Designed by Apple in California. Assembled in China. But the iPhone actually provides a better illustration of the importance of local jobs that
can't be easily shopped around to the lowest bidder. "Designed" actually
encompasses an array of local jobs that have to be done near Apple's home
base in California. It includes the work of thousands of engineers and scientists who scour the globe developing new materials; the product managers, who conduct market research and generate product requirements;
and the retail staff trained to introduce and explain the devices to end
consumers. "Apple creates value, and thus U.S. jobs, through the design
and development of its products, not because of where they're built," a recent analysis in *Bloomberg Businessweek* concluded. "All these aspects are
part of the iPhone's product design, and explain how Apple can charge
significant mark-ups and take the lion's share of the industry's profits.
Its 38 percent gross margin puts the rest of the smartphone market to
shame."

19. According to data from the World Bank, global net foreign portfolio
investments (FPI) were approximately $173 billion. These investments
are more short-term, liquid, and volatile. FPIs target equities, bonds, and
other financial assets. The absolute value (inflows and outflows) totaled
just under $2.4 trillion. So, even if we accounted for the shorter-term
FPI, it is clear that the amount of cross-border investments is a very small
percentage of the global assets under management.

20. Matt Harding, "Op-Ed: The Internet will fail and the TV will never
compete with the radio," *Digital Journal*, April 25, 2010, http://www.digital
journal.com/article/291152.

21. A study conducted by Christopher Blattman at Columbia University
and Jeannie Annan of the International Rescue Committee suggests that
providing job training and employment opportunities could help curb
crime in a region. On the surface, it makes sense. The more legitimate
opportunities people in a community have to solve the problems that engaging in crime enables them to solve, such as providing the resources
necessary to live a comfortable life, the less likely they are to engage in

crime. If you look at some of the most crime-infested areas in our world, even in the United States, they are often areas where many are devoid of opportunity. While this is not the only reason people engage in crime, it is often a major one. The study found that a wage boost of as little as 40 cents a day was enough to entice former Liberian mercenary soldiers to shift more time toward their new (honest) occupation and away from violence or other criminal activities. And the assurance that more earnings would arrive in the future was particularly effective in combating illegal activity.

Gillian B. White, "Can Jobs Deter Crime?," *The Atlantic*, June 25, 2015, https://www.theatlantic.com/business/archive/2015/06/can-jobs-deter -crime/396758/.

22. Ibid.

23. Milton Friedman, "Milton Friedman on Charlie Rose," video, 53:57, https://charlierose.com/videos/19192.

Chapter 3

In the Struggle Lies Opportunity

The real voyage of discovery consists not in seeking new landscapes but in having new eyes.

—MARCEL PROUST

The Idea in Brief

You may be thinking that it's one thing to say market-creating innovations are important to creating prosperity, but how in the world do you *spot* these opportunities, much less go after them? If it were so easy, wouldn't everyone be doing this already? The problem is, it is very difficult to "see" what you're not looking for. Many of our economic forecasts don't necessarily help—they typically focus on what we call the "consumption economy," the part of the economy that is most visible through conventional metrics. But they do not factor in what's less obvious, and perhaps the richest vein to mine for growth—the "nonconsumption economy."[1] To see opportunity in nonconsumption, you have to change what you're looking for.

In his first job, working in the insurance industry in London, Richard Leftley was fascinated and puzzled by two tables in the annual statistical analysis published by Swiss Re, the leading global reinsurer. The first one was the number and location of people who died as a result of natural disasters. The second was the total cost of insurance payouts in those areas. "There was a total mismatch between the two lists," Leftley recalls now. "The human toll was enormous in places like Bangladesh, Pakistan, and India. But those countries were never even on the 'total payouts' rankings." It made no sense, Leftley thought, that the people who need insurance most in the world are least likely to have it.

A few years later, using his two-week vacation to do volunteer work in Zambia, Leftley saw an opportunity to change that. He was placed in the home of a widow and her child in a poor village, as part of his volunteer experience. Leftley was unprepared for just how painful her daily life was: she lived hand-to-mouth, at best. But Leftley learned during that stay that her life had not always been so bleak. She had previously lived in Lusaka, the capital of Zambia, working as a schoolteacher while her husband made his living as a security guard. They had risen above their poor childhood economic circumstances and were living a life of relative comfort, with a decent home and a motorcycle to get around. In what Leftley calls the "chutes and ladders" of life, her husband contracted HIV at the height of the epidemic in Zambia, and the family's downward spiral began. Not only was he too ill to work, but they spent all of their savings on medicine—both legitimate and "hocus pocus" that offered false hope—and, eventually, on his funeral. Broken, she and her child returned to the village to start again.

Leftley was profoundly moved by the widow's story and returned to London determined to find a way to use his professional expertise to help people in poor economies who most needed it. When he started telling his insurance colleagues his idea for a new type of business, much like Mo Ibrahim a decade before, he was greeted with guffaws. "They laughed at me," he recalls now. "I was talking about going to Zambia and selling insurance to people who had HIV. People thought I had lost my marbles."

They're not laughing now. As of this writing, MicroEnsure, the company that Leftley went on to found, has registered more than fifty-six million people for insurance in emerging economies (eighteen million in 2017 alone), paying out $30 million in claims by finding enormous opportunity in nonconsumption—and radically innovating the insurance business model to make that possible. The company, which has been awarded the *Financial Times*/IFC Transformational Business Award four times in recent years, is already profitable in 80 percent of the markets it has entered. More than 85 percent of MicroEnsure's customers had never purchased an insurance product until MicroEnsure came to the scene.

This is what sets market-creating innovators apart—the ability to identify opportunities where there seem to be *no customers*. "It's difficult to run a ruler over things you can't see," Leftley says now. But Leftley and his team had a revelation that completely changed how they approached their innovation. "We realized we weren't competing with giant insurance companies; we were competing with apathy." Apathy, it turns out, is a fierce competitor. But a well-thought-out innovation that responds to a struggle that potential consumers are facing can eventually win out. Therein lies some of the greatest potential to create markets that will lead to prosperity—first for the entrepreneur, and then, over time, for the region.

A Tale of Two Economies

I have often wondered how we can better describe economies in a way that points to their potential for growth and development. To many of us, the "economy" is simply an abstract hodgepodge of money and businesses, products and advertisements, laws and regulations, and buyers and sellers that interact with one another in some fashion. We typically categorize countries and their economies as monolithic entities. As such, many of the projections and analyses, such as GDP growth, per capita income growth, and even sector-specific statistics, offer a high-level view of what's going on in the economy as a whole. Although these sorts of analyses are informative and useful, they may not always tell the whole story.

From an innovation point of view, we see the world a bit differently: countries are made up of consumers (the "consumption economy") and nonconsumers (the "nonconsumption economy"), a distinction that helps identify fertile territory for market-creating innovations. Seeing an economy this way helps cut through the noise of GDP growth and a host of other metrics that we tend to use to determine an economy's health and potential.

The consumption economy is composed of customers who have the income, time, and expertise to purchase and use existing products or services in the market. It is the part of the economy that economists, forecasters, and marketing managers often use to predict the growth of a product or a region.[2] The most common type of innovations, sustaining innovations, are targeted at the consumption economy because it's relatively easy to see the potential for growth. When you already know who your customers are, you can find ways to make your products or services better for them so they'll spend more with you.[3]

Not surprisingly, capital, being risk-averse by its very nature, tends to chase sustaining innovations in hopes of a predictable return on investment (ROI) because it can more easily see and understand the potential using existing financial tools and theories. To appreciate the degree to which capital chases the consumption economy, consider the global Foreign Direct Investment (FDI) flows. In 2016, approximately $1.1 trillion of the total $1.5 trillion of global FDI flowed to the richest countries in the world, that is, the thirty-five member countries in the Organization for Economic Cooperation and Development (OECD).[4] In other words, more than 73 percent of global FDI went to just 35 of the 196 countries in the world. Or consider the billions of dollars of investments that flowed to the mobile telecommunications industry in Africa after Mo Ibrahim created a market and turned millions of nonconsumers into consumers.

As we've noted, the potential of market-creating innovations is significant relative to even the most robust efficiency or sustaining innovations. But innovating for a market that does not yet exist can feel risky. Think about the conventional art of product development, which focuses on segmentation: identifying groups of customers that are similar enough that the same product or service will appeal to all of them. Since investments are necessary to develop and market products, investment decisions are typically made based on similar segmentation decisions. Questions like "How much disposable income do people in Country A have?" or "What is the average expenditure on entertainment in Country B, and is that number growing or shrinking?" typically drive investment decisions. Marketers, research analysts, and investors often segment markets by product type, by price point, or by the demographics and psychographics of the individuals or companies who are their customers. This is about focusing on the consumption economy—the opportunity we can most easily see and segment.

But this method leaves billions of people out of consideration because they are deemed too poor, too uneducated, or too uninteresting to develop products for. History has shown us time and again that that way of thinking is very limiting.

Consider, for example, how AT&T missed the chance to lead a mobile phone revolution. Just a few decades ago, AT&T asked a prominent consulting firm to estimate how many cell phones there would be in the world at the turn of this century. The consulting firm estimated just under one million. And so AT&T did not invest since the market would not be big enough to warrant its investment.[5] All the existing data AT&T had access to pointed to "low opportunity." Cell phones at the time were heavy, bulky, and expensive. Most people could not afford them. Not investing made sense, at least on paper.

Fast-forward to the present day and it's impossible to imagine any place in the world without them. By the year 2001, there were almost one billion cell phones in the world. Today, there are more than 7.5 billion cell phone subscriptions globally.[6] Just try making eye contact with your fellow passengers on a New York—or New Delhi—subway. It's impossible. You'll find people of all ages and demographic backgrounds looking down, transfixed by something on their phones.

Nonconsumption offers a powerful clue that there is enormous potential for innovation. But spotting nonconsumption requires putting on a new set of lenses to see what others might be missing.

Identifying the Barriers

How do you go about identifying high-potential pockets of nonconsumption? In their book *The Innovator's Guide to Growth: Putting Disruptive Innovation to Work,* my colleague Scott Anthony and his coauthors dedicate a whole chapter to how to identify nonconsumption. There are primarily four barriers or constraints that prevent people from consuming a solution that will help them make progress. They are: skill, wealth, access, and time. Sometimes, solutions on the market exhibit similar constraints that prevent would-be consumers from consuming those particular solutions. Let us explore each briefly.[7]

> SKILL: Often, nonconsumers do not have the skills necessary to consume existing solutions on the market, even though they would benefit from doing so. For example, fifty years ago, computers required immense skill to operate, and those who used them, mostly technicians at large universities and big corporations, had to be able to operate a very large and complex machine. This created an extra barrier to consumption, in addition to the price tag.

> WEALTH: Wealth is usually the most easily identifiable constraint. This is when nonconsumers cannot economically afford existing solutions on the market that would help them

make progress, if they exist. For example, most Americans could not afford a personal computer until Apple, IBM, Microsoft, and Intel, innovating over time, made access to computing more affordable for the average nonconsumer. Today, most of us have computers in our pockets.

ACCESS: Access is when nonconsumers would benefit from a particular solution, but existing solutions are not within reach in their particular location or context. Remember the photocopying centers in many large organizations? Those big and complicated-to-use machines were in centralized locations, and if you were not connected to one of them, you were not able to print. But Canon and Ricoh developed smaller, simpler, and more affordable printers that we now have in our homes and offices. Their innovation removed the access barrier. Today we can print thousands of pages from our mobile phones connected to wireless printers in our homes.

TIME: Time-related constraints are when nonconsumers would benefit from using a solution, but the time required is prohibitive. In my sixty-five years of life, I have yet to meet a person who just loves waiting, or wasting time. Clinicas del Azúcar, a Mexican chain of clinics that provides an integrated solution for the treatment of diabetes (which we will discuss in detail in chapter 7), developed its solution with this barrier in mind. Many existing solutions to treating diabetes in Mexico required patients to go to different hospitals or clinics, and visit with different specialists—this required a significant amount of time just traveling. Clincas del Azúcar's solution is different. Patients visit one clinic, where they see several different specialists in a timely manner. Because the more patients the clinic sees the more revenue it generates, there is an incentive for the clinic to be efficient with its treatment.

The Struggle Is Real

Identifying the barriers that lead to nonconsumption is a vital *clue*, but it's not the only thing innovators should be looking for. People are nonconsumers because they're struggling to accomplish something, but none of the available solutions is a good option for them.

We believe that innovation is too often hit-or-miss because it relies on existing data about the consumption economy—using information about what customers have done in the past to predict what they'll do in the future. But that data is missing something fundamental. It doesn't explain why people make the choices they do—and it doesn't necessarily predict what they will do in the future. And it doesn't capture why someone has chosen to not purchase a product or service at all—which is where the nonconsumption economy exists.

Instead, this can be explained by the Theory of Jobs to Be Done, which we believe explains why people make the purchasing choices that they do.[8] Many marketers focus on identifying demographics or putting prospective customers into segments, but we believe this misses what fundamentally causes each of us to make a choice to buy a product or service. There's something else going on that demographics can't explain.

Everyday jobs arise in my life that I need to get done. Some are little jobs, some are big ones. Some jobs surface unpredictably. Some are an everyday affair. When we realize we have a job to do, we reach out and pull something into our lives to help us get the job done. When we buy a product, we essentially "hire" something to help us solve that job. If the product we hire does the job well, when we are confronted with the same job again, we hire that same product. And if the product does a crummy job, we "fire" it and look around for something else we might hire to solve the problem.

Let me illustrate what I mean. I might choose to buy the *New York Times* newspaper on my way to work one morning. I am sixty-five years old, I'm six feet eight inches tall, and my shoe size is sixteen. My wife and I have sent all our children off to college. I drive an SUV to work. I have a lot of characteristics and attributes, but none of them has *caused* me to go out and buy the *New York Times*. My reasons for buying the paper are much more specific. I might buy it because I need something to read on a plane and I don't want to be forced to chat with the gabby passenger beside me. I might be buying it because I'm a basketball fan and I want to look in the sports section and tease one of my sons about his favorite team's chances of making it to the playoffs. Marketers who collect demographic or psychographic information about me—and look for correlations with other buyer segments—are not going to capture those reasons. They won't have understood the Job I was hiring the newspaper to do that day. Or if I don't purchase a newspaper on a given day because I won't have time to read it, there will be no data about my choice at all.

Until you understand the Job your customers are hiring your product or service to do, in all its rich complexity and nuance, you can never be certain that your innovations will be successful. Successful market-creating innovations emerge from unfulfilled Jobs to Be Done; they solve problems that formerly had only inadequate solutions—or no solution at all. Celtel's Mo Ibrahim knew that someone who wanted to talk to his mother in a village far away would have to travel for days to make contact. For most people, that was an inadequate solution. MicroEnsure's Richard Leftley knew that people who desperately wanted to protect their families from unforeseen difficulties had few options. Neither one of those opportunities would have been apparent through the lens of the consumption economy.

People would rather go without any product—stay as nonconsumers—than "hire" a product or service that solves their Job in an unsatisfactory way. This is what happened when Leftley realized that his insurance product was not competing with other insurance products on the market. It was competing with apathy. His product was actually competing with *nothing*. Once you understand the real Job people are looking to get done—and in the case of nonconsumption, that people are *choosing to go without* rather than solve that Job with existing options—the market suddenly seems full of potential. Nonconsumption is simply a clue that there is enormous potential to solve a struggle with innovation.

"No One Wakes Up in the Morning and Wants to Buy Insurance."

Innovators need to walk in the shoes of their prospective customers to create a product that is so much better than the existing alternatives that people hire it—even when the competition is *nothing*. Once innovators understand the Job to Be Done well enough, they will be able to create a solution that will cause nonconsumers to "fire" apathy or whatever workaround they have created, and hire their solution instead. That might seem easy on the surface (isn't *something* better than nothing?), but a customer's decision-making process about what to fire and hire for their Job is complicated. There are always two opposing forces battling for dominance within us in that moment of choice, and they both play a significant role in our decision to "hire" something.

> THE FORCES COMPELLING CHANGE TO A NEW SOLUTION: First of all, the "push" of the situation—the frustration or problem that a customer is trying to solve—has to be substantial enough to cause them to want to take action. A problem that is simply nagging or annoying might not be enough to trigger someone to do something differently. Secondly, the "pull" of an enticing new product or service to solve that problem has to be pretty strong, too. The new solution to their Job to Be Done has to help customers make progress that will make their lives better.

THE FORCES OPPOSING CHANGE: There are two unseen, yet incredibly powerful, forces at play at the same time that many innovators often ignore: the forces holding a customer back. First, "habits of the present" weigh heavily on consumers. I'm *used* to doing it this way, or living with the problem. I don't love it, but I'm at least comfortable with how I deal with it now. This is where nonconsumers tend to live, stuck in the habits of the present—the thought of switching to a new solution is almost overwhelming. Sticking with the devil they know (in this case simply living with their struggle) is bearable. I refused to upgrade my mobile phone for years, in spite of all the whizbang things my assistant assured me the new phone could do, because I was *comfortable* with the one I had. This is largely because—as Nobel Prize winner Daniel Kahneman has shown—the principal allure of the old is that it requires no deliberation and has some intuitive plausibility as a solution already. Loss aversion—people's tendency to want to avoid loss—is twice as powerful psychologically as the allure of gains, as first demonstrated by Kahneman and Amos Tversky.[9]

On top of that, anxieties that come into play with hiring a new solution are powerful: anxiety about the cost, anxiety of learning something new, and anxiety of the unknown can be overwhelming. I'm guessing you probably have at least one old mobile phone gathering dust in a junk drawer or closet somewhere in your home. You're not alone. Many consumers hang on to their old mobile phones, even when they might get some trade-in value toward a new one. Why? Anxiety about the new solution. *What if the new one fails at some point? What if I find myself in some kind of unanticipated situation where I need a backup phone? What if . . .* Innovators all too often focus exclusively on the forces pushing for change—making sure that the new solution for resolving a customer's struggle is sufficiently alluring to cause them to switch, but ignore the powerful forces blocking that change.

MicroEnsure's Leftley found this out the hard way. It took Leftley and his team a few tries to get their offering right. Initially Micro-Ensure focused on trying to draw people in simply by offering insurance. MicroEnsure doesn't fund the insurance it sells, but rather works as a middleman between the mobile phone companies and mainstream insurers. The company makes money by getting a small cut from new and existing mobile phone subscribers who spend up to a certain amount of money purchasing cell phone minutes monthly. In addition, when insurance companies want access to new customers, they sometimes contract out consulting and product development services to MicroEnsure. This means the burden is on MicroEnsure to understand the prospective customers and find a way to appeal to them. At the outset, MicroEnsure created programs that allowed mobile phone companies to offer free insurance to customers who spent a bit more topping up their prepaid mobile minutes. All a customer needed to do to sign up for insurance was provide his or her name, age, and next of kin. Just three questions stood between a potential customer and "free" insurance ("free" as a bonus for buying more mobile minutes). It should have been a slam dunk.

But it was not. Even after spending lots of money on advertising, for a *free* product (the company would hope to make its money upselling once it had registered customers), the company had only recruited ten thousand customers in more than a year, a tiny dent in the market. Even though MicroEnsure tried to make it simple to sign up for insurance, the product itself made little sense in the circumstances in which many customers found themselves. It wasn't solving *their* Job to Be Done. It was essentially traditional insurance, just priced for an emerging market economy. "I had to print brochures that said things like 'Skydiving and water polo are excluded,'" Leftley recalls of the insurer's requirement that he specifically exclude participating in expensive sports that the non-consumers they were targeting would never even contemplate. "It was mad."

Seeing through the lens of what Job *these* nonconsumers were really trying to do caused Leftley and his team to rethink not only what they were selling—but how. "No one wakes up in the morning and wants to buy insurance," Leftley realized, but they do wake up worrying about what could possibly go wrong that day that could ruin their lives. Risk of getting sick that day and not being able to work. Risk of their market stall burning down. Risk of being robbed. Risk of a flood wiping out all their supplies. Risk of the cruelties of fate swiping them off the board altogether. The Job to Be Done was not "sell me insurance"; the Job was something like "help me continue to earn a living for my family—in my particular circumstances—without worrying about things outside of my control." Their strategy at this stage had to be *emergent*, not *deliberate*. They had to learn how to first create the market before scaling their solution.

To respond to what they were learning, MicroEnsure had to change virtually everything about the traditional insurance model. Even asking three simple questions to get customers to sign up was too much. "We could track where people gave up in the process," Leftley recalls. "Those three questions caused 80 percent of the people to not complete the process." In many lower-income countries, questions such as age and next of kin are not simple—people don't often know or care so much about their age, and choosing a next of kin in a complex family structure is difficult. So MicroEnsure had to radically innovate its business model to address the forces opposing change in prospective customers' minds.

What would happen if they didn't ask customers *anything*? At all. MicroEnsure and its partner insurers would only have one piece of information about a customer: his or her mobile phone number. And with that one piece of information, insurance companies would agree to provide insurance and make payments directly to that phone number without paperwork, questions, or proof of *anything*. "This was very freaky for insurance companies," Leftley recalls. Not knowing a customer's age, in an industry built on data, forecasting, and predictable actuarial tables, was a truly radical thought. But with that innovation, "Buying insurance became as simple as signing up for a ringtone." Now free insurance became a powerful marketing tool—once a customer was educated about the concept of insurance, it was easier to upsell and cross-market other insurance products.

"We had cracked the code," Leftley says. So much so that Micro-Ensure signed up one million customers *on the first day* they offered a new life insurance product in India—one that had no age limit and no exclusions, and only required a mobile phone number. The company wasn't prepared for just how successfully they had cracked it. In the next three months, another nineteen million customers followed suit. "We hadn't built systems that could deal with that kind of volume!" Leftley recounts. "We were plugging in hard drives and thumb drives, and were right on the edge of what was physically possible."

That's not to say that MicroEnsure's success came easily. Creating markets in emerging economies is difficult. MicroEnsure actually began as a not-for-profit organization before Leftley and his team realized that they couldn't possibly keep up with the growth relying on donated funds and grants in the glacial process by which they are often bestowed. MicroEnsure came close to folding several times while they waited for grants to be approved. By the time MicroEnsure was signing up millions of customers every week, it was clear that relying on funders was not a strategy for long-term growth and sustainability. "We'd think about approaching a major foundation, for example, and going through that whole process. If we were lucky, six months later we'd get a check. But in six months, we might be out of business. We couldn't wait that long."

With a clear market and untold potential opportunity, Leftley and his team were eventually able to attract a consortium of backers, including AXA insurance company, Sanlam, Omidyar, IFC, and Telenor and converted to a for-profit venture. The company could now afford to experiment and create new products and services in markets that other insurance companies simply couldn't see. In each location, MicroEnsure would hire and set up a local team to run operations on the ground, creating a battery of new local jobs.

To be clear, it's not that existing companies aren't looking for opportunities to grow. They are, but, unfortunately, they are often blinded by their existing business models and the market research tools they use. This causes them not to see opportunity in the struggle of millions of people. The vastness of the nonconsumption economy in many regions in our world is simply an indication that, while major struggles exist for hundreds of millions of people, an entrepreneur has yet to build a viable business model to address these particular struggles. The interesting thing about developing a business model that targets this struggle is that, once done successfully, all of a sudden, the opportunity looks obvious.

Consider the case of appliance maker Galanz.

Just Because You Can't See It, Doesn't Mean It's Not There

Liang Zhaoxian, founder of Galanz, built what has become one of the world's largest home appliance companies. Barely a blip on anyone's radar twenty-five years ago, today, roughly half the microwave ovens sold globally are made by Galanz. That's a lot of microwave ovens. But Zhaoxian didn't build that empire by focusing primarily on exploiting China's low wages to create exports for the world. He focused first on the struggle he saw *in* China.

This was an opportunity his competitors initially couldn't see. In 1992, for example, only two hundred thousand microwave ovens were sold in China, a majority of which were sold in cities. The average price of a microwave oven was around 3,000 yuan (approximately $500 at the time), well beyond the reach of the average

Chinese citizen. Most Chinese people saw the microwave oven as a luxury they didn't need, and so did many microwave manufacturers who saw the average Chinese nonconsumer as "too poor" to even consider purchasing a microwave oven. The largest producers of microwave ovens for the local Chinese market had annual sales of around 120,000 units.

But Galanz's founder saw something else: he saw people who lived in tiny apartment buildings with either no stoves or cumbersome ones. Many used hot plates, which often heated up their small and cramped apartments. He saw a growing number of Chinese people who were, now more than ever, pressed for time. He also saw that the last thing anyone living in a small apartment, who does not own an air conditioner and is pressed for time, wants to do is cook, thereby emitting more heat into the room. Zhaoxian saw this struggle as a huge market-creating opportunity.

Galanz chose to focus on the microwave oven market in China for precisely the same reasons many recognized global brands chose to ignore it. To them, *the existing demand was small, microwave ovens were expensive, and the average Chinese consumer could not afford one.*

So Galanz developed a business model that focused on *creating a market* in China. Even though Galanz took advantage of lower labor costs in China, as did many other brands and manufacturers, it would be incorrect to suggest that Galanz was just a low-cost manufacturer of microwave ovens. Galanz started from scratch, with the average Chinese customer in mind.

In order to successfully target the average Chinese customer, company executives at Galanz had to think differently than other microwave manufacturers in China. For example, in the mid-1990s, the capacity utilization rate for most microwave manufacturers in China was around 40 percent, but Galanz ran its plants 24/7 in order to maximize its asset utilization.[10] While other manufacturers advertised their products on TV, Galanz opted for newspapers, where it introduced "knowledge marketing." With "knowledge marketing," companies provide consumers with information about how to use their products and include details about new models. This strategy drastically reduced Galanz's advertising and marketing costs as companies with similar sales volumes were spending almost ten times as much as Galanz on advertising.

An article in *China Daily*, a popular English-language Chinese newspaper, credits Galanz with educating many first-time consumers in China on how to use microwave ovens. "In 1995, the company [Galanz] popularized the knowledge of the use of microwave ovens nationwide. It started running special features such as 'A Guide to Microwave Oven Usage,' 'A Talk on Microwave Ovens by an Expert' and 'Recipes for Microwave Oven Dishes' in more than 150 newspapers. It spent nearly 1 million yuan ($120,481) in publishing books like 'How to Choose a Good Microwave Oven,'" the article stated.[11] These efforts not only educated the Chinese population about microwaves, but also created brand awareness for Galanz.

Galanz also developed new capabilities that other contract manufacturers focused primarily on low-wage exports did not need to develop. Where the company needed new engineers, salespeople, and marketing experts, it recruited them; where it needed new distribution channels, it developed them; where it needed new offices, factories, or showrooms, it built them. In order to serve the Chinese market, Galanz had to create many *local jobs*. Just two years after Galanz began production, the company had a national sales network of almost five thousand stores.[12]

Today, Galanz has the world's largest microwave research and development center. In addition, the company actively seeks partnerships with research institutions and R&D centers in several countries, including the United States, Japan, and South Korea. Galanz now has distribution centers in nearly two hundred countries and regions around the world. If Galanz had focused exclusively on exporting low-cost microwave ovens, it would not have had to make many of these investments.[13]

With Galanz, we can begin to see the development impact of targeting nonconsumption. For instance, in 1993, Galanz had twenty employees; by 2003, it had grown to more than ten thousand. From a production standpoint, Galanz was producing approximately four hundred units per day on a single line in 1993; by 2003, Galanz was running twenty-four lines, producing fifty thousand units a day. About a decade later, Galanz was producing approximately one hundred thousand microwave ovens a day.

Galanz had been so successful that the company posted over $4.5 billion in revenues and employed more than forty thousand people in 2013. The company now enjoys greater than 40 percent market share in the global microwave market, and its founder, Liang Zhaoxian, is sitting comfortably on *Forbes*'s list of the world's richest people, worth a whopping $1.01 billion. Zhaoxian's wealth and Galanz's success, however, were built on a foundation of market-creating innovations, in China, for China. After successfully targeting nonconsumption in China, Galanz was well positioned to go after global markets.

Nonconsumption Everywhere

Armed with the understanding that there is vast opportunity in creating businesses that target nonconsumption, it is possible to develop market-creating innovations in the same way these entrepreneurs below have done. As a consequence, many of the innovators who build companies that address the struggles of millions in our world will begin to transform their local economies in the process.

"Seeing" What Cannot Be Seen

Conventional wisdom suggests that we look for growth and prosperity in the consumption economy. That is certainly where a majority

Organization/Innovation	Nonconsumption and Impact
Safaricom/M-PESA—a mobile money platform that enables the storage, transfer, and saving of money without owning a bank account	**Nonconsumption:** More than 85 percent of Kenyans did not have access to banking services before M-PESA. It took the Kenyan banking system more than one hundred years to build roughly 1,200 bank branches in the country. **Impact:** More than twenty-two million Kenyans have pulled M-PESA into their lives since its release in 2007. The service currently transacts upward of $4.5 billion monthly. More than forty thousand M-PESA agents now exist across Kenya, increasing their incomes as a result. Millions of Kenyans can now access other financial services products, such as loans and insurance. These products were historically unavailable to them.
Tolaram/Indomie noodles—a tasty, inexpensive, and easy-to-cook meal that can be prepared in less than three minutes	**Nonconsumption:** With tens of millions of Nigerians living on less than $2 a day, the ability to afford three meals a day is difficult for many in the country. **Impact:** Tolaram now sells more than 4.5 billion packets of noodles in Nigeria annually. The company runs thirteen manufacturing plants, has enabled tens of thousands of jobs, has invested over $350 million in Nigeria, and contributes tens of millions of dollars to the Nigerian economy annually. Before the company began selling noodles in Nigeria, few Nigerians had heard of the food.
Celtel/mobile telephony—a pay-as-you-go mobile phone service that enables customers to purchase cell phone minutes for as little as 25 cents	**Nonconsumption:** In 2000, of the eight hundred million people who lived in Africa, approximately 2.5 percent, fewer than twenty million, had mobile phones. The Democratic Republic of Congo, for instance, with a population of more than fifty-five million people, had only three thousand phones. There were fewer than one million telephone lines for Nigeria's 126 million people. **Impact:** The telecommunications market in Africa today adds more than $150 billion to the African economy annually. By 2020, the industry is forecast to support 4.5 million jobs, provide $20.5 billion in taxes, and add more than $214 billion of value to African economies.[14] The proliferation of mobile telephony has also enabled other technologies, such as M-PESA's mobile money platform and MicroEnsure's insurance services. It is now being leveraged as an education platform and used to provide mobile health services as well.

Organization/Innovation	Nonconsumption and Impact
Galanz/microwave ovens—an inexpensive microwave oven (~$45) for the average Chinese citizen	**Nonconsumption:** In the early 1990s, there were fewer than one million microwave ovens in China. China's population then was over 1.1 billion people. **Impact:** From fewer than one million microwaves in the early 1990s in China, today more than thirteen million microwave ovens are sold domestically in China. Galanz has a 43 percent market share of the microwave oven market. The company employs more than forty thousand people and has now ventured into air conditioners, refrigerators, washing machines, dishwashers, and several other household appliances. As a result of the proliferation of microwave ovens in China, the frozen foods industry has also boomed. Some estimates suggest it has reached more than $10 billion. Think about all the jobs, productivity, income, regulations, and development that supports.
Fyodor Biotechnologies/urine malaria test (UMT)—a nonblood malaria test that costs less than $2 and gives results in less than twenty minutes	**Nonconsumption:** More than two hundred million people annually contract malaria globally. In the regions still susceptible to malaria, whenever most people get a fever, they immediately assume it is malaria and take malaria medications. In order to properly diagnose the disease, sick patients must visit a doctor for a blood test, something many cannot afford. Annually, over five hundred million laboratory blood tests are performed globally. **Impact:** The Fyodor UMT solves this problem by providing a simple noninvasive way to diagnose malaria so that people don't falsely medicate fevers that don't end up being malaria. Even though Fyodor is new and recently released the UMT, the company is already ramping up the production and distribution of this test so it can reach millions of people for whom a simple malaria test is not possible.
Ford Motor Company/Ford Model T—an affordable car for the average American	**Nonconsumption:** In 1900, there were only eight thousand cars registered in the United States. Typical cars back then were very difficult to drive and only wealthy Americans could afford them. **Impact:** From 1909 to 1924, Ford sold more than ten million cars, fundamentally changing the landscape of America. He created tens of thousands of jobs, paid better wages than the competition, and initiated some social programs for employees. The Model T also spurred other industries, such as insurance, distribution, and home and road construction, as people were able to move out to suburbs. It was a game changer.

Organization/Innovation	Nonconsumption and Impact
EarthEnable/earthen floors—affordable hardened floors that are one-fifth the cost of cement	**Nonconsumption:** More than 80 percent of homes in Rwanda have dirt floors. These floors are breeding grounds for mosquitoes and many other parasites. Concrete floors would be a solution, but they are just too expensive for most Rwandans, where the GDP per capita is just $703. **Impact:** Although just a few years old, Earth-Enable has already provided more than half a million square feet of flooring in over three hundred villages in Rwanda.
Clinicas del Azúcar/diabetes treatment—affordable and convenient diabetes treatment in Mexico	**Nonconsumption:** Today, diabetes is the number one cause of death and amputations in Mexico, claiming the lives of more than eighty thousand people annually. Since 1990, the number of Mexicans with diabetes has more than tripled from 5.6 million to more than 16 million. But the $1,000-a-year treatment is too expensive for most Mexicans, and the health-care delivery system is also very inconvenient. **Impact:** Clinicas del Azúcar has reduced the cost of diabetes treatment from $1,000 to roughly $250 a year. Their integrated solution has also resulted in a 60 percent reduction in diabetes-related complications, such as blindness, amputations, and kidney failure. 95 percent of the more than fifty thousand patients they have treated had never received specialized diabetes care. They are opening two new clinics every three months.
Grupo Bimbo/bread—affordable, quality bread	**Nonconsumption:** Quality affordable bread was hard to find in Mexico before Grupo Bimbo, the world's largest bakery, decided to create a new market for different breads that targeted the average Mexican. **Impact:** Today, Grupo Bimbo grosses more than $14 billion annually, operates 165 plants in 22 countries, and employs more than 128,000 people globally. With a market capitalization of over $11 billion, Bimbo also owns more than one hundred brands and sells its products in Ecuador, Colombia, and Peru, as well as in the United States, the United Kingdom, and China. The company pays its lowest-paid employee more than double the minimum wage in Mexico.

Organization/Innovation	Nonconsumption and Impact
Opticas Ver De Verdad/prescription lenses—affordable prescription lenses and eye-care services for the average Mexican	**Nonconsumption:** Approximately 43 percent of Mexicans have a visual deficiency for which they need corrective eyeglasses. Existing solutions, which on average cost $75, are too expensive. So many Mexicans go without glasses, effectively living without good sight. **Impact:** Since opening its first store in December 2011, Ver De Verdad has performed more than 240,000 eye tests and has sold over 150,000 pairs of glasses. With an average sale price of approximately $17 per frame, the company is making bad eyesight a thing of the past in Mexico. It plans to operate over 330 stores across the country by 2020.
MicroEnsure/insurance—affordable insurance for millions of people living on less than $3 a day	**Nonconsumption:** Insurance is grossly underconsumed by many in low-income countries. North America, Western Europe, Japan, and China (fewer than 34 percent of global population) are responsible for more than 81 percent of premiums. The Middle East and Africa, for instance, are responsible for just 1.6 percent, while Asia (excluding China and Japan) is responsible for 11 percent. There were practically no insurance products in their current form designed for those in low-income countries. **Impact:** MicroEnsure is a misnomer; it is a misleading name for a company whose innovation, in just over a decade of operation, has insured more than fifty million nonconsumers of insurance in Bangladesh, Ghana, Kenya, India, Nigeria, and several other countries. More than 85 percent of its customers had never purchased an insurance product until MicroEnsure came to the scene.

of capital spends its time, chasing new and exciting growth opportunities. Understandably, these opportunities are easier to assess with the market research tools companies have come to rely on. But focusing on nonconsumption provides what we believe to be the best opportunity to ignite new growth engines for companies. In turn, these new growth engines help communities provide jobs and income, both of which ultimately help people make progress in their lives.

As counterintuitive as it may seem, it is possible to develop market-creating innovations amid the nonconsumption that exists in many poor countries. It is often through the arduous work of innovators who can see the opportunities in nonconsumption, spot a struggle, and conceive of a future that is different from the past that the seeds of prosperity get planted.

That's exactly what Leftley and his team continue to do at Micro-Ensure. After spending time in some poor neighborhoods in Dhaka, Bangladesh's capital city, Leftley saw the opportunity for another product that might seem inconceivable to others: very basic hospitalization insurance. Any customer who signs up—for free—for this insurance gets $50 if they spend two or more nights in a hospital. No matter their age or underlying health condition, a $50 payment will be made to a mobile phone number as soon as the claim is filed. No questions asked.

The idea for the product came after a heartbreaking conversation Leftley had with a mother who had lost her child to illness. She had brought her sick child to the local hospital, but without money to pay for private medical care, her child just waited, for two days, without seeing a single medical professional. When she realized that her child was not going to be seen at that hospital, she turned up at the private clinic down the road to see if they would treat her child. Yes, they would, if the woman would pay them $5—half up front. Desperate, the woman raced home, leaving her child alone in the hospital, so she could sell all her possessions to raise the money. When she returned to the hospital the next day, her child had died.

"She was inconsolable. Broken. And I felt it, too," Leftley recalls. "I came away from that conversation with my team saying we have to fix this. We have to come up with a product that addresses this market failure." Her struggle was beyond description, but not beyond repair.

According to Leftley, 24 percent of people who enter a hospital in India, for any reason, leave the hospital below the poverty line, the toll of both lost wages and hospital bills. Through trial and error—the initial product offering was too clunky and relied on hospitals to submit paperwork and claims—MicroEnsure got to the simple product it has now. It didn't need to be cash in advance of hospitalization—MicroEnsure learned that even patients required to find cash up front, as this woman was, could borrow and raise enough money knowing they could repay any loans within a couple of days. "To end up with a product that really works, you have no idea what that does to you," Leftley says now. He's wished many, many times that he could tell the woman how meeting her changed the fate of many other people in her heartbreaking situation. "I've spent years trying to find that family again and tell that mother that her experience caused us to come up with a product that millions of people have and has saved so many lives. I'd love to have a chance to do that."

———

We do not have all the answers to the struggles in our world. But we do know that one rarely finds what one is not looking for. We are hopeful that with the lenses of searching for nonconsumption opportunities through the struggle people encounter on a daily basis, and by creating better solutions for the Job to Be Done, we can begin to chip away at them. And, in turn, begin to create the markets that will help struggling communities march toward prosperity.

NOTES

1. In his seminal work, *The Fortune at the Bottom of the Pyramid: Eradicating Poverty through Profits*, the late business school professor C. K. Prahalad explains the vast potential in developing products and services for those at the bottom of the pyramid (BoP). The BoP represents some of the poorest people in our world, most of whom earn less than $2 a day. Professor Prahalad helped us understand that serving the poor can be profitable for many companies that often overlook them as consumers. Although many who are poor are often nonconsumers of existing products and services on the market due to cost, the cost of a product represents just one constraint to nonconsumption. Since nonconsumption is characterized by struggle and not income bracket, this highlights a couple of things. First, the income bracket of a person can be a proxy for struggle, but they are not the same thing. Second, focusing on nonconsumption characterized by struggle allows you to develop solutions that are useful for high-income, low-income, and middle-income people who struggle with the same problem. This subtle difference in developing innovations exclusively for the poor and developing innovations to target nonconsumers is important to consider.

C. K. Prahalad, *The Fortune at the Base of the Pyramid: Eradicating Poverty through Profits* (Upper Saddle River, NJ: Prentice Hall, 2006).

2. From the World Bank's website on methodologies for calculating growth: "Growth rates are calculated as annual averages and represented as percentages. Except where noted, growth rates of values are computed from constant price series. Three principal methods are used to calculate growth rates: least squares, exponential endpoint, and geometric endpoint. Rates of change from one period to the next are calculated as proportional changes from the earlier period." It is clear that these future calculations are dependent on past economic data, which is primarily based on demographics of a region. For example, one of the methods, "least-squares growth rate," is used when there is a "sufficiently [historical] long-time series" in order to ensure accuracy. But since the nonconsumption economy is hard to see, it is difficult to include it in these calculations.

"Data Compilation Methodology," Data, The World Bank, accessed February 19, 2018, https://datahelpdesk.worldbank.org/knowledgebase/articles/906531-methodologies.

3.   We do not imply here that there are exactly two distinct parts of an economy and once you belong in one, the consumption economy, for instance, you belong to every consumption economy that exists within that economy. For example, if we decided to categorize based on income, we could say that individuals who made over $75,000 in the United States were part of the consumption economy. However, within that, there are likely people for whom certain products on the market are still too expensive, even though they would benefit from owning the products. As a result, this model is helpful from the innovator's perspective because it helps her understand why potential consumers— nonconsumers—are not purchasing her product.

4.   "FDI Flows," Data, OECD, accessed February 19, 2018, https://data .oecd.org/fdi/fdi-flows.htm.

5.   "Cutting the Cord," *The Economist*, October 7, 1999, http://www .economist.com/node/246152.

6.   "Number of mobile phone subscriptions worldwide from 1993 to 2017 (in millions)," Statista, accessed February 19, 2018, https://www .statista.com/statistics/262950/global-mobile-subscriptions-since-1993/.

7.   Scott D. Anthony, Mark W. Johnson, Joseph V. Sinfied, and Elizabeth J. Altman, *The Innovator's Guide to Growth: Putting Disruptive Innovation to Work* (Boston: Harvard Business Press, 2008), 45–60.

8.   In our book *Competing Against Luck: The Story of Innovation and Customer Choice*, my coauthors, my longtime collaborator, Bob Moesta, and I provide a more detailed overview of the Theory of Jobs to Be Done.
    Clayton Christensen, Taddy Hall, Karen Dillon, and David Duncan, *Competing Against Luck: The Story of Innovation and Customer Choice* (New York: HarperCollins, 2016).

9.   Daniel Kahneman and Amos Tversky, "Prospect Theory: An Analysis of Decision under Risk," *Econometrica* 47, no. 2 (March 1979): 263–92.

10. Galanz served as a contract manufacturer for several microwave companies. As part of the contract manufacturing agreements, Galanz was able to run the manufacturing lines for its own purposes after it had delivered on its contract obligations. On the one hand, this gave Galanz a low-cost entry into the microwave business. The company did not have to invest in much manufacturing technology. But this was not enough to sell to the average Chinese customer. Galanz also had to develop the local sales, distribution, and support in order to successfully target nonconsumption in China.

11. De Xian, "Innovative firm leads in microwave market," *China Daily News*, December 19, 1996, http://www.chinadaily.com.cn/epaper/html /cd/1996/199612/19961219/19961219010_1.html.

12. As detailed in a Samsung Economic Research Institute study conducted by the Beijing office, Galanz did many other things to ensure its product was affordable for the average Chinese. For example, when the average company spent roughly $800 million to $1 billion developing a magnetron, the main component in a microwave oven, Galanz spent around $400 million. The company also focused on efficient management practices that reduced its costs of operation by 5–10 percent when compared with competitors. In addition, Galanz's purchase practices, where it purchased supplies in bulk and paid immediately, helped reduce its costs of parts and supplies. Altogether, Galanz focused on making its operations cost effective because it was targeting nonconsumption in China.
"Microwave Oven Maker Needs Reheating: Galanz's Low Pricing Stalls," Samsung Economic Research Institute (Beijing Office), February 29, 2008.

13. "About Galanz: Profile," Galanz, accessed April 6, 2018, http://www .galanz.com/about/about_detail.html.

14. "Number of unique mobile subscribers in Africa surpasses half a billion, finds new GSM study," GSMA, accessed February 1, 2018, https:// www.gsma.com/newsroom/press-release/number-of-unique-mobile -subscribers-in-africa-surpasses-half-a-billion-finds-new-gsma-study/.

Chapter 4

Pull Versus Push

A Tale of Two Strategies

I run a food company, but I know more about electricity generation than food.

—DEEPAK SINGHAL, CEO TOLARAM AFRICA

The Idea in Brief

Every year we spend billions of dollars in an attempt to help low- and middle-income countries develop. These funds are primarily used to *push* resources into poor countries in order to help them begin their march toward prosperity. But even after pushing trillions of dollars' worth of resources over the past seventy years, too many countries are still poor, with some even poorer today. Why is development so hard to attain and then sustain?

We believe that many of these attempts are missing a critical component for development: *innovation*. Development and prosperity take root when we develop innovations that *pull in* necessary resources a society requires. Once a new innovation that is profitable to the stakeholders in the economy (including investors, entrepreneurs, customers, and the government) is introduced, the stakeholders are often incentivized to help maintain the resources the innovation has *pulled in*—such as infrastructures, education, and even policies. Pull strategies ensure a ready market is waiting. This, we believe, is essential for long-term and sustainable prosperity.

One of the most popular movies in India in 2017 was not a high-budget Hollywood blockbuster or a shiny Bollywood extravaganza. It was a film called *Toilet: A Love Story*, which chronicled the trials and tribulations of a young bride who is devastated to learn that her new groom's family does not have a toilet. The village divides into those who understand her perspective and those who don't, and much chaos and laughter ensue. Eventually, the husband builds his beloved a toilet and they live happily ever after.

Toilet: A Love Story may sound like an unlikely sleeper hit, but the plot clearly hit a nerve for its intended audience in India, where more than half of households don't have access to a toilet. In reality, the lack of toilets is no laughing matter. One in ten deaths in India can be attributed to poor sanitation, according to the World Bank. Children pick up chronic infections from contaminated groundwater, and diarrhea is the leading killer of Indian children, causing more than three hundred thousand deaths annually. Millions more are impaired by stunted growth as a result of contaminated water. Many people wait until dark to use public spaces for defecation—a circumstance that has created its own set of problems, including reports of rape and violence against women. The quest for better sanitation is profoundly important for the country, so much so that Mahatma Gandhi once declared sanitation to be sacred and "more important than political freedom."

The solution, of course, seems obvious. Build more toilets. So obvious, agrees India's current prime minister, Narendra Modi, that he has declared building toilets a priority over temples as part of his "Clean India" mission. To that end, the Indian government built more than ten million toilets in 2014 and 2015—with plans to add an additional *sixty million* toilets by 2019. How can this not be a good thing in the context of India's serious sanitation problem?[1]

Well, it turns out that *building* toilets is not enough. By mid-2015, the government found that a majority of the toilets were not being used. "Even as we accelerate toilet construction now, much more needs to be done to persuade people to use them," noted Chaudhary Birender Singh, India's minister for rural development, sanitation, and drinking water. "Persuading" has taken a number of forms. In some rural parts of India, teams of government employees and volunteer "motivators" roam villages publicly shaming people who opt to relieve themselves out in the open rather than use a newly installed public or private toilet. In some villages, little children have been taught to chase people who appear to be headed for a field to relieve themselves and blow whistles at them. The government itself has resorted to financial incentives to help motivate villages to support the use of toilets. "For long, we assumed that if the toilets are built, people will automatically use it," Singh observed. "But we have to diligently monitor the use over a period of time and reward them with cash incentives to the village councils at every stage. Only then will it become a daily habit."[2]

"Motivators" and children with whistles following, goading, and shaming people? A *cash incentive* to use a free toilet? Something is wrong here. No matter how well intended the efforts, "pushing" a solution like this without understanding the underlying causes of why people make particular decisions can lead to such painful distortions. In some of the rural villages where people have been shamed into compliance, drought conditions actually make it virtually impossible to keep toilets clean—the scarce water is essential for drinking and bathing. It would be a luxury to use it to clean a toilet. In other locations, toilets have been so hastily installed that they are not actually connected to anything—quickly becoming so fly-ridden and smelly that no one will use them.

After years of working with and studying many communities that struggle with this problem, Kamal Kar, a development consultant, pioneered the Community-Led Total Sanitation (CLTS) approach. On the CLTS website, they note, "Merely providing toilets does not guarantee their use, nor result in improved sanitation and hygiene. Earlier approaches to sanitation prescribed high initial standards and offered subsidies as an incentive. But this often led to uneven adoption, problems with long-term sustainability and only partial use. It also created a culture of dependence on subsidies." The CLTS approach does not believe the solution to a sanitation problem is simply the provision of the hardware.[3] And neither do we. But this is easier said than done. Here's why.

Poverty is painful, and almost always shows itself as a lack of resources, such as food, sanitation, safe water, education, health care, and public services in poor communities. As such, it is reasonable to assume that poverty is primarily a resource problem. Based on that assumption, over the past several decades, we have been executing an expensive *push strategy* of development that is almost exclusively resource-based. With good intentions, we push the resources that wealthy communities have, and that poor communities lack, in order to solve a problem. But as the efforts to push toilets into India at a rapid pace shows, push strategies don't always take root. They often are temporarily successful at best. A school, a hospital, a road, an airport, and even a toilet are all good investments, but when made in the wrong sequence, they can unintentionally cause more harm than good. Cambridge University economist Ha-Joon Chang explores this phenomenon with regards to building rich-country-style institutions in poor countries, in his book *Kicking Away the Ladder*.[4]

To be clear, there can be real value in providing resources for those who lack. But in many circumstances, the expense outweighs the value we get when they are merely pushed into a region. Another way to think of it is like this: push strategies treat poverty as a chronic disease that must be managed, and for which there seems to be no cure. But this is a very expensive approach; in the United States alone, more than 80 percent of the nation's $2.7 trillion health-care expenditures is spent on treating chronic diseases.[5] The diseases are treated but not cured. And for some, this may mean lifelong suffering. It is hard to believe that there isn't a better way. With poverty, it's possible we are doing the same thing— treating the pain by pushing a lot of resources, but not curing the disease, because treating the pain seems like the most obvious approach to making the patient better. But our current approach might be blinding us to what's possible.

Push Versus Pull

Push strategies are often driven by the priorities of their originators, typically experts in a particular field of development, and generate solutions that are recommended to low-income countries. It is important to note that many of these resources being pushed are good things and are often welcome by people in poor countries. Unfortunately, however, they are often pushed into a context that isn't quite ready to absorb them. And that can turn what started out as a good thing into something profoundly disappointing, very quickly.

Consider, for example, the fierce competition that occurs every few years to host the FIFA World Cup, one of the most prestigious sporting events in the world. National federations around the globe launch ambitious campaigns to convince their local citizens that spending millions, and even billions, to prepare the region to host the World Cup would be hugely beneficial. There is always a flashy media event in which the winning host is announced, to the jubilant cheers of local crowds. Flooding their local region with new resources and infrastructure as they prepare for such a vaunted international event will surely attract a huge influx of foreign visitors and money, create lots of jobs, and ultimately benefit the city's economic development, the thinking goes.

But in reality, those original promises almost never bear out.

South Africa, for example, did a wonderful job hosting the 2010 World Cup—defying critics' expectations that the country would fail to finish the needed infrastructure and security improvements. But even so, the country ended up recovering only 10 percent of the $3.12 billion it invested on transportation, telecommunication, and stadiums.[6] In the years after the World Cup, the visible reminders of that spending—perhaps most notably a purpose-built stadium near Cape Town—have come to symbolize "the worst of FIFA's legacy in South Africa," according to the *New York Times*. "It is a superfluous megastructure unwanted by the wealthier, mostly white residents nearby, and it is far away from the areas where soccer fans, who are mostly black and colored, live. The stadium has also become a strain on the public purse, costing the city at least $32 million since 2010. These funds could be better spent on the city's more urgent priorities, such as providing sanitation and houses for the poor. The lack of such services continues to be the spark that periodically ignites protests." The spending on the World Cup did not move the needle—at least not enough—in South Africa. Nearly a decade later, South Africa still tops the World Bank's list of countries with the most income inequality, with more than half the country still living below the national poverty line.

By contrast, what we will call ***pull* strategies** are different from *push* strategies in almost every way. Consider the case of education, for example, and more specifically our investment in human capital, which is often far more successful at taking root when it is pulled into a society as a response to demand. This demand is brought about by an economy that can absorb the knowledge and skills being taught to students.

I became acutely aware of this after I began serving on the board of Tata Consultancy Services (TCS), one of the world's largest IT companies. With almost four hundred thousand employees, TCS is one of the largest private-sector employers in India. Over the past several years, in order to meet the demands of many of its clients, who are asking for more and more digital services including data analytics, mobility, cloud computing, and Internet of things, TCS has pulled "digital education" into its business model. The company has trained two hundred thousand employees on more than six hundred thousand competencies in digital technologies, and it doesn't seem to be slowing down. When TCS trains employees—new hires or existing hires—it is usually based on market demand or project specifications. This way, the education is relevant almost immediately. The employee understands why she is learning, and the company understands why it is investing.[7]

Our research suggests that pull strategies, over time, are far more effective at triggering sustainable prosperity.

First, they are often originated by innovators on the ground who are responding to the struggles of everyday consumers or specific market demands. Second, pull strategies have more of an investigative or inquisitorial approach to problem-solving as opposed to a more advocacy or assertive approach. The innovators are there to learn and then solve problems in a sustainable manner, as opposed to pushing, however well intentioned, what they believe to be the right answers to particular development puzzles. Every quarter, for instance, TCS takes stock of the skills it needs to pull into the organization and invests accordingly.

Third, pull strategies focus on creating, or responding to the needs of, a market first. It is then the job of the market to pull in the resources it needs to survive. In essence, pull strategies emerge from a burning need to make something work—they almost *will* a solution into existence, however imperfect at first, because it is a critical part of creating or sustaining a market. Market-creating demands breathe life into a pulled-in solution, allowing them to take root. Consider, for example, the extraordinary impact one noodle company has had on Nigeria's economy.

4.5 Billion Packs of Noodles and Counting

Perhaps the most beloved consumer product in Nigeria is also one of the humblest: Indomie instant noodles. Sold in single-serving packets for the equivalent of less than 20 US cents, the brand enjoys near-universal name recognition in the country, maintains a 150,000-member fan club with branches in more than three thousand primary schools, and sponsors Independence Day Awards for

Heroes of Nigeria to celebrate the accomplishments of exemplary Nigerian children.

You may not have heard of it, but Indomie is a household brand name in Nigeria.

In 2016, I was honored to speak at the annual conference of Harvard Business School's Africa Business Club. With approximately 1,500 attendees, it is the largest student-run conference on business in Africa in the world. In my talk, I referenced Tolaram, a fascinating company we had been studying, only to receive blank stares in the auditorium.[8] But when I said, "These are the guys that make Indomie noodles," the crowd went wild. Why would noodles cause a crowd to erupt in raucous cheers? And more important, what in the world does that have to do with development and prosperity?

What Tolaram, through Indomie noodles, has done in Nigeria is astonishing. Since its entry into Nigeria in 1988—when Nigeria was still under military rule—Tolaram has invested more than $350 million to create tens of thousands of jobs, developed a logistics company, and built infrastructure including electricity and sewage and water treatment facilities. In addition, Tolaram has built educational institutions, funded community organization programs, and provided millions of dollars in tax revenues. Perhaps the most visible evidence of this strategy is that the company has taken a lead role in developing a $1.5 billion public-private partnership to build and operate the new Lekki deep-water port in the state of Lagos, Nigeria's commercial capital. Without overstating it at all, Indomie noodles *is* development.

Tolaram has shown that out of very little, a market can be created—and with the birth of a market come the attendant benefits that can lead to development.

Indomie noodles are so woven into Nigerian society that it might even surprise Nigerians to recall that noodles are not among their traditional foods. Tolaram has only been selling the product in the country for about thirty years. The company's growth track turns the conventional wisdom about development on its head.

In 1988, the year Tolaram began selling Indomie noodles in Nigeria, the country was far from an investment magnet: Nigeria was under military rule; life expectancy for its ninety-one million people was forty-six years; annual per capita income was barely $257 (approximately $535 today); less than 1 percent of the population owned a phone; only about half had access to safe water; just 37 percent had access to proper sanitation; a staggering 78 percent lived on less than $2 a day. But even in these dismal circumstances, brothers Haresh and Sajen Aswani saw a huge opportunity to feed a nation with an affordable and convenient product. For them, this represented an enormous market-creating opportunity.

Indomie noodles can be cooked in less than three minutes and, when combined with an egg, can be a nutritious, low-cost meal. But in 1988, the vast majority of Nigerians had never eaten or even seen noodles. "Many people initially thought we were selling them worms," recalls Deepak Singhal, currently the CEO of Tolaram Africa. The Aswani brothers were convinced, however, that they could create a market in Nigeria because of the country's growing and urbanizing population, and the convenience their product offered. Instead of focusing on Nigeria's unfavorable demographics, they focused on developing a business model that would enable them to *create* a noodle market.

The decision to target the needs of average Nigerians who were very poor compelled Tolaram to make long-term investments in the country. In 1995, the company made the decision to shift noodle manufacture to Nigeria to better control its costs. In order to do so, Tolaram had to pull infrastructure such as electricity, waste management, and water treatment into its operations. "I run a food company, but I know more about electricity generation than food," Singhal says now.

Tolaram, just like TCS, also got into the "education" business, through company-sponsored training in electrical and mechanical engineering, finance, and disciplines relevant to the business.

Tolaram had to make these specific investments because the underlying infrastructure in Nigeria was either nonexistent or subpar. So Tolaram "pulled" them in instead.

And that, in turn, created more opportunity for prosperity to begin flourishing. Consider, for example, what happens when Tolaram pulls a recent graduate from a local university into its operations and provides employment and training for the new employee. First, the company increases the productivity of its own operations and, by extension, that of the region. Second, it reduces unemployment and, as a result, indirectly reduces crime, since people with jobs are less likely to engage in criminal activities to try to meet their basic needs.[9] Third, it contributes additional income taxes and consumer spending. All of these things might have been core regional development objectives, but for the executives at Tolaram, they were just the natural result of operating their growing business.

36 Percent Growth, 17 Years in a Row

Like many other emerging and frontier markets, Nigeria has virtually no thriving "formal" supermarket sector, and the path from factory to consumer contains many potential points of failure—or "leakage" (the process in which products are stolen or disappear before the point of sale). So Tolaram's managers chose to invest in a supermarket supply chain. This was by no means trivial, as the supermarket supply chain investment required Tolaram to build an entire distribution and logistics business. This meant the company built distribution warehouses and storefronts, purchased hundreds of trucks for its fleet, and hired thousands of drivers who would drive into neighborhoods selling cartons of Indomie noodles to retailers in both independently owned and Tolaram-owned stores.

Tolaram's investments in distribution may have seemed like overkill, but Tolaram's executives knew they would never succeed if they couldn't get the product into customers' hands. In many poor coun-

tries, companies might spend an inordinate amount of time thinking about how to make their products affordable, but may spend little
time thinking about making their products available. This is, in part,
because these companies don't see distribution as a core part of their
business model. But at this stage of development in poor countries,
it must be; in fact, investing in *both* affordability and availability is
paramount to the success of a market-creating business.

It is through this process of making one's product available, affordable, and therefore accessible that innovators create the right
solutions for new markets. A market-creating innovation, then, isn't
simply a product or a service—it is the entire solution: the product
or service coupled with a business model that is profitable to the
firm. In creating this solution, organizations do what is necessary,
including building infrastructures, factories, distribution, logistics, sales, and other components of their business model. These,
in turn, begin to lay down a foundation of a region's infrastructure.
This is what Tolaram did, and continues to do, in Nigeria.

The company now controls 92 percent of the supplies essential
to manufacture Indomie noodles and operates thirteen manufacturing plants in Nigeria. This is no different from what the Ford
Motor Company, Celtel, or Galanz did when the circumstance
called for it.

It has been a tough journey, but that's to be expected because development, by its very nature, is hard. Tolaram's investments, however, are paying off handsomely by any measure—and Nigeria is
reaping significant developmental gains. Today the company sells
more than 4.5 billion packs of noodles in Nigeria annually, making Nigerians the eleventh-largest consumers of instant noodles in
the world, a product they barely knew existed thirty years ago. Tolaram directly employs more than 8,500 people, has created a value
chain with one thousand exclusive distributors and six hundred
thousand retailers, and has revenue of almost $1 billion a year, all
the while contributing tens of millions of dollars in taxes to the Nigerian government. Tolaram also created a logistics company that

owns and operates more than one thousand vehicles. The logistics company now serves both Tolaram and other Nigerian companies, with 65 percent of its revenues coming from external clients. Today, it is one of the largest corporate transporters in the country.[10]

If Tolaram had taken a different and more common approach, to invest only when the circumstances were right, or when the situation on the ground improved, it would likely not have achieved its stunning 36 percent year-over-year growth—in a market it created—seventeen years in a row, a market that has attracted investments from sixteen other noodle companies and many other supplier and raw materials companies responsible for things like packaging, flour, palm oil, salt, sugar, and chili, and also distribution, advertising, sales, and retail. All these companies are now responsible for directly creating tens of thousands of other jobs in Nigeria.

In order to build a market in Nigeria, and other environments like it, Tolaram had to, and continually has to, internalize the risks that others perceive. This is one of the reasons behind the $1.5 billion public-private partnership to build and operate the new Lekki deep-water port in the state of Lagos. Once Tolaram is successful in building the port, the company will further reduce its costs and provide port services to other companies.

If Tolaram had waited for the Nigerian government to address the "infrastructure" and "institutions" challenges before investing, the company would still be waiting and would likely not be operating in Nigeria today.

Ankur Sharma, former head of corporate strategy for Tolaram Africa, summarized the company's approach to self-reliance in February 2016: "As we create a market, we do what is necessary to ensure success. In some countries we have built power plants; in others we have invested millions of dollars in transportation infrastructure just to move our products from the factory to the retail sites, in line with our theme of controlling our own destiny by driving costs down. We are committed to whatever market we enter and will do whatever it takes to be successful there."

A pack of Indomie noodles is simply a 20-cent packet of instant noodles. How can it matter so much? It matters because Indomie noodles represent the *process* by which poverty, through innovation, can become prosperity.

Tolaram's investments in Nigeria illustrate a fundamental principle that, when applied in a context of nonconsumption and poverty, has a powerful impact on development and prosperity. It illustrates the immense potential of market-creating innovations to pull many resources into an economy. In addition, it also shows that, in some circumstances, localizing an innovation is necessary for success. Although the Aswani brothers are not native Nigerians, they are Nigerian by function. In fact, Haresh Aswani has been honored with a chieftaincy title in Ogun state, one of the highest honors a community can bestow on a person, because of his commitment to the economic development of Nigeria.

Because of its investments and success in Nigeria, Tolaram has begun attracting hundreds of millions of dollars of foreign direct investment from major international companies into Nigeria. In 2015, Kellogg's, the American multinational food company, bought half of Tolaram's distribution operations in Nigeria for $450 million, and both companies commissioned a 6-billion-naira (~$17 million) cereal manufacturing plant in December 2017.

Tolaram's Impact on the Nigerian Economy (Currency Values in Nigerian Naira[11])

- Total value added to the economy—N 241 billion annually
- Staff income—N 7.6 billion annually
- Government revenue—N 4.5 billion annually
- Investment in manufacturing sector—N 70 billion
- Direct jobs created—8,570
- Total jobs created throughout the economy—42,850

- Number of manufacturing plants—13
- Number of warehouses—13
- Number of distributors—2,500
- Number of subdistributors—30,000
- Number of network and convenience stores—290
- Number of trucks and other vehicles—1,000 plus
- Number of *other* noodle companies—16

And Specifically, Look at What Tolaram Is Pulling into the Nigerian Economy

- Electricity generation
- Water and sewage treatment plant
- $1.5 billion deep-sea port
- Education—specialized technical training on finance, engineering, and marketing for employees
- Logistics—Tolaram now runs one of the largest logistics companies in Nigeria
- Foreign direct investment—Kellogg's $450 million purchase of half of Tolaram's distribution operations
- Sustainable social development projects—the Tolaram Foundation owns 25 percent of the Tolaram Group and invests in a wide range of social programs that benefit Nigerians, including providing prosthetic devices for Nigerians who have lost limbs, caring for orphans, and providing scholarships for students to attend school, to name just a few.

The Power, and the Necessity, of *Pull*

Tolaram was able to *pull* many components into the Nigerian economy that would otherwise have been impossible or, at the very least, incredibly difficult to sustain without the creation of a noodle market. The noodle market, in some ways, acts as a magnetic force that ensures educated students get employed, government revenues are generated to fund other projects, and new technologies get developed and used productively. All these things are pulled into the economy in order to grow the noodle market that Tolaram created. If we create a market that successfully serves a growing population of nonconsumers, that market is likely to pull in many other resources an economy requires. This is the simple, yet powerful, mechanism of *pull*.

The question still remains, why does Tolaram need to invest in electricity, water, education, logistics, and so on, in order to deliver a pack of noodles to the average Nigerian? Surely, it wouldn't need to do this if it were operating in, say, the United States. The answer to that question—on when and whether a company should internalize and integrate certain costs even though they don't seem core to the company's business—can be explained by one of the management theories I teach my students.

The decision on whether a company should integrate certain aspects of its business model (bring them in-house and do it by themselves) or whether it should outsource them depends on a theory we call interdependence and modularity. A company should develop an interdependent (integrated) business model when it cannot depend on suppliers for specifiable, verifiable, and predictable inputs. In some cases, this can be access to constant electricity, quality raw materials, or even well-educated employees. Inputs cover anything an organization needs to ensure it properly accomplishes the Job to Be Done for which customers "hire" its product.

In other words, if the company cannot reliably depend on a particular input from a supplier to accomplish the customer's Job to Be Done, then the company must integrate its operations—create and manage all those "inputs" itself. For example, when Tolaram began operating in Nigeria, it had partnerships with several other companies for its packaging and logistics needs. Tolaram also depended on suppliers for wheat, flour, and oil. But because supplies from these companies weren't reliable, Tolaram had to integrate these components into its business model.[12] It had to do these activities itself.

If other companies were able to provide these supplies reliably, Tolaram would have been able to more easily outsource these activities to these companies. In this case, Tolaram would not have had to integrate as many aspects of its business model and would have developed something more modular. The company would have partnered with reliable suppliers in the same way many companies in the United States partner with UPS or FedEx for their logistics and shipping needs, or with other suppliers of things like electricity, water, raw materials, and so on.

It was precisely because Tolaram could not find reliable companies that it decided to integrate many aspects of its business model. An interesting thing happened after Tolaram successfully integrated these other aspects of its business model, including logistics, packaging, electricity, and others. When other companies, many of which also needed these things, saw that Tolaram could *reliably* provide them, they began asking if Tolaram could sell those services to them. And just like that, a cost center was transformed into a profit center for Tolaram.

That is the power of pull.

Tolaram's Infrastructure Is Nigeria's Infrastructure

Market-creating innovators do what is necessary, core competency or not, in order to create a new market that serves those who have historically been unable to purchase a product. The investments these companies make are not just the company's infrastructure; they become the country's as well. But perhaps most important of all is that market-creating innovations instill in citizens a culture that *innovation* is possible, even in dire circumstances. This is crucial because it is often in the *process* of developing market-creating innovations, which are simpler, more affordable, and therefore more accessible to the broader population, that a company necessarily pulls in the many things currently pushed onto poor countries in hopes of spurring innovation, development, and growth.

Unfortunately, when these things are pushed before there is a market demanding them or willing to absorb them, the countries are seldom ready to maintain them. And so what we see with push initiatives are brand-new schools that lose their value and deliver subpar education; new roads that become difficult to maintain; and "institutions" that are copied and pasted from prosperous nations that end up hitting the undo button. As a result, nothing remains permanent, except perhaps the never-ending stream of well-meaning but unsustainable projects designed to help poor countries. But when a market pulls these resources in, they tend to stick.

A Noodle Economy?

We are under no illusions; a 20-cent pack of noodles, no matter how many are sold, cannot single-handedly develop Nigeria. But the principles behind Tolaram's success can.

Consider, for example, the sanitation problem in India through the lens of identifying a vast market-creating opportunity. That is the approach of the Toilet Board Coalition (TBC), a global consortium of companies, social investors, and sanitation experts that are attempting to catalyze market-creating solutions to the problem. In what the TBC refers to as the "sanitation economy," they've identified what they say is a $62 billion opportunity in India alone. Here are the three subsectors of the sanitation economy as identified by the TBC:

The Sanitation Economy	Description	Type of Work
Toilet economy	Product and service innovation that provides toilets suited to all environments and incomes	Household and public toilet fixtures, maintenance, repair; hygiene products
Circular sanitation economy	Toilet resources (human waste) feed into a system that replaces traditional waste management	Collection, transportation, processing of human waste, and turning it into products like organic fertilizers, protein oils, and more
Smart sanitation economy	Digitized systems that ensure operating efficiencies and maintenance, besides consumer use and health information insights	Consumer and health data collection, analysis, and distribution; sensors and data transmission

Source: The Toilet Board Coalition 2018

"This is the biggest opportunity in a century to transform sanitation systems into a smart, sustainable, and revenue-generating economy," Cheryl Hicks, executive director of the TBC, believes. Hicks notes that each year over 3.8 trillion liters of human waste are generated, which companies can use to produce treated water, renewable energy, organic fertilizers, protein products, and so on. "Innovation can really effect transformational change," Hicks says. "Just look at all the ways people are exploring creating 'product' out of the system, in the form of capturing biological resources, energy, fertilizers, plastics, protein, even data to help us understand, digitally, a community's health." For example, she says, innovation is helping create data trackers that can help identify, early on, outbreaks in a community—long before hospitals and clinics are flooded with seriously ill people. Similarly, smart technologies can help shape business and health decisions, as well as influence policy-making. Moreover, various other industries could also participate in the emerging sanitation economy. One market can be created, Hicks predicts, which will, in turn, generate other related markets. Identifying the opportunity and then innovating around a market-creating solution may just help India pull in the sanitation infrastructure it desperately needs.

Banking Without Banks, Movies Without TVs

We have observed the power with which pull strategies can serve as catalysts for long-term change. Consider how this played out in Kenya when twenty million people adopted the mobile money platform M-PESA into their lives in a very short time. Before M-PESA, the traditional banking system in Kenya served fewer than 15 percent of the population. Also in 2007, the year M-PESA was founded, Kenya had just over one thousand bank branches for its thirty-eight million people. But M-PESA, an innovation built on top of the mobile phone, was pulled into millions of Kenyan homes and today transacts more than $4.5 billion a month.[13] A traditional push approach would have meant setting up many more bank branches in Kenya, hoping it then spurred people to join the existing banking economy. But that would have likely been significantly more expensive, reached far fewer people than M-PESA, and taken longer to have any kind of impact.

Or what about Nigeria's "Nollywood" industry? You may not have known that Nigeria has a thriving movie industry, but that's probably because Nigerian movies are created to serve nonconsumption, for Africans and Africans in the diaspora. In terms of number of movies produced annually, Nollywood's 1,500 movies is second only to India's Bollywood—a surprising statistic in a country where fewer than 60 percent of people have access to electricity and only 40 percent of households have a television.[14] Nollywood has been able to thrive precisely because it targets nonconsumption. Before the advent and proliferation of Nigerian movies, most Africans consumed Hollywood- and Bollywood-produced movies. There were few movies that spoke to the lives of average Africans, taking into consideration their cultures and experiences. As such, while Western and Indian movies were interesting, they were not relatable. Nollywood changed that.

Nollywood's annual revenue of roughly $1 billion pales in comparison to Hollywood's projected $35 billion in 2019, but that doesn't mean that Nollywood isn't having a significant impact on the Nigerian economy. The industry currently employs more than one million people, second only to the agriculture industry.[15] In addition, Nollywood has been able to pull in better governance as it relates to piracy and copyright laws. Appreciating the importance of the industry as a major source of employment and potential income from the sale and export of Nigerian movies, the Nigerian Export Promotion Council, the Nigerian Copyright Commission, and the National Film and Video Censors Board are now collaborating on programs to reduce piracy in the industry.

No One Gets Fired for Building a Well

If *pulling* seems to be a more effective strategy than *pushing*, then why don't we dedicate more of our resources toward pull strategies? There are several reasons for this, one of which is that no one really gets fired for *pushing*. Think of it this way: no one gets fired for building a well in a poor community. There are few more satisfying images in poor countries than gushing fresh well water, students in fresh school uniforms seated in a shiny new classroom, or ribbon-cutting ceremonies for fabulous new roads or hospitals.

By contrast, there are also few more depressing images than broken wells, school-aged children on the streets, or abandoned infrastructure projects.

What could happen if we changed our emphasis from push to pull? What if much more of the $143 billion spent on official development assistance in 2016 was channeled to support direct market-creation efforts in poor countries, even when the circumstances seemed unlikely? Imagine how many markets could be created; imagine how many Tolarams, Nollywoods, M-PESAs, and other new-market creators could emerge; imagine how many jobs could be created.

As I think about this problem, I can't help but wonder how many fathers and mothers would be afforded the dignity of work and the resources to provide simple things for their families—like food, health care, and quality education. Imagine how many people would have a renewed sense of hope and purpose when they begin to see their suffering can become a thing of the past.

"We are the first generation in human history that can end extreme poverty," Jim Kim, president of the World Bank, often says. He may be right—but this will not happen if we continue focusing our efforts on ending poverty.[16] That's the paradox at play.

NOTES

1. Rama Lakshmi, "India is building millions of toilets, but that's the easy part," *Washington Post*, June 4, 2015, https://www.washingtonpost.com/world/asia_pacific/india-is-building-millions-of-toilets-but-toilet-training-could-be-a-bigger-task/2015/06/03/09d1aa9e-095a-11e5-a7ad-b430fc1d3f5c_story.html?utm_term=.d28251385c4e.

2. Ibid.

3. "The CLTS approach," Community-Led Total Sanitation, accessed March 15, 2018, http://www.communityledtotalsanitation.org/page/clts-approach.

4. In his book *Kicking Away the Ladder: Development Strategy in Historical Perspective*, Chang shows that many of the investments that poor countries are making in hopes of generating economic growth are being made at a different stage of development than was the case for countries that are now prosperous. They are often made too soon and as a consequence, are not yet sustainable.
   Ha-Joon Chang, *Kicking Away the Ladder: Development Strategy in Historical Perspective* (London: Anthem Press, 2007).

5. "Chronic Diseases; The Leading Causes of Death and Disability in the United States: Chronic Disease Overview," Centers for Disease Control and Prevention, accessed February 5, 2018, https://www.cdc.gov/chronicdisease/overview/index.htm.

6. Mirele Matsuoka De Aragao, "Economic Impacts of the FIFA World Cup in Developing Countries," Honors Theses, Paper 2609, April 2015, https://scholarworks.wmich.edu/cgi/viewcontent.cgi?article=3609&context=honors_theses.

7. Madhura Karnik, "TCS is quietly transforming itself to take on India's emerging tech scene," *Quartz*, July 3, 2017, https://qz.com/1000424/tcs-is-quietly-transforming-itself-to-take-on-indias-emerging-it-scene/.

8. The Tolaram Group was founded in Malang, Indonesia, in 1948. It began by trading textiles and fabrics and has since evolved into a manufacturing, real estate, infrastructure, banking, retail, and e-commerce conglomerate.

9. Gillian B. White, "Can Jobs Deter Crime?," *The Atlantic*, June 25, 2015,

https://www.theatlantic.com/business/archive/2015/06/can-jobs-deter
-crime/396758/.

10. Tolaram is also creating other new markets in Nigeria for other fast-moving consumer goods, such as bleach and vegetable oil. Before Tolaram released its Hypo bleach product, fewer than 5 percent of Nigerians used bleach to wash their clothes. Tolaram reports that over the past few years, leveraging its manufacturing and distribution prowess, it has expanded that market sixfold, reaching 30 percent of the population.

11. Many of these investments were made over the span of three decades, unless otherwise stated. The exchange rate for the Nigerian naira to the US dollar has changed drastically during this period. In 1995, for example, one US dollar exchanged for approximately 22 Nigerian naira. At the time of writing, one US dollar exchanged for about 360 Nigerian naira.

12. In their paper "The Educator's Dilemma: When and how schools should embrace poverty relief," Michael Horn and Julia Freeland Fisher provide an excellent example of how Gustavus Franklin Swift integrated his operations in order to make beef more affordable and accessible to tens of thousands of people at a time when it was not common practice to move meat across state lines in the United States. They explain, "For centuries, companies have been driven to integrate activities that were not at their core in order to reach new heights of performance and distribution. Gustavus Franklin Swift's approach to marketing and selling beef, for example, reflected his willingness to integrate beyond the late 19th-century's model of raising, butchering, and selling beef on an exclusively local basis. At that time, because there was no technology for transporting meat long distances, the beef industry lacked significant economies of scale. Swift saw an opportunity to integrate backward and forward: he centralized butchering in Kansas City, which meant he could process beef at a very low cost. Then Swift designed the world's first ice-cooled railcars. He even made and sold ice cabinets to retail shops throughout the Midwest and Northeast so that once the beef arrived, it would stay fresh. One key to Swift's ability to market beef in far flung regions was the ability to assure customers that the beef was still safe to consume, given that it had traveled all the way from the stockyards of Chicago to the market. Because a clear understanding of refrigeration and meatpacking processes did not exist at the time, Swift had to control the entire process to ensure that the temperature and storage practices remained sound. In other words, Swift had to expand beyond his so-called core competencies and introduce new, interdependent lines of business in order to revolutionize the beef industry."

Michael B. Horn and Julia Freeland Fisher, "The Educator's Dilemma:

When and how schools should embrace poverty relief," Clayton Christensen Institute for Disruptive Innovation, accessed May 1, 2018, https://www.christenseninstitute.org/wp-content/uploads/2015/06/The-Educators-Dilemma.pdf.

In *The Innovator's Solution: Creating and Sustaining Successful Growth*, my coauthor Michael Raynor and I dedicate a whole chapter (Chapter 5) to the interdependence and modularity theory.

Clayton M. Christensen and Michael E. Raynor, *The Innovator's Solution: Creating and Sustaining Successful Growth* (Boston: Harvard Business Review Press, 2003), 125–126.

13. Elvis Ondieki, "M-Pesa transactions rise to Sh15bn daily after systems upgrade," *Daily Nation*, May 8, 2016, https://www.nation.co.ke/news/MPesa-transactions-rise-to-Sh15bn-after-systems-upgrade/1056-3194774-llu8yjz/index.html.

14. "World Development Indicators: The information society," The World Bank, accessed February 20, 2018, http://wdi.worldbank.org/table/5.12.

15. Rebecca Moudio, "Nigeria's film industry, a potential gold mine?," *U.N. AfricaRenewal Online*, May 2013, http://www.un.org/africarenewal/magazine/may-2013/nigeria%E2%80%99s-film-industry-potential-gold-mine.

16. Efosa Ojomo, "Obsession with ending poverty is where development is going wrong," *Guardian*, February 8, 2017, https://www.theguardian.com/global-development-professionals-network/2017/feb/08/obsession-with-ending-poverty-is-where-development-is-going-wrong.

How Innovation Created Prosperity for Many

Chapter 5

America's Innovation Story

The century of revolution in the United States after the Civil War was economic, not political, freeing households from an unremitting daily grind of painful manual labor, household drudgery, darkness, isolation, and early death. Only one hundred years later, daily life had changed beyond recognition.[1]

—ROBERT GORDON, *THE RISE AND FALL OF AMERICAN GROWTH: THE U.S. STANDARD OF LIVING SINCE THE CIVIL WAR*

The Idea in Brief

Imagine a country where average life expectancy is just forty-five years, infant mortality a staggering two hundred deaths per one thousand births, and fewer than 5 percent of people have access to indoor plumbing. In this country, the average person spends approximately 52 percent of their hard-earned income on food. There's little help from the government, and corruption is rife at all levels— from local to federal; cronyism, not merit, determines most civil service jobs. What impoverished country would you guess this is?

It's the United States of America, in the nineteenth century. Though we usually don't think of it this way, America was once desperately poor—poorer than some of today's most underdeveloped economies. Considering where it once was, America's transformation into an economic powerhouse is extraordinary. But as we will explore, at the heart of America's transformation story is the same force that has driven many economies around the world from poverty to prosperity: market-creating innovations.

In spite of being impoverished, unregulated, and poorly infra-structured, America became fertile territory for scores of inno-vators and entrepreneurs seeing opportunity where others saw nothing. In this chapter, we profile the innovators behind several of the most spectacular market-creating innovations in Ameri-can history—Isaac Merritt Singer, George Eastman, Henry Ford, and Amadeo Giannini. Of course these innovators did not single-handedly develop America—the country has benefited from the innovation of scores and scores of entrepreneurs whose work im-proved our lives. But collectively they demonstrate the transforma-tive power of a culture of innovation that allows prosperity to take root and flourish.

––––––

We have an old-fashioned Singer sewing machine in our base-ment. One of my neighbors left it out for trash and I couldn't help rescuing it. It's rusted and worn, but it's still a beautiful piece of equipment. The pedals alone are works of art. I made it a personal passion project to refinish and restore it to its former glory.

When I look at that sewing machine, I see more than just quality craftsmanship. I'm reminded of what it stands for. Isaac Merritt Singer may not be the most famous American innovator—he's not even credited with actually inventing the sewing machine—but Singer's impact on American culture cannot be overstated.

We may forget now, but in Singer's time, America was not a pros-perous country. Not only were most Americans poor, but many, especially in urban centers, lived in squalor.[2] In the tenements of many large cities, sewage spewed out onto alleyways, garbage was dumped outside apartments and left to rot, and horse manure lined the streets. The typical North Carolinian woman walked 148 miles and carried more than 36 tons of water in a year, just fetching the daily water for her family.[3] We may all lament our current fears of increasing crime rates in some American cities, but for many of us, our grandparents were not only much poorer than we are today, but also less safe. The murder rate in 1900 was far worse than it is now, double what it was in 2016.[4]

America's governments in the nineteenth century shared many of the characteristics of poor-country governments today. Local, state, and federal government officials engaged in rampant corruption, taking kickbacks and bribes from legitimate businessmen and illicit actors alike. "Bosses" ran big-city political organizations and indirectly controlled city services such as utilities, police protection and security, trash collection, and transportation. Some gave handouts to the poor in exchange for votes.[5]

For most, working conditions were deplorable and industrial accidents were all too common. In December 1907 alone, close to seven hundred miners lost their lives.[6] Many children, some as young as eleven years old, began their "careers," in factories and mines, where they were paid a pittance. In 1904, we actually had a National Child Labor Committee to lobby for the rights of children. As many as fourteen thousand children worked (legally) in coal mines. Women were paid a little more than children. Wages at the time, even for men who were better paid, were seldom enough to rise out of poverty.[7] Workers frequently went on strike. Sometimes the state militias were sent in to quell these protests, and other times wealthy business owners conscripted their own private militias to do the same. There were sometimes deaths. This was not the relative peace and stability of America today. America was ad hoc and chaotic—at one point the country had more than eighty time zones. Noon in Chicago was 11:27 a.m. in Omaha and 12:31 p.m. in Pittsburgh.[8]

But a generation of American innovators and entrepreneurs began to change America's circumstances (including how the country kept time, a change brought about by the proliferation of the railroads), succeeding against what might have seemed staggering odds, by pioneering market-creating innovations, with new business models that allowed those products to become simple and affordable. In their day, the innovators we profile in this chapter—Isaac Singer, George Eastman, Henry Ford, and Amadeo

Giannini—were entrepreneurs and innovators who just wanted to see their market-creating innovations take hold. But their impact on American prosperity would be far more profound. It's almost impossible to calculate the exact impact that these innovation pioneers had on the prosperity of America, but by any measure, it was enormous. When you view not just what they built, but the culture of innovation they *inspired*, it becomes clear that the real revolution in America after the Civil War was not political, but economic. In their stories of survival, we see the story of America's remarkable transformation.

With Isaac Singer, we will illustrate the immense **power of market-creating innovations**. With George Eastman, the poor high school dropout who created Kodak, we will focus on the opportunity found in **targeting nonconsumption**. We will revisit Henry Ford's story to demonstrate just how much the **Model T was able to pull into American society**. From gas stations to roads to how we earn and spend our money, Ford played a role in changing how we live, work, and play. Finally, we will look at how Amadeo Giannini fundamentally **changed the dominant business model** of banking at the time—and all of our lives in the decades since then. A bank that lent to poor immigrants became what we now know as Bank of America, creating some of the essential banking practices that we all count on today. The success of these four innovators (and scores more) had enormous ripple effects across the American, and even global, economy. As a culture of innovation began to emerge in America, one in which entrepreneurs looked to serve more and more nonconsumers, a virtuous cycle of prosperity creation was set in motion.

An Industry Is Born

Isaac Singer's impact on the world might have been difficult to predict when he was a young man. Born in New York in 1811 to poor

German immigrants, the uneducated Singer wanted nothing more than to become an actor.[9] A short stint as an apprentice in a machinist shop when he was nineteen gave him a career fallback plan, but he had no intention of earning his living that way. He tried to find his fortune on the stage, without much success. Until one day he found himself tinkering with an existing, but imperfect, sewing machine design. On paper, the idea of a sewing machine made sense—at the time even a skilled seamstress could produce only forty stitches a minute by hand—but no one had yet been able to produce a reliable machine that could do much better.

Singer saw an opportunity to improve the machine. With mechanical improvements that made the sewing machine simpler, less expensive, and more reliable, Singer's sewing machine enabled an *unskilled* person to produce *nine hundred* stitches a minute. That meant that the average time it took to stitch a shirt went down from about fourteen hours to just one.[10]

Experts who knew much more about tailoring and clothing predicted he would fail.[11] Who would buy it? It seemed inconceivable that American households that could barely find money for fabric for a new shirt would find money for a fancy sewing machine. "Would women even be able to *operate* such a machine?" skeptics asked.

But Singer was not daunted. His success eventually came after teaming up with lawyer Edward Clark to create "I.M. Singer & Co." Together, they innovated not only their product, but also their business model to ensure they could survive in a challenging business and legal environment.[12] These innovations included creating branch offices, sending out door-to-door sales and service staff, offering lessons to customers on how to use the product, and extending credit to cash-strapped customers. A typical Singer sewing machine retailed for $100 (roughly $1,400 in 2017 dollars), but with as little as $5 down and a monthly payment of $3, a family who earned just $500 a year could own a sewing machine.

Though familiar to modern-day Americans, these business

model innovations were unprecedented in Singer's time—and they led to extraordinary growth. In 1858, the company had annual sales of just three thousand units. By 1863, when a tailor named Ebenezer Butterick began selling dress patterns in standard sizes, making it easy for anyone to copy a dress design to make at home, the Singer sewing machine had become America's most popular sewing machine and was on its way to a worldwide monopoly. By 1873, demand was so high that Singer had to build the United States' largest sewing machine factory, with a manufacturing capacity of seven thousand units *per week*. Ten years later, the company built Europe's largest sewing machine factory, where it produced ten thousand units a week.[13] The Singer sewing machine would eventually build an international organization[14] that manufactured more than half a million sewing machines in Europe and almost four hundred thousand in the United States annually.[15] This led to vast numbers of jobs in sales, distribution, maintenance, manufacturing, advertising, training, bookkeeping, and beyond.

While Singer's direct economic impact was impressive, its indirect impact was arguably even greater—catalyzing other innovations and industries, and also spurring the construction of new infrastructures. For example, small shops began to open in the poorest districts of New York and Chicago to serve as subcontractors to larger manufacturers who had developed a standardized, task-oriented production system—a predecessor of the modern-day supply chain. All a manufacturer had to do was cut and mark the cloth with a particular design, and then package and ship it to the small shops with instructions on how to sew the pieces. Entire families took part in this process, leading to higher incomes and better life prospects.[16] Singer's sewing machine was also an unexpected boon to the closet or wardrobe industry. Where were people going to put all their new clothes? First they needed wardrobes, and then they needed bigger wardrobes. Another industry was born.

Perhaps most notably, the Singer sewing machine revolutionized the clothing industry—which doubled in size between 1860 and

1870, eventually reaching a *billion dollars* by 1890 ($26 billion in 2018 dollars)—making it possible for a customer, knowing his or her size, to shop at the newly emerging department stores of the late nineteenth century.[17] Increasing demand for sewing machines also led to booms in the steel, wood, and cotton industries—and the creation of several others. It also, in turn, impacted the shoe industry, which could then sell its wares at those department stores, too.

As these new industries and markets were created, they began to pull in the infrastructure and institutions they required to survive. The I. M. Singer company actually built rail lines to more efficiently transport the company's sewing machines; the company also built a turbine power station for their factory in Podolsk, Russia, which eventually provided electricity to the whole town; in Moscow, their foundry shop supplied pig iron to nearby cotton mills; and in Scotland, they built a railway station that is still functioning to this day.[18] This all happened without the direct help of governments. In fact, the I.M. Singer company actually helped the governments by generating taxes that would fund many public services.

In 1890, for instance, Americans didn't expect much from their federal government. The United States federal government managed the military, foreign policy, land, the treasury, and tariffs. They didn't do much else.

For example, there were no federal agencies for Labor (that would not come until 1913), Veterans Affairs (1930), Health and Human Services (1953), Housing and Urban Development (1965), Transportation (1967), Energy (1977), and Education (1979) until well into America's life as an independent nation. These agencies would form and evolve over time in response to public outcry of some sort, or to manage the affairs of a new and thriving market. The Department of Transportation, for instance, came almost sixty years after Henry Ford's Model T. In many instances, there were precursors to the federal departments, but they were smaller, were less of a priority, and thus wielded much less influence. But that didn't matter to innovators like Singer.

The same was true for George Eastman, whose innovation has enabled millions of us to preserve precious memories and communicate and connect through images.

George Eastman's Kodak—Picturing the Future

Today we take for granted how simple it is to take pictures and preserve memories. From pictures of our unforgettable family vacations to photos shared with us of faraway lands we may never visit, we are bombarded daily with images. By some estimates, we upload more than 657 billion photos every year. One writer put it this way: "Every two minutes, humans take more photos than ever existed in total 150 years ago."[19]

But images weren't always so widely accessible. Photography was invented in the 1830s, but even fifty years after its invention it was still a practice limited to highly skilled professionals and to those who could afford its high cost. This is because photography required knowledge of chemistry and expertise working in wet labs.[20] In addition to the camera, photographers required lots of additional equipment like chemicals, glass tanks, and heavy-duty plate holders and tripods. Photography was very expensive and impractical until George Eastman set up the Eastman Kodak Company, which targeted the vast nonconsumption of photography that we can now see in retrospect.

Born on July 12, 1854, George Eastman was a high school dropout, and, according to schooling standards at the time, he was not particularly bright. To make matters worse for Eastman, he was born into a poor family and had to support his widowed mother and two sisters, one of whom suffered from polio. Eastman began his professional career as a bank clerk, a job he took to help pay his family's bills. It was through the work and ingenuity of this former clerk that millions of nonconsumers of memories, pictures, and photography became consumers. Eastman's innovation, and the vast market it created, led to immense economic prosperity, job creation, and the development and expansion of many billion-dollar industries, including advertising and motion pictures.

When Eastman was twenty-three, a colleague suggested that he take a camera on an upcoming vacation, an idea that thrilled him. Eastman quickly learned, however, that cameras were heavy, awkward, and expensive, and that the set of gear required to develop photographs was expensive, too. So he began to work at finding a better way to take pictures and develop photography, and spent three years experimenting at his mother's kitchen table until he got it right. Eastman believed that one of our most precious resources, our experiences, should be preserved more easily, and that the average American—the nonconsumer—should be able to take pictures whenever he wanted, and do so affordably.

This led him to set up the Eastman Kodak Company. "The idea gradually dawned on me that what we were doing was not merely making dry plates, but that we were starting out to make photography an everyday affair . . . to make the camera as convenient as the pencil," Eastman noted.[21] Eastman's decision to target nonconsumption caused him to engineer an entirely different business model. He intuitively understood the Job to Be Done, that people wanted to capture the precious moments of their lives. While they might not spend a lot of their time looking at the pictures they took, the notion of stopping, capturing, and having the possibility of going back to the pictures was enough for them to consume photography.

Kodak's 1888 camera set the stage for transforming the photography industry. The easy-to-use $25 camera was preloaded with enough film for one hundred pictures. Once done with taking pictures, customers sent the camera to the Eastman Kodak Company, where they were developed and sent back to the customer with a fresh roll of film for more pictures. This service—developing the pictures and resending empty film—cost an additional $10. Eastman popularized the slogan, "You press the button, we do the rest." Eastman's business boomed.

In fact, the idea of taking pictures caught on so well that twelve years later Kodak developed the Brownie, a camera that sold for just one dollar (a mere $27 in today's dollars); the film was an additional 15 cents. An advertising campaign followed. And before long, the phrase "a Kodak moment" became mainstream.[22]

Unprecedented success and prosperity for the man who once lived on less than a dollar a day followed. Over the next several decades, Eastman Kodak would sell hundreds of millions of cameras and film, forever transforming an industry once limited to the rich.

In order to accomplish this, Eastman developed a business model that focused on the following core principles: *the customer, mass production at low cost, worldwide distribution*, and *extensive advertising*. This was in the 1890s, when fewer than 10 percent of Americans were in secondary school and fewer than 10 percent of America's roads were constructed (that would happen after Henry Ford's Model T), and shipping containers were not yet mainstream. But these facts didn't stop Eastman from building Kodak into a multibillion-dollar empire and one of the most successful American companies at the time.

By 1966, Kodak employed more than one hundred thousand people and combined sales of all Kodak units around the world surpassed $4 billion (more than $30 billion in today's dollars). Eastman's impact on the development of the United States was immense. From the inputs and technologies necessary to develop the camera to the multibillion-dollar industries that emerged as a result, few could have predicted Eastman's impact.[23] But that's almost always true with targeting nonconsumption.

Taking a picture today, and even recording a video, might seem mundane and ordinary, but this was not so 150 years ago. Eastman's innovation and his decision to target nonconsumption created markets that many other innovators have improved and further developed. In so doing, Eastman not only generated vast amounts of wealth for himself, but also created a market that pulled in jobs and business opportunities for many people all around the globe.

Henry Ford's Model T

As we write this, Ford Motor Company is more than 115 years old, generates more than $150 billion in revenues annually, employs over two hundred thousand people globally, and has assets of more than $200 billion. But when Henry Ford first boldly decided to build a car for the average American, he was met with intense skepticism. Critics predicted he would be out of business in six months.[24] But Ford was not deterred. "I will build a car for the great multitude. It will be large enough for the family but small enough for the individual to run and care for. It will be constructed of the best materials, by the best men to be hired, after the simplest design that modern engineering can devise. But it will be so low in price that no man making a good salary will be unable to own one—and enjoy with his family the blessing of hours of pleasure in God's great open spaces," he declared.

For transformative development to happen, innovators must first imagine a different world, one that is filled with possibilities that many others can't begin to imagine. It's not hard to understand why critics thought Ford's prediction was crazy. Think of the America into which Ford introduced his cars.[25] By the early 1900s, GDP per capita had reached about $7,800 in 2018 dollars, almost the level of the United Kingdom's $8,800, but life was still difficult for the average American. Most people still had no access to electricity; relatively few children made it to secondary schools; life expectancy was around forty-seven years; and America's road infrastructure was not developed, at least not for the automobile. At the time, the average American did not even see the need for cars or the way they could impact America. Most people lived close to where they worked and played. Much like many emerging markets today, only wealthy Americans could afford cars. But Henry Ford set about to change that.

Born in 1863, Henry Ford had a penchant for innovation. His father owned a farm in Dearborn, Michigan, where Ford made little contraptions that would ease some of the more laborious farming tasks. Like other innovators we have written about, Ford was not formally educated.[26] After he became a mechanic's apprentice, Ford became increasingly fascinated with building a horseless carriage. He worked on it in his spare time for more than twelve years, until he quit his full-time job at the Edison Illuminating Company to join a fledgling start-up, the Detroit Automobile Company. The Detroit Automobile Company did not succeed, and Ford was ousted from the company, but his determination to build a successful automobile company remained strong.

In 1903, after winning a race against a prominent Ohioan automaker, Alexander Winton, with a car Ford had designed himself, he and a small group of investors formed the Ford Motor Company. It was there that the seeds of the "democratization of the automobile" in America were planted.[27]

In order to build a successful business model that targeted nonconsumption, Ford did many things that may seem not "core" to building a car today. In other words, his company had to pull in many resources and components that, today, would seem an unreasonable expenditure. But in particular circumstances—especially those in which a new market is being created—pulling in what may seem to be "non-core resources" to successfully accomplish a Job to Be Done is necessary. Today, we call this vertical integration, but back then innovators simply understood it as doing what was necessary to succeed in creating a new market. That's effectively what Ford did. Because a majority of car manufacturers at the time focused on the consumption economy and targeted only wealthy individuals, they remained small and didn't have to pull in extensive resources to produce their custom-crafted vehicles.

By contrast, Ford had to figure out how to make a lot of things work. By the 1920s, the auto assembly plant was just one in a long line of significant investments Ford made to get his car to American nonconsumers. Ford's company also ran blast furnaces for steel, timberlands, coal mines, rubber plantations, a railroad, freighters, gas stations, sawmills, and glassworks.[28] This was a first in the auto industry. No one had ever quite seen anything like this. These investments were not just Ford's infrastructure, they became America's infrastructure, too.

Ford's Model T changed the landscape of America—quite literally. In 1900, the number of registered cars in the United States totaled 8,000; by 1910, just ten years later, it reached 458,000; in 1920, it was 8 million; and by 1929, there were more than 23 million registered motor vehicles in the country.[29] The Model T was a significant reason for the adoption of automobiles in the United States and other parts of the world. In 1922, for instance, of the approximately 2.5 million new cars registered, roughly 2 million were Ford Model T automobiles.

As cars were made more affordable, fewer horses were needed both for city travel and for work on farms. Many farmers also retrofitted the Ford Model T for their farming needs, further reducing the need for horses and mules. By the early twentieth century, it was costing America more than $2 billion to maintain *horses* annually, about the same as it cost to maintain the railroads. In New York City, for example, city officials had to deal with more than forty-five thousand tons of horse manure monthly. The problem was so pervasive—and vile—that one motoring advocate claimed, "all wars together have not caused half the deaths that may be traced to the horse." That may be a bit of an exaggeration, but it certainly captures the fears at the time. One critic went so far as to suggest that by 1930, horse manure would reach "the level of Manhattan's third-story windows." Luckily, Henry Ford's automobile took off before that could happen.[30]

Ford's decision to target nonconsumption and create a new market for the automobile in America and the market's need to develop and pull in many new resources were critical to the development and prosperity of America, including roads. In his book *The Big Roads: The Untold Story of the Engineers, Visionaries, and Trailblazers Who Created the American Superhighways*, Earl Swift explains that by 1909, only 8 percent of America's 2.2 million miles of roads were "improved in any way." And half of the 8 percent of "improved roads" were gravel. At the time, America had just nine miles of concrete roads. But as the car became ubiquitous, improved roads followed, and Americans benefited immensely.

The economic and social impact of road building in America was enormous. "Each billion dollars spent on construction provided the equivalent of 48,000 fulltime jobs for a year and consumed an almost inconceivable vast pile of resources; 16 million barrels of cement, more than half a million tons of steel, 18 million pounds of explosives, 123 million gallons of petroleum products, and enough earth to bury New Jersey knee-deep. It also devoured 76 million tons of aggregate," notes Swift.[31]

But as important as roads were, what's even more important is what they enabled. Rural school attendance in the US stood at around 57 percent before the emergence of good roads. Once good roads were built, daily attendance spiked to 77 percent. The cost of moving a ton of freight was around 22 cents a mile on an unimproved road, but dropped drastically to 12 cents on better roads. The reduction in transport expenses enabled further travel and trade to thrive within and between cities.[32]

Roads and their attendant benefits, however, were not the only things Ford's innovation pulled into America. Consider how the company impacted wages and incomes, one of the most important determinants of development, prosperity, and the efficacy of a democracy.[33] When Ford instituted the assembly line in his factories, work became monotonous. Unskilled men did the same thing over and over again for nine hours a day, six days a week, and for approximately $2.34 a day ($60 in today's dollars). As a result of the work's monotony, turnover at Ford's manufacturing plant skyrocketed to a whopping 370 percent annually. This meant that for every one job, Ford had to hire four people to keep his factory running smoothly. It was unsustainable. In order to combat this problem, in 1914, Ford instituted a $5 per day minimum wage, essentially doubling the pay for his factory workers. Critics and other automobile manufacturers thought Ford crazy for increasing wages. The *Wall Street Journal* editorial page at the time implied that in doing so, Ford was not only betraying his fellow business owners, he was jeopardizing the whole of American enterprise. "To double the minimum wage, without regard to length of service, is to apply Biblical or spiritual principles where they do not belong," the *Journal* wrote, adding that Ford had "in his social endeavor committed blunders, if not crimes. They may return to plague him and the industry he represents, as well as organized society."[34]

Luckily, Ford did not agree with many of the prevailing sentiments at the time. His decision is frequently discussed as part of his efforts to turn his own workers into customers—with higher wages, they could afford his cars, the thinking goes. But in reality, Ford was focused on keeping his factory open. Ford later remarked that the wage increase was the "smartest cost-cutting move [the company] ever made." Other manufacturers, too, saw the payoff in the move and followed suit, opting for higher wages in their operations.[35]

Ford was also largely responsible for changing what had been a six-day workweek into a five-day one—a move his critics also feared would undermine the entire economy. Somehow, Ford saw things differently: he saw a reduced workweek as essential for keeping (and even improving) his workers' productivity and understood the potential ripple effects on the economy as a whole. "It is high time to rid ourselves of the notion that leisure for workmen is either 'lost time' or a class privilege . . . The people who work only five days a week will consume more goods than the people who work six days a week," he said at the time. "People who have more leisure must have more clothes. They eat a greater variety of food. They require more transportation facilities. This increased consumption will require greater production than we now have. . . . This will lead to more work. And this to more wages."[36]

With such moves helping improve his plant's efficiency, the Ford

Motor Company was able to reduce the price of the Model T from $950 in 1909 (approximately $25,000 in 2018 dollars) to $260 in 1927 ($3,700 in 2018 dollars), making it even more affordable for the average American, including Ford factory employees. Sales of the Model T boomed as a result.[37]

By 1923, there were just over 15 million cars registered in the country—approximately 135 cars per 1,000 people. Economists predicted that the industry's growth just couldn't continue. They could not see how Americans would keep buying cars. Most people who could afford cars, they thought, had already bought at least one. Some households even had two. But their projections grossly missed the mark. In 2014, there were 816 vehicles per 1,000 Americans.[38] More than 260 million cars roamed US streets, roadways, and highways.

When I think about Ford, or the Model T, I think about how this *one* innovation changed so many American lives. I think about the culture of innovation Ford fostered, and the possibilities he created for many of us to lead better lives. That kind of impact, much like the kind we see in the story of Bank of America, is often hard to predict with the economic tools we have today.

From the Bank of Italy to the Bank of America

Like many products in the late nineteenth and early twentieth centuries, financial services, such as loans and bank accounts, existed mostly for the wealthy. When Amadeo Giannini suggested that his bank lend to credit-worthy working-class Americans, he was ungraciously rejected.[39] Determined to change things, in 1904 he went on to found the Bank of Italy in San Francisco. He would focus on the "little fellows," whom the other banks wouldn't serve.[40] That's how Bank of America, the onetime largest commercial bank in the world, was born.

Some historians have hailed Giannini as the "greatest innovator in modern banking," explaining that "he probably did more to democratize and popularize banking than any other individual."[41] Judging not only from Bank of America's ultimate success, but also the new business models Giannini's bank executed, it is hard to disagree with the assertion. Amadeo Giannini is responsible for converting millions of Americans from nonconsumers of financial services to consumers. To do that, however, he had to change the dominant business model of banking at the time.

Market-creating innovations are not simply the products or services themselves. At the core of any market-creating innovation is a business model that profitably democratizes an innovation so that many more people—nonconsumers who can benefit from using the innovation—gain access to it. That's where the transformative power comes into play.

As a high school dropout who joined his stepfather's produce company when he was fifteen, Giannini's decision to go into banking stemmed from his disdain for conventional banking practices that primarily targeted the rich—a group from which he was decidedly excluded. But how could one blame the bankers? At the time, Americans were not as wealthy as they are today, and there was no established business model for targeting those who were not rich. It made sense for bankers to lend money to big corporations for railroad and skyscraper projects, but not to the poor, no matter how hardworking they were. Similar to the situation in many poor countries today, it was incredibly difficult for the average American to get a bank loan. They were considered high risk—how would they ever repay the loans? In fact, the banking industry did everything it could to discourage poor Americans from even asking. And in the event they got a loan, interest rates were often in *high double digits*.

But it was in this "undesirable" segment of the population that Giannini saw opportunity. "The 'little fellow' is the best customer that a bank can have," Giannini reasoned. "He starts with you and stays with you until the end."[42] Giannini believed that he could develop a profitable banking business that provided lower interest rates to the average Californian, offering customers in Central Valley loans at just 7 percent—a fraction of what they would be able to get from any other bank (and an even smaller fraction of what they'd have to pay if they resorted to the "gray market" for a loan). Offering loans of $10 to $300 to anyone who had a job, Giannini also convinced nonconsumers that they should stop stuffing their hard-earned money into mattresses or tin cans and turn it over to a bank, where it would be protected and earn interest.

But Giannini couldn't afford to do this unless he ripped up the conventional rule book for banking—so he "began knocking the starch out of tried, true and conservative banking," as the *San Francisco Chronicle* later observed.

Giannini would literally stop people on the street and solicit would-be customers to open accounts with the bank. It was a practice that was looked down on by other banks and bankers who relied on one-on-one meetings in august buildings with private bankers to impress wealthy clients. Giannini didn't just offer his bank's services. He also had to educate his customers about the benefits of banking in general. He set up local advisory committees in his banks, advised his customers to purchase the bank's stock, and created a national system of branches that catered to the poor and working class. Although branch banking may seem obvious today, it wasn't one hundred years ago. Giannini introduced the model for banking that most of us know today.

Giannini also didn't see Bank of America as just a bank. He integrated the bank's services to meet the needs of its customers. For example, in the devastation of the great San Francisco earthquake of 1906—just two years after he founded his bank—Giannini managed to remove $80,000 in gold from the deposit vaults of his Bank of Italy with the help of two quick-thinking employees, loading the gold onto a horse-drawn cart, hidden under loads of vegetables, before fire ravaged the building. Other banks that had not thought to do that would find their vaults too hot to open for weeks. The day after the earthquake ravaged the city, his fellow bankers proposed a six-month banking moratorium until their banks could recover. But Giannini broke ranks. "In November," he argued, "there will be no city or people left to serve."[43] He was open for business the next day at a makeshift desk in North Beach and offered to extend credit "on a face and a signature" to small businesses and individuals in need of money to rebuild their lives. His actions spurred the city's redevelopment.

The gesture reflected Giannini's philosophy: the money in the vaults wasn't there to serve banks. It was there to serve customers. By the mid-1920s, Giannini's Bank of Italy was already a misnomer, as he had started lending to "little fellows" in the Yugoslavian, Russian, Mexican, Portuguese, Chinese, Greek, and several other immigrant communities. In 1930, Bank of Italy became Bank of America, and by 1945, it had become the largest commercial bank in the world.

Giannini also lent to other undeveloped and nascent industries at the time, including the California wine industry, Hollywood, and the high-tech industry. After Walt Disney went over budget on his production of the first fully featured animation movie, *Snow White and the Seven Dwarfs*, Giannini stepped in with a $2 million loan to Disney. Giannini also provided initial capital to William Hewlett and David Packard, founders of Hewlett-Packard Inc. While these are all multibillion-dollar industries today, each attracting billions of dollars of investments annually, few would have predicted their success at the time. Even Charlie Chaplin, one of the world's most prominent actors, directors, and producers, once declared that "the cinema is little more than a fad. It's canned drama. What audiences really want to see is flesh and blood on the stage."[44]

While the market that Giannini created for the average American to access capital was important, what's even more important are the institutions and the infrastructure the market helped put in place. When lending to a few rich people in society, banks did not need to invest in much infrastructure to ensure that their loans would be repaid. When lending to hundreds of thousands of people, these systems were not only important, but essential. Giannini had his staff check on the business practices of people they lent money to, to ensure that they were running their firms as well as possible. For example, senior bank officials realized that for many of their agribusiness customers to succeed in marketing their products in faraway markets, they would need to establish cooperatives.[45] Bank of America helped with this, and by 1919, California farmers grossed $127 million in sales through marketing cooperatives. (The next largest, at the time, were Minnesota farmers at $82 million.)

Giannini's dedication to the "little fellows" gave us Bank of America. But it also changed our lives. Our parents and grandparents were able to understand the value of saving money, of compounded interest, of making investment choices. Entire generations of Americans reaped the benefits of that knowledge. It's hard to imagine that the same sea change isn't possible for the "little fellows" in poor economies, too. Thanks to Giannini, and others who followed in his path, we know what's possible.

Innovation Becomes the New Normal in America

Identifying just a few American market-creating innovators was difficult for us—not because we couldn't find them, but because there were so many great stories from which to choose. American history is replete with tales of innovators whose work played a role in America's march to prosperity. Not every innovator succeeded in creating a new market; not every entrepreneur got his or her business model right. History is also littered with painful tales of failure. Thomas Edison failed many more times than he succeeded—electric pen, anyone? "I have not failed 10,000 times," he famously declared, "I've successfully found 10,000 ways that will not work." But he got several innovations spectacularly right, including the incandescent light bulb, phonograph, and motion picture camera, a process that ultimately gave us General Electric. There are dozens and dozens of others who did as well. For example:

Samuel Insull, a colleague of Thomas Edison, targeted nonconsumption of electricity when he developed a way to deliver inexpensive electricity throughout America. His company, Commonwealth Edison Company, combined technological innovations with business model innovations—charging customers based on time of day and use, wiring homes cheaply, and giving away electrical appliances in order to increase demand. He started out in 1892 with just five thousand customers in Chicago. By the 1920s, he was serving more than four million customers in thirty-two states.

Sarah Breedlove Walker, popularly known as "Madam C.J.," embodied this spirit when she founded a business that targeted nonconsumption of cosmetic products in African-American communities. In the early 1900s, when few thought a business that served the African-American community could be viable, Madam C.J. saw opportunity— not just for herself but for others. As she explained in 1914, "I am not merely satisfied in making money for myself, I am endeavoring to provide employment for hundreds of women of my race."[46] She did end up making money for herself— becoming the first African-American woman to become a millionaire. But more important, she achieved her ambition of creating employment for thousands of women. She was not formally educated, and once earned barely $1.50 a day.

Charles Goodyear, after enduring years of poverty—living on fish he caught in the harbor off Staten Island, New York—and spending time in jail for not being able to pay his debt, gave us vulcanized rubber. At a time when many advised him that "rubber was dead" in America after many Americans saw smelly rubber melt in the hot summer months and become hard like rock in the winter, Goodyear continually experimented with it, trying to make it more durable and affordable. After many years of failure, he succeeded. In 2018, global demand for industrial rubber products topped $150 billion.

Georges Doriot institutionalized America's innovation culture when he founded American Research and Development Corporation (ARDC), the world's first publicly owned venture capital firm. One of the start-ups his company backed was Digital Equipment Corporation—at one time a successful computer company with more than 140,000 employees and $14 billion in sales. He also advised Fred Smith, the founder of FedEx.

No one innovator single-handedly changed America's fate, but the ripple effects of their work certainly did.

In Praise of Fixer-Uppers

When we bought our first house, I optimistically saw it as a *fixer-upper*. That was probably too diplomatic. My wife, Christine, would tell you it was a wreck. At the time I was working at my first job, and we stretched everything we had to buy a home for our growing family. But it was a shell of a home. We couldn't afford to pay any tradesmen to improve the house for us. So whatever needed fixing had to be fixed by us. And everything needed fixing. There wasn't a room in the house that didn't need *something*. Some of it was minor, like painting a room. Some of it was truly fundamental, like making sure the windows kept out the rain or the plumbing didn't leak. Though I might never have predicted it the day we were first handed the keys, little by little that wreck did truly become our home. Converting our house from a fixer-upper to the home that it is today was a process that took time, financial resources, patience, and resilience. But our home, over time, came to reflect who we are as a family: our values, our abilities (or lack thereof), and our willingness to roll up our sleeves and find ways to solve problems.

America was once a fixer-upper, too, but through trial and error, and investments in market-creating innovations, we've built a culture of innovation. Singer, Eastman, Ford, Giannini, and the other innovators we mentioned above are just the tip of the iceberg. They represent a *spirit* of innovation in America that has become a foundation of American culture. Many more followed, each, in turn, helping crank the wheel of prosperity a little bit further. As Henry Ford once said, "Every success is the mother of countless others." Collectively, they changed America's destiny.

NOTES

1. Robert J. Gordon, *The Rise and Fall of American Growth: The U.S. Standard of Living Since the Civil War* (New Jersey: Princeton University Press, 2016), 1.

2. In 1890, more than half of New Yorkers lived in "crowded, small, poorly ventilated apartments from which windows looked out on stinking air shafts." Children often urinated on the walls in many apartment buildings and plumbing pipes were infested "with holes that emitted sewer gasses so virulent they were flammable."

   Robert J. Gordon, *The Rise and Fall of American Growth: The U.S. Standard of Living Since the Civil War* (New Jersey: Princeton University Press, 2016), 97, 103.

3. Ibid., 57.

4. "Rate: Number of Crimes per 100,000 Inhabitants," 2016 Crime in the United States, Department of Justice: FBI, accessed March 8, 2018, https://ucr.fbi.gov/crime-in-the-u.s/2016/crime-in-the-u.s.-2016/tables/table-11.

5. Faith Jaycox, *The Progressive Era* (New York: Facts on File, Inc., 2005), 79.

6. Ibid., 267.

7. Ibid., 22.

8. Jack Beatty, *Age of Betrayal: The Triumph of Money in America, 1865–1900* (New York: Alfred A. Knopf, 2007), 3.

9. Isaac Merritt Singer was not, by all accounts, a very nice man. He fathered twenty-four children with his wife and various mistresses. He repeatedly pushed backers and partners aside in his ascent, and he was known for his personal flamboyance. But his drive also played a role in pioneering business practices where he saw opportunity, including translating Singer owners' manuals into fifty different languages. As we describe, what Singer's innovation enabled changed the world.

10. A popular song at the time of Singer's rise was this ditty about the stressful life of women seamstresses before the sewing machine's proliferation.

Song of the Shirt
With fingers weary and worn,
With eyelids heavy and red,
A woman sat, in unwomanly rags,
Plying her needle and thread—
Stitch! Stitch! Stitch!
In poverty, hunger, and dirt
And still with a voice of dolorous pitch—
Would that its tone could reach the rich!—
She sang this "Song of the Shirt!"

11. Many experts who knew a whole lot more about tailoring and the industry than Singer did, thought Singer would fail. Who could blame them? Edwin Wildman writes in his book *Famous Leaders of Industry*, "People were skeptical of the sewing machine . . . and quite often [Singer] was 'shown the door' the moment he mentioned his business. He [Singer] was advised by Mr. Blodgett, who was a tailor by trade and knew more about sewing than Singer possibly could, to give up manufacturing . . . Blodgett further told Singer that he was positive that sewing machines would never come into use . . ."

Edwin Wildman, *Famous Leaders of Industry: The Life Stories of Boys Who Have Succeeded* (Boston: The Page Company, 1921), 251–252.

12. There were many sewing machine "inventors" jockeying for market dominance in Singer's era, and they were quick to grab patents (from a largely undiscerning patent office) to stake their claims. Legal battles flourished, threatening to bankrupt virtually all of the sewing machine companies at the time, including Singer. Eventually many patent holders of specific innovations on sewing machines pooled together and agreed to allow the use of their patents in exchange for a share of the proceeds of any sales generated. This is how Elias Howe, who is credited with the first patent of a sewing machine, finally became wealthy. Previously, he had utterly failed to commercialize his invention, showing that perhaps even more important than technical innovation is business model innovation.

13. Geoffrey Jones and David Kiron, "Globalizing Consumer Durables: Singer Sewing Machine before 1914," Harvard Business School Case 804-001, October 2003. (Revised January 2017.)

14. Singer's story is especially noteworthy because in the late 1800s, he created a truly global company, setting up manufacturing, distribution, and sales offices in America, Russia, Scotland, England, Germany, Austria, and several other countries. Note that these countries were at

varying levels of development, each with its own unique infrastructures, institutions, and culture. Russia, for instance, was considered an "undeveloped wasteland" at the time. But Singer's firm was able to internalize a lot of risk and pull in the necessary infrastructure to sell his products in the region. As a result, his firm succeeded in Russia without government help and despite the government's efforts to impose high tariffs on the company. His focus, however, remained clear—to create a new market by getting as many sewing machines into the hands of Russian nonconsumers as possible.

Consider how Singer's strategy of targeting nonconsumption enabled the company's success in Russia. The country was so poor that Singer would have had to sell almost all its machines on credit; Russia's legal system, capital markets, and credit institutions were underdeveloped even for that era; Russia was also experiencing economic and political turmoil; the country did not have the skilled labor force that was important to Singer's operations; and the country's landmass was large, with a dispersed population. Does that remind you of any poor countries or emerging markets today?

But Singer not only built a factory in Russia, he also created Russia's largest commercial enterprise with thousands of stores and a staff of more than twenty-seven thousand. Through a series of managerial and organizational innovations, including hiring unskilled workers and training them (building an education infrastructure), the Singer operation in Russia became one of the most successful within the Singer corporation.

15. Building an international organization is no small feat today, even with how globally connected we are, considering improvements in telecommunications and transportation technology. Singer, however, was able to accomplish this in the 1800s, when no such technologies existed. Similarly, many emerging markets today have at least comparable or better infrastructures than America did during Singer's rise. The question remains, what business model innovations should innovators in these regions execute in order to target nonconsumption?

16. Quentin Skrabec, *The 100 Most Significant Events in American Business: An Encyclopedia* (Santa Barbara: Greenwood, 2012), 39.

17. Ibid., 38.

18. "Singer Railway Station," Overview, Gazetteer for Scotland, accessed February 24, 2018, http://www.scottish-places.info/features/featurefirst 11985.html.

19. Rose Eveleth, "How Many Photographs of You are Out There in the World?," *The Atlantic*, November 2, 2015, https://www.theatlantic.com /technology/archive/2015/11/how-many-photographs-of-you-are-out -there-in-the-world/413389/.

20. Wet labs are labs where chemicals are handled in liquid and some-times volatile forms.

21. "About us: George Eastman," Heritage, Kodak, accessed February 27, 2018, https://www.kodak.com/corp/aboutus/heritage/georgeeastman /default.htm#.

22. "George Eastman, Easy-to-Use Cameras," Who Made America?, PBS, accessed February 27, 2018, http://www.pbs.org/wgbh/theymadeamerica /whomade/eastman_hi.html.

23. As impressive as George Eastman's prowess for business and inno-vation was, his generosity was perhaps even more noteworthy. George Eastman gave. The first act of generosity Eastman displayed was an out-right gift of a "substantial sum of his own money" to all his employees in 1889. More acts followed, including a "wage dividend," where employees benefited beyond their wages in accordance with the company dividend. That was not normal practice during that time. Eastman truly believed that organizations rose and fell on the backs of the loyalty and ingenuity of employees. He exemplified this belief in 1919 by giving a third of his stock, worth $10 million (or $146.3 million in 2017 dollars), to his employ-ees. Soon after, he instituted retirement annuity programs, life insurance plans, and disability benefits for his staff. But generosity was in his blood and, as such, was not limited to his employees. Eastman gave up to $20 million to the Massachusetts Institute of Technology (MIT) and millions more to the University of Rochester, Hampton University, and Tuskegee University. He also financed many dental clinics in various cities in the US and Europe, including Rochester, London, Paris, Rome, and Brussels.
   "About us: George Eastman," Heritage, Kodak, accessed February 27, 2018, https://www.kodak.com/corp/aboutus/heritage/georgeeastman /default.htm#.

24. Henry Ford, *My Life and Work* (New York: Garden City Publishing, 1922), 31.

25. Although we go into more detail on the relationship between inno-vation and infrastructures and institutions later, consider the following. American intellectual property law was not advanced (and this is even overstating it) in the mid-1800s. Cambridge economist Ha-Joon Chang

notes that "patents were granted without proof of originality," leading to importation of already-patented technologies and rent-seeking by racketeers who sought to profit from already-existing innovations. Bankruptcy law in America was also nonexistent, or immature at best. It wasn't until 1898 that Congress adopted a lasting federal bankruptcy law. Earlier attempts created significant stress on the court systems. Additionally, most manufacturing in the 1860s was done by unincorporated firms as there was not yet a federal law granting limited liability for entrepreneurs.

26. Ford would later attend Goldsmith, Bryant & Stratton Business College (now called Detroit Business Institute) in Detroit. Whatever "education" Ford received growing up was contextual in nature. He learned to fix things around the farm until he moved to Detroit, where he found work as a mechanic's apprentice.

27. In retrospect, the idea of an affordable car is sensible. However, at the time it was considered nonsensical. Several of Ford's investors pulled out because they couldn't see how he could succeed. Only rich people drove, and mainly for the purposes of joyriding. Long-distance transportation was largely by rail or sea. Shorter-distance transportation was by horse and carriage. Most people lived around where they worked. But Ford foresaw a future that many didn't.

28. "Is the recession heralding a return to Henry Ford's model?," *The Economist*, March 27, 2009, http://www.economist.com/node/13173671.

29. "State Motor Vehicle Registrations (1900–1995)," U.S. Department of Transportation Federal Highway Administration, accessed March 1, 2018, https://www.fhwa.dot.gov/ohim/summary95/mv200.pdf.

30. Earl Swift, *Big Roads* (New York: Houghton Mifflin Harcourt, 2011).

31. Ibid., 255.

32. Even as cars were making their way all across America, many states still had a hard time building roads. Swift points out that "just about every state [in America] was desperate for better roads but exasperated by its inability to provide them. The cost of bringing highways up to even minimal surface standards was beyond the means of most and the technical capabilities of many." We discuss the relationship between innovation and infrastructures in Chapter 10.
     Ibid., 24, 38.

33. Adam Przeworski's study on this is quite comprehensive and clear. As citizens gain economic independence, political liberties and democratic freedoms follow. Summarizing Przeworski's research, Fareed Zakaria

notes in his book *The Future of Freedom: Illiberal Democracy at Home and Abroad,* "In a democratic country that has a per capita income of under $1,500 (in today's dollars), the regime on average had a life expectancy of just eight years. With between $1,500 and $3,000, it survived on average for about eighteen years. Above $6,000 it became highly resilient. The chance that a democratic regime would die in a country with an income above $6,000 was 1 in 500. Once rich, democracies become immortal." And so, on the one hand, one could applaud the American government for its ingenuity in promoting democratic values, or one could applaud the innovators who work tirelessly to increase incomes that, thereafter, render democracies stable.

Fareed Zakaria, *The Future of Freedom: Illiberal Democracy at Home and Abroad* (New York: W. W. Norton & Company, Inc., 2007), 69–70.

34. Daniel Gross, "Henry Ford Understood That Raising Wages Would Bring Him More Profit," *The Daily Beast,* January 6, 2014, https://www .thedailybeast.com/henry-ford-understood-that-raising-wages-would -bring-him-more-profit.

35. Steven C. Stanford, "Henry Ford—An Impact Felt," Henry Ford Heritage Association, March 1, 2018, http://hfha.org/the-ford-story/henry -ford-an-impact-felt/.

36. "Henry Ford Quotations: Popular Research Topics," Collections & Research, The Henry Ford, accessed April 7, 2018, https://www.the henryford.org/collections-and-research/digital-resources/popular-topics /henry-ford-quotes/.

37. It is no coincidence that the price of steel dropped significantly during the late 1800s and early 1900s. In 1872, a ton of steel cost $56, but by 1900, steel prices had dropped to $11.50. As market-creating innovations spread in the United States, transportation became more important to move products around. For instance, the number of miles of railroad track, of which steel is a major component, increased from 30,626 in 1860 to 193,346 in 1900. This resulted in a significant drop in freight costs from 20 cents per ton-mile in 1865 to 1.75 cents per ton-mile in 1900. As more Americans pulled steel into their lives (railroads, automobiles, buildings), innovators were incentivized to make the product cheaper. Andrew Carnegie, one of the most influential innovators of the nineteenth and twentieth centuries, was responsible for a majority of the efficiency innovations in this industry. He consolidated the industry and took advantage of economies of scale.

Michael Dahlen, "The Rise of American Big Government: A Brief History of How We Got Here," *The Objective Standard,* January 28, 2014,

https://www.theobjectivestandard.com/issues/2009-fall/rise-of-american
-big-government/.

38. "Fact #962: January 30, 2017 Vehicles per Capita: Other Regions/
Countries Compared to the United States," Vehicle Technologies Office,
Office of Energy Efficiency & Renewable Energy, January 30, 2017, https://
energy.gov/eere/vehicles/fact-962-january-30-2017-vehicles-capita
-other-regionscountries-compared-united-states.

39. Daniel Kadlec, "America's Banker A.P. Giannini," *TIME*, March 8,
2017, http://content.time.com/time/magazine/article/0,9171,989772-2,00
.html.

40. "A. P. Giannini, Branch Banking," Who Made America?, PBS, accessed March 1, 2018, http://www.pbs.org/wgbh/theymadeamerica/who
made/giannini_hi.html.

41. Ralph J. Christian, "Statement of Significance," form for United States
Department of the Interior, accessed March 2, 2018, https://npgallery
.nps.gov/pdfhost/docs/NHLS/Text/78000754.pdf.

42. Alex E. McCalla and Warren E. Johnston, "Giannini: A Retrospective,"
Giannini Foundation for Agricultural Economics, accessed March 2, 2018,
https://s.giannini.ucop.edu/uploads/giannini_public/7b/9e/7b9e282b
-f8dd-4250-bdd7-9cd42235c269/apgiannini-book-a-retrospective.pdf.

43. Jerry Useem, "20 That Made History," *Fortune*, June 27, 2005.

44. Richard Morin, "UNCONVENTIONAL WISDOM," *Washington Post*,
November 15, 1998, https://www.washingtonpost.com/archive/opinions
/1998/11/15/unconventional-wisdom/24f94e64-5010-4ca1-9786-8c5c30b
f6a68/?utm_term=.a3c06a9278ea.

45. Farmers, pickers, and canners were very important to Bank of America's business. In 1919, more than half of the $74 million the bank loaned
out went to farmers.

46. Henry Louis Gates Jr., "Madam Walker, the First Black American Woman to Be a Self-Made Millionaire," *PBS*, accessed March 9,
2018, http://www.pbs.org/wnet/african-americans-many-rivers-to-cross
/history/100-amazing-facts/madam-walker-the-first-black-american
-woman-to-be-a-self-made-millionaire/.

Chapter 6

How the East Met the West

The mission of Sony is to design products for markets that don't exist yet.

—AKIO MORITA, COFOUNDER OF SONY

The Idea in Brief

After World War II and the subsequent Korean War, Japan, South Korea, and the whole East Asia region were desperately poor. Whatever industries these nations had were decimated by the wars, and prospects for economic development were bleak. Fast-forward to today, and Japan and South Korea have each achieved a remarkable level of prosperity. As these nations emerged from poverty, not only were the efforts of some entrepreneurs supported by the government, but several companies also leveraged their low-cost advantage and ultimately targeted export markets.

Although each of those factors was critical, when we assess the rise of these nations through our lenses, we also see a spectacular tale of innovation. Many of the most successful firms, some of which are household names today, invested in innovations that either created new markets or connected to large and growing ones. The trajectory of these firms would have been impossible to predict considering their humble beginnings. One of Sony's initial products was an electric blanket that often caught fire. Kia began as a bicycle company. And Samsung once sold dried fish.

In this chapter, we shine a light on the triumph of innovation in helping Japan and South Korea sustain their rise to prosperity. What we learn from these nations is that prosperity is a process, not an event, one that requires a continuous commitment to innovation.

————

In the years after the end of World War II, Japan was in dire economic straits. In 1950, the per capita income of Japan was less than those of Mexico and Colombia—and just 20 percent of that of the United States. Most of the country's industry was destroyed during the war, and it experienced a severe food shortage that lasted several years afterward. Food was rationed and millions starved. Raw materials, such as rubber, magnets, electric motors, and other metals, were virtually impossible to come by. In fact, many homes didn't have cooking utensils and doorknobs because they were used toward the war effort as raw materials. Four years before the war, Japanese streets were teeming with six times as many horse-drawn cargo vehicles as motorized cars. After the war, motorcycles were a luxury for civilians, also cars—and many cars had been converted to run on wood, the only fuel Japan could be sure to replenish during the war. In 1949, Japan had only 9,306 kilometers of roads, of which just 1,824 kilometers were paved. To put that into perspective, today Japan has approximately 1.2 million kilometers of roads, most of which are paved.

The Japanese—much like the Americans in the 1800s and billions of citizens in low-income countries today—were very, very poor.

As if that weren't bad enough, Allied Forces occupied Japan from 1945 to 1952 and dictated manufacturing and industrial policy appropriate for peacetime. For example, at the outset of the occupation, Government Headquarters (GHQ) limited monthly production of trucks and passenger vehicles to just 1,500 and 350 respectively. Japan faced an enormous uphill battle to rebuild.

The prospect of Japan's economy recovering swiftly from the shock of war seemed unlikely. So unlikely, in fact, that US Secretary of State John Foster Dulles famously declared that the country "should not expect to find a big U.S. market because the Japanese don't make the things we want."[1] In other words, don't look to the export markets to solve your problems. Whatever Japan was selling, America wasn't buying. In some ways, Dulles was right. Many of us are old enough to remember that the label "Made in Japan" once signaled dubious quality.[2]

The nascent innovations being developed at that time by Tokyo Tsushin Kogyo (TTK) cofounders Akio Morita and Masaru Ibuka, out of what was initially a radio repair shop set up in a bombed-out department store, were part of the generation of low-quality Japanese products. The twenty-person company had no support from the government and no obvious demand for the innovations they had begun to create, but they remained undeterred. Though he didn't have our language for it at the time, it's clear that Morita was a master at instinctively identifying opportunity in struggle and nonconsumption. Morita and his colleagues began to build a market-creating innovation powerhouse—a company you now know as Sony Corporation. Today, Sony is worth an estimated $49 billion and employs more than 128,000 worldwide, and the company is synonymous with technology and innovation in Japan and across the world.

Sony is just one of the plethora of Japanese companies that focused on developing innovations for markets that did not yet exist. By then, the world had begun to hear about Toyota, Nissan, and a very young Honda. What the world did not know, however, was that this was simply the tip of the innovation iceberg, which would impact citizens of both Japan and the rest of the world. With these companies and the market-creating innovations they developed, the country's economy would grow so fast that war-ravaged Japan was in a position to host the world in Tokyo at the 1964 Olympic Games—less than two decades after the end of World War II. Fifty years after World War II, Japan's GDP of $42,500 had eclipsed those of the United States and the United Kingdom. Today, Japan is the world's third-largest economy, responsible for approximately 6 percent of all global economic activity.

Japan's neighbor, South Korea, shares a similar story of economic transformation through innovation. And as was true for Japan, a few decades ago, no one would have predicted that South Korea would develop, much less develop as quickly as it did. The country's transformation has frequently been dubbed a "miracle" because it seemed to defy logic. But that's exactly why both Japan's and South Korea's rise from poverty to prosperity offers us several important lessons. We will focus on three here.

The first is that investing in innovation, regardless of the circumstances in which a country finds itself, is possible. The markets that these innovations create and sustain pull other much-needed resources into society. And because those components are pulled in to support a market, their likelihood of sustainability is very high.

The second lesson is that entrepreneurs with an eye for local needs are necessary to drive market-creating innovations. Because locals are immersed in the struggles of average everyday citizens, they can translate those struggles into viable innovations and economic opportunity. And local entrepreneurs are able to instill a sense of pride in their citizens—a belief that "we too" can innovate, create, and prosper. This, to us, seems to be one of the most valuable things that can happen in a nation: driving home the fact that locals can solve their own problems.

And finally, as we showed in the last chapter, we see that integration is necessary when countries are at an early stage of development. By definition, poor countries do not have the requisite education, transportation, and business and governance infrastructures that are already present in wealthy economies. As such, innovators that seek to engage in business in these countries often have to integrate their operations in order to be successful. By pulling in the resources and the support they need for their businesses to thrive, be it infrastructures, education, or other things, they are inadvertently engaging in nation-building.

Few examples illustrate these lessons better than Sony.

Sony: The Market-Creating Machine

Before Sony became Sony, when it was still Tokyo Tsushin Kogyo (TTK), the company might have deserved Dulles's harsh words. It didn't start out making world-class innovations that would wow the world. In fact, it would have been impossible to predict Sony's trajectory from its humble beginnings. In the early years, TTK manufactured and sold electric heated cushions that often caught fire, "scorching blankets and futons."[3] The floors in the company's manufacturing plants were peppered with potholes, and since the company could only afford buildings that had been damaged during the war, the exteriors also had cracks. This made for very interesting working conditions: whenever it rained, the factory floors were dotted with pools of water.

As was true for so many of the innovation pioneers in America in the previous century, the tale of Sony's humble start-up years is filled with hardscrabble survival strategies, workarounds, and sheer ingenuity in the face of seemingly impossible survival odds. Sony had so few resources that the company couldn't afford machinery and equipment, so engineers created their own. They made soldering irons, electrical coils, and even screwdrivers, often working into the early hours of the morning, sometimes being mistaken for thieves by the local police, as they tried to get in and out of the building at odd hours. Several times, Sony almost couldn't make payroll. On one particular occasion, the company had to pay salaries in two installments, instead of the usual one.

None of that, however, stopped company founders Akio Morita and Masaru Ibuka, who instinctively did what large corporations, many of which were propped up by the government, found difficult to do—target nonconsumption and create new markets.

Many people would think of Sony's major innovation triumph as the Walkman, which went on to sell over four hundred million units and created a worldwide culture of personal music devices. But it was actually a much humbler product that started Sony on its trajectory to the innovation powerhouse it is today: the G-type tape recorder, a portable magnetic reel-to-reel tape-recording device, what Morita called a "tape corder" at the time. "Before tape corders were invented, 'recording' was something very remote from our daily lives," Morita would write in a 1950 book trying to explain the value of personal recording. "Previously it required special, complex technology and was very expensive. Now, however, with Sony's new tape corder, recordings can be made quickly, cheaply and accurately by anyone anywhere anytime."

Morita saw the enormous potential of helping customers record moments and memories of their own lives, not unlike Eastman's photographs had done decades before. "It's such a revolutionary product, the first of its kind in Japan. And it is so convenient. How could anyone resist buying it?" was how Akio Morita saw it. Yet people did resist. At least at first. People were fascinated by the portable recorders, but they weren't selling like hotcakes, and Sony executives knew they had to do something different. After experiencing tepid sales for a while, Ibuka and Morita mobilized virtually all of the company's engineers into sales roles. Sony learned through this process that, as Nobel laureate Ron Coase observed, markets don't just appear or happen; "markets have to be created."

To create this new market, the company had to build its own sales and distribution channels, and so in 1951, Sony established a subsidiary called the Tokyo Recording Company for this purpose, triggering the creation of a battery of *local jobs* (sales, distribution, advertising, training, service and support, and so on). Once, Ibuka asked the head of Tokyo Recording Company to go on a nationwide tour to demonstrate the product in schools. So many schools ended up putting in orders as a result of this tour that Sony couldn't produce the recorders fast enough to meet the demand. Additionally, Ibuka redirected some of the company's engineering effort to after-sales support in order to improve the customer experience. Sales flourished, and Sony learned never to underestimate either the effort required to create a new market or the potentially huge reward that comes with it.

Thankfully, Sony kept innovating, focused on creating new markets—first in Japan, and then for exports. In 1955, Sony introduced the world's first battery-powered pocket transistor radio, a product that targeted the hundreds of millions of people for whom vacuum tube radios were too large and expensive. Although Sony's battery-powered transistor radio was not as good in terms of sound quality compared to the vacuum tube radios on the market, it was small, inexpensive, and "good enough." The customers Sony targeted—typically teenagers, few of whom could afford big vacuum tube radios—were very happy to listen to music with their friends in new places out of earshot of their parents.

I remember being thrilled to purchase and listen to my own transistor radio. For me, it represented progress, and, quite frankly, my alternative was no radio at all. Before the end of the 1950s, the battery-powered transistor radio market was worth hundreds of millions of dollars, with many other companies developing the product. The battery-powered transistor radio created jobs, generated profits for Sony, and provided Sony, and Japanese citizens, with more proof that they could innovate their way to prosperity. Sony would replicate this formula time and again, with market-creating innovations that initially took root in local markets before traveling around the world.

Between 1950 and 1982, Sony successfully built twelve different new markets. These included the original battery-powered pocket transistor radio, the first portable solid-state black-and-white television (by 1959, so many Japanese families owned a television that the royal wedding of the crown prince became a media spectacle, with a record fifteen million people watching it live on TV), videocassette players, portable video recorders, 3.5-inch floppy disk drives, and, of course, the now-famous Sony Walkman.

Sony cofounder Morita built an empire on his instinctive understanding of the opportunity found in struggle. The Walkman cassette player was actually temporarily put on hold when market research indicated that consumers would never buy a tape player that didn't have the capacity to record and that customers would be irritated by the use of earphones. But Morita ignored his marketing department's warning, trusting his own gut instead. Rather than relying on market research, he urged his team to "carefully watch how people live, get an intuitive sense as to what they might want, and then go with it." Morita's instincts were right: others shared in his struggle to make music portable. The Walkman found a ready market in Japan, where Sony executives initially thought they would sell roughly five thousand units a month. Instead, they sold more than fifty thousand in the first two months. All of a sudden, walking, running, reading, and writing while listening to music became possible. In forty years, Sony sold more than four hundred million units. The Walkman became one of the most successful portable consumer products to ever be released.

A market was born—and others were quick to jump in. With every new market Sony created, many other companies, including Toshiba, Panasonic, and several others, followed suit and capitalized on the opportunity. The Walkman helped other companies see that "mobile music" was possible. To be clear, a market does not revolve around any individual company—it revolves around creating new consumers and continually innovating and refining the understanding of their struggle and Job to Be Done. Sony later missed the boat on the MP3 and iPod, but the company had already planted the seeds for the industry to grow and flourish. What's truly amazing is how many times Sony identified and created new markets that others then jumped into.

That's in part because with each product Sony released—from the electric heated cushions to the Walkman—and each market the company created, Sony found a way to develop a profitable business model that targeted the struggles of average Japanese people. To be successful, Sony needed to create local jobs. With each job the company created, Sony was inadvertently helping rebuild Japan, and pulled in the resources necessary to develop it into a prosperous nation. When I come across a Sony product these days, I don't just see a cool innovation, I see something much more powerful and enduring: the process by which one of the most prosperous nations in the world developed.

Even though there are other prominent consumer electronics companies today, Sony is still synonymous with Japanese innovation. From war-torn Japan, two friends with modest means and with no government support were able to build one of the world's most recognizable companies by creating new markets that targeted nonconsumption. And that, of course, was just one of the innovation success stories that fueled Japan's economic ascendancy. There were many more.

Toyota: From Japanese Nonconsumption to Global Powerhouse

Consider the Japanese automaker Toyota, whose low-cost, compact Corolla is the bestselling car of all time. That didn't happen primarily because Toyota was able to employ cheap labor or receive government support. Those things certainly helped, but Toyota was onto something far more significant and enduring—in the years after World War II.

When Toyota Motor Corporation was first founded in 1937, the company focused on nonconsumption locally in Japan and the East Asia region. Few would have thought that it would someday become the fifth-largest company in the world by revenue. At the time, there were close to 310,000 horse-drawn vehicles and another 111,000 ox-drawn vehicles still circling the streets of Japan.[4] Most of Japan's roads were unpaved, which made driving both an expensive and risky adventure. Bad roads lead to broken cars, and with only 20 percent of roads paved, broken cars were a common sight in postwar Japan. Toyota vehicles were therefore designed with that local context in mind: the then-president of Toyota, Kiichiro Toyoda, declared that Toyota cars should be developed as "economical vehicles that can withstand poor roads and are more practical for the peoples of East Asia."[5]

The cars Toyota made in Japan back then would not have been good enough for an American consumer. But that didn't matter. His intent was to capture the vast nonconsumption in both Japan and neighboring Asian countries before focusing on exporting to more advanced countries. It wasn't until 1980 that Toyota exported as many cars to North America as it sold in Japan.[6] But even when Toyota began exporting to North America, it still employed a strategy of targeting the lower end of the American market, people who couldn't afford Detroit's gas-guzzling vehicles.

The importance of Toyota first targeting nonconsumption, as opposed to competing with incumbent automobile companies in richer countries, such as Ford, General Motors, and Chrysler, cannot be overstated, especially in the context of a developing Japan. First of all, Toyota was able to create a local market in Japan that pulled in marketing, sales, distribution, training, servicing, and supporting products pertaining to the auto industry. For example, Toyota invested heavily in the Chubu Nippon Drivers' School in Nagoya and spent as much as 40 percent of the company's capital on the school. It became a model for other driving schools in the country, promoted motorization in Japan, and helped Toyota sell more vehicles. This differs greatly from a purely low-wage strategy where products are manufactured in a factory and exported to another country. If it had followed that strategy, Toyota would not have chosen to invest in a driving school, which, in 1958, housed a Toyota sales college for training new employees on the Toyota sales method (now called Nisshin Education and Training Center). Targeting nonconsumption requires more than technical knowledge of how to efficiently make and ship a product. It requires knowledge of the local context.

Second, targeting nonconsumption successfully creates a vibrant market that pulls in long-term employment. As Toyota built new plants and sold more cars to Japanese customers, it needed more employees. For example, as more companies set up automobile manufacturing in Toyota City—a city that was given its new name after Toyota built a plant and offices there—the ratio of job openings to job applicants rose from 2.7 in 1962 to 7.1 in 1970.[7] Toyota had only twenty-nine dealerships in 1938; by 1980, it had more than three hundred across Japan. From an employment standpoint, Toyota's growth was exponential. In 1957, Toyota employed approximately 6,300 people. Ten years later, employment at Toyota had quintupled, reaching more than 32,000. Today, Toyota employs more than 344,000 people worldwide, with more than 70,000 in Japan. Eiji Toyoda summarized Toyota's attitude toward training and providing relevant education for its workforce: "It is people who make things. So we must first make people before we make things." This thinking led Toyota to build an education and training department and a Toyota trade school for training "middle-rank skilled shop employees."[8]

Third, targeting nonconsumption can help a region create a more relevant and contextual regulatory and institutional framework. As Jeffrey Alexander writes in his book *Japan's Motorcycle Wars,* as more and more vehicles found themselves on Japanese roads, "[there became] a pressing need for coherent government policies on road traffic, vehicle and driver licensing, and the policing of city streets."[9] In other words, the proliferation of the innovation (vehicles) led to policies that made sense in Japan's specific circumstances. These circumstance-specific regulations further helped the country develop its regulations more sustainably. Innovations, as we have found, often precede regulations. It's hard to properly regulate what you don't yet have.

Fourth, targeting nonconsumption, especially for the automobile industry, built up other industries in the Japanese economy. For example, not only did jobs in selling and servicing cars increase, but jobs in the logistics and transportation sectors increased as well. More Japanese began to travel and tour their country as transportation became less expensive. Additionally, access to schools and hospitals, and the expansion of cities in Japan, were also enabled by the automobile.

Sliding Doors: What if Toyota Went after Consumption?

Imagine if this had all played out differently. What if postwar Toyota had consistently focused on competing with the big three US auto giants at the time (Ford, GM, Chrysler)? Would the company—and the country—have fared as well? As it turns out, Toyota did, but only very briefly.

In 1958, after Toyota experienced success in the Japanese market, the company set its eyes on the US market with its leading model, the Toyopet Crown. The car had done very well in Japan, and executives felt the success would be replicated in the United States. Instead, the Crown was a spectacular failure. One observer commented, "While the Crown was purpose-built for Japan's poor quality road network, it struggled to keep pace on America's smooth, fast-flowing black-top. When it eventually got to 60 mph—a speed that was rare in Japan—the car apparently shuddered so much the driver couldn't see out of the rear-view mirror." By 1961, defeated Toyota executives packed their bags and left the US market. But not for good.

After studying the US market and better understanding the Job to Be Done of US consumers, Toyota built the Corolla, which would go on to become the most successful car in history by sales volume. Instead of building something that competed with the big three, Toyota pursued a different strategy. "We can avoid direct competition with the Big 3, and small cars are very good for second or third cars," one of Toyota's top executives, Shotaro Kamiya, later explained about the Corolla strategy.[10]

Toyota's success as a Japanese car manufacturer affected other Japanese companies as well. While Toyota is the largest Japanese car manufacturer, and currently among the top three largest car companies in the world, the company is not alone. Nissan, Honda, Mitsubishi, Suzuki, and Mazda are just several other Japanese auto manufacturers that have played a significant role in shaping the Japanese economy as well.

Small Motorcycles, Big Development

As impressive as the Japanese entry into the global automobile industry was, even more impressive was their entry into the motorcycle market, largely because they did it in spite of the lack of government support. After the war, the Japanese government supported investments in heavy industries, such as shipbuilding and the manufacturing of larger vehicles, because it assumed growth would come from those industries.[11] As such, many motorcycle manufacturers were often denied the raw materials they needed to develop their products, which were referred to as toys.

As we mentioned earlier, government support, when channeled properly, can help an industry and an economy grow, but it is usually not the main reason for success. And we can all point to well-intentioned and well-designed but ultimately unsuccessful government-led economic development programs. Many governments pursue one economic agenda or another, but only a few succeed. So when new companies enter a market and swiftly become dominant players in it, as Japanese companies did in the motorcycle industry—without the support of the Japanese government—it provides compelling evidence of the power of market-creating innovation.

Before the emergence of the Japanese motorcycle industry, motorcycles were very expensive in Japan. "No motorcycles were made domestically at the time, so all of ours were imported . . . We brought in ten units of this 'Rolls Royce of Motorcycles,' but they sold for roughly 2,000 yen, while a Ford Model T sold for only 1,900 yen, so motorcycles were more expensive," recalls Ozeki Hidekichi, one of the pioneers in the industry. "I think my monthly wage was 3 yen or 5 yen at that time, and from the age of twenty I was paid 7 yen or 10 yen, so a motorcycle was absurdly expensive, and as a result we only sold one or two in a year."[12] Understandably, the industry was just too small and unimportant to attract any sort of attention or help from the government. Nonetheless, several companies began to see the need for Japanese people to move around more freely, and more cheaply. Over time, as more and more motorcycle companies sprang up in Japan, these firms created the Hamamatsu Motorcycle Manufacturers' Association.[13]

From a group of more than two hundred motorcycle makers in the 1950s, Honda, Kawasaki, Suzuki, and Yamaha emerged to captain the industry's development at home and abroad. As tempting as it was, these "big four" motorcycle firms did not seek growth by stealing market share from existing leaders in motorcycle manufacturing. Rather, they created new markets by targeting nonconsumption. When the National Diet (Japan's legislative body, known as Kokkai) passed an amendment to the country's Road Traffic Control Law in 1952 to allow younger drivers to ride motorcycles, Suzuki was one of the first companies to see the opportunity to create a new market. It swiftly adapted its offerings for younger consumers, with its low-end 60cc Diamond Free bike.

Similarly, Honda launched the 1952 50cc Cub F-Type to target the growing number of small businesses that needed delivery vehicles but couldn't afford large ones. Honda positioned the motorcycle at a more affordable price of 25,000 yen (about $70 at the time)[14] and provided a twelve-month installment financing plan. Domestic competition among firms vying for the business of consumers

with little disposable income caused them to invest in not just manufacturing, but also distribution, marketing, sales, support, and,
in some cases, training. This created jobs in Japan beyond the big
four themselves, and after years of improving their products, it also
gave them the ability to export their motorcycles to nonconsumers
in the United States and Europe, serving the markets there as well.

The same pattern of targeting nonconsumption was seen with
Panasonic, Sharp, and Nintendo in consumer electronics, and
Canon, Kyocera, and Ricoh in office equipment. These firms often
targeted nonconsumption in Japan first, and then globally.[15] Focusing on nonconsumption has significant development potential
for countries, because it forces companies to develop not just their
manufacturing capabilities, which create *global jobs*, but also their
sales and distribution capabilities, which create much-needed *local
jobs*, a critical factor in producing and spreading prosperity.

Japan rose out of the ashes of the war's destruction with ideals and goals that created a culture of innovation and opportunity.
"The losers wished to both forget the past and to transcend it," John
Dower wrote in his Pulitzer Prize–winning analysis of Japan in the
wake of World War II. "The ideals of peace and democracy took root
in Japan—not as a borrowed ideology or imposed vision, but as a
lived experience and seized opportunity."

Where you start is not where you finish, and Japan is not the only
Asian country that makes that clear. South Korea does as well.

South Korea: Pulling Its Way to Prosperity

In the years following the Korean War, South Korea was in tatters.
"[In] 1953 . . . The nation's capital, Seoul, had changed hands four
times and each time there was bitter fighting between rival parties.
There was little to no electricity and just about the only industry the
country had was textiles,"[16] according to Harvard emeritus professor
Ezra Vogel. In fact, at the time North Korea was more industrialized

than South Korea. With a GDP per capita of $155 in 1960, South Korea was desperately poor.

But when I visit South Korea these days, it's hard to reconcile it with the impoverished country I grew to love a few decades ago. Today, with a GDP per capita of more than $27,500, South Korea's *Korea Aid* is active in assisting many other poor countries in meeting the UN Sustainable Development Goals. How did South Korea orchestrate such an astonishing turnaround?[17]

Many factors, such as culture, visionary leadership, heavy industries, foreign trade, aid from the United States, and geography, have played an important role in what's been dubbed "The Miracle on the Han River." But the story of innovation in South Korea, one not often told, has also been critical in the country's transformation.

Companies such as Samsung, Hyundai, LG, and Kia Motors, which have been engines of economic growth in South Korea, are today recognized as some of the world's most innovative companies. Samsung, for instance, is responsible for approximately a fifth of South Korea's $1.1 trillion GDP. When these firms were founded, however, the notion that they would someday become major global powerhouses was unthinkable. But South Korea's story tells us that it is possible.

Consider Kia's modest beginnings. The company was founded in 1944 as Kyungsung Precision Industry, makers of steel tubing and bicycle parts. Kia then saw the opportunity to help Koreans move around much more easily, and fully integrated to manufacture bicycles. By 1952, Kia developed its first bicycle, called the Samchully. A few years after the Samchully, Kia began building Honda-licensed motorcycles. In 1962, Kia built the three-wheeler K-360 pickup; that was the company's first foray into automobile manufacturing. With the K-360, Kia made mobility more affordable for Koreans. It soon followed that with the T-600, another three-wheeler pickup vehicle but with larger storage space and better fuel efficiency. It was not until 1974 that Kia released the Kia Brisa, its first passenger vehicle, a good thirty years after the company was founded.[18]

Kia's strategy of first targeting nonconsumption prevented it from competing head-on with established auto manufacturers. By 1944, automobile manufacturing technology was well under way. Ford had been around for more than four decades; General Motors had acquired Oldsmobile, Cadillac, and Pontiac; Mitsubishi had been manufacturing automobiles for almost thirty years; and Toyota released its first passenger vehicle in 1936. People knew what cars were and had embraced them as part and parcel of modern society. Wealthy countries had vibrant auto markets where many citizens understood the value of owning a vehicle. Many businesses revolved around the car. Kia could have easily made the decision to leverage its low-cost labor and target existing consumption of cars by competing head-on with other car manufacturers.

But instead, the company started with bicycles, then graduated to three-wheelers, and then, only years later, passenger vehicles—a product targeted at nonconsumption. The impact Kia has had and is still having on the Korean economy is astounding. From makers of bicycles and three-wheeler vehicles, Kia has grown into one of the world's largest auto manufacturers. Today, the company employs more than thirty thousand people directly and grosses revenues of approximately $50 billion. In June 2015, forty years after the company's first exports of ten units of Kia Brisa vehicles to Qatar, Kia exported its fifteen millionth vehicle.

Samsung, which began in 1938 selling dried fish, flour, and vegetables in a depressingly poor South Korea, has a similar story. After the war, Samsung ventured into other sectors such as insurance, retail, textiles, and in 1969, electronics. Samsung Electronics' first product, a black-and-white television, was known for such fuzzy picture quality that it was often "thrown in free with magazine subscriptions."[19] Soon after, the company produced its first cheap electric fans, followed by low-cost air conditioners, and in 1983 it launched its first personal computer.

Much like Sony's initial products, many of Samsung's early products were also poor quality. So poor, in fact, that Samsung CEO

Lee Kun-hee told his executives in 1993 that *everything* needed to be improved. "Change everything but your wife and children," he famously declared, ordering more than 150,000 electronics products, including phones and fax machines, to be burned in front of the employees that made them. This served as a wake-up call to Samsung employees that low-cost doesn't mean low-quality. It worked.

In 1994, Samsung developed the world's first 256-megabit DRAM chip, and by 1998 the company introduced the world's first mass-produced digital TV. Samsung became the largest and most profitable consumer electronics company in the world in 2006. Its digital research center alone had floor space equivalent to the size of thirty football fields. In 2017, Samsung spent $12.7 billion on research and development, more than any other company except Amazon and Alphabet (Google's parent company).

Today, Samsung makes everything from washing machines and refrigerators to smartphones and smart TVs. By launching a continuous stream of innovations, it is widely recognized as an industry leader in technology and ranks as a top-ten global brand.

These innovations have not only propelled Samsung to global dominance but have also had a significant impact on the South Korean economy.

Most people outside of South Korea really only know Samsung for its laptop computers or its line of Galaxy smartphones. But Samsung is so much more than just an electronics gadget maker to the average South Korean consumer. Today, Samsung not only is South Korea's leading electronics manufacturer, but also has significant market presence in numerous industries through its subsidiaries and affiliates—home appliances, securities, life insurance, construction, packaged foods, and chemicals, just to name a few. If you live in South Korea, there's a good chance that you consume products and services that are either directly or indirectly produced by Samsung on a daily basis.

If you're still having a hard time picturing just how pervasive the Samsung brand is throughout South Korea, here's a good example. Nate Kim, who has helped us with research for this book, visits his family in Seoul every year. Nate tells me that when he arrives at Incheon International Airport, his parents come to pick him up in their Renault Samsung SM5 sedan (which, by the way, is insured by Samsung Fire & Marine Insurance). They then bring him back home to their apartment, which was built by Samsung Construction and Trading Corporation. Most of the appliances in their apartment—such as their refrigerator, washer and dryer, air conditioner, and television—are Samsung-made. One of Nate's cousins is a doctor at the Samsung Medical Center, while another works at Samsung Heavy Industries, one of the largest shipbuilders in the world. While millions of parents in the United States take their kids to Disney World for family vacations, Nate's parents took him and his brother to Everland, a theme park owned and operated by Samsung.

From its humble beginnings in 1938, when the company had just forty employees, Samsung has grown to more than $220 billion in revenues and approximately half a million employees today.

Innovation is contagious, and it often feeds other innovations. Other South Korean companies have followed suit, and companies such as Hyundai, LG, POSCO, and many others have been instrumental in fueling prosperity in South Korea.

Consider POSCO—formerly Pohang Iron and Steel Company, a critical supplier to many South Korean companies and now a major steel exporter—and how it has impacted development in South Korea. In 2016, POSCO produced approximately forty-two million tons of steel and is now one of the world's largest steel manufacturers. Forty-five years ago, this would have been unthinkable.

When the World Bank assessed the economic feasibility of building an integrated steel mill in South Korea in the 1960s, it concluded that the project would be premature. Who could blame them? At the time, South Korea was not only poor, but also lacked iron ore (a critical input for steelmaking), and the country was not close to any easy-to-access supply. In addition, South Korea didn't have the technical capabilities necessary to build and maintain such a heavy industry. Then there was the question of markets: in the unlikely event that South Korea could build all this steel, to whom would it sell? Japan may have been the logical choice, but that country already had some of the world's most efficient steel companies.[20]

So POSCO looked inward. POSCO's initial strategy of meeting domestic demand for steel helped the company get on its feet. As the South Korean economy grew, several local industries emerged that would need steel as an input. For example, POSCO supported the auto and construction industries as they grew. Today, the South Korean auto industry accounts for roughly 25 percent of the steel production while the construction industry accounts for 28 percent. From its humble beginnings—when employees slept in makeshift shelters at the company site and actually ate rice mixed with sand to help themselves feel more full—POSCO has grown to become one of South Korea's largest companies. Today the company grosses more than $60 billion annually.

POSCO's impact on South Korea had a ripple effect on other industries because the company had to integrate many of its operations. Observing that "you can import coal and machines, but you cannot import talent," POSCO's founder, Park Tae-joon, led the company to establish the Pohang University of Science and Technology (POSTECH) and Research Institute of Industrial Science and Technology (RIST) to provide needed education in science and technology. The schools were "established to meet the needs of self-developed technology for technology independence, creating a firm connection between academia and industry," according to POSCO's leadership.

Although POSTECH began as a training ground for future engineers and technicians, to meet the technical demands of South Korea's growing economy, it has evolved into a full-fledged university with more than twenty different departments, including mathematics, computer science, life sciences, and so on. As South Korea's economy grew and evolved, so did POSTECH. The school morphed itself to respond to the demands of the economy. POSTECH now consistently tops domestic and international university rankings and has been rated number one by the London-based Times Higher Education's "100 Under 50," a ranking of the top one hundred universities under fifty years old.[21]

Because POSCO had to develop a school to train its workers, South Korea now benefits from having a top-notch institution. But this institution had to be *pulled* into South Korea to accomplish a very specific task. If it had been *pushed* onto the country, it would likely not have had the same impact. To remain sustainable, educational institutions need to be connected to the needs of a market, local or global; POSTECH was.

South Korea today is not the same country it was right after the war, or even when I was there in the early 1970s. Many things have helped South Korea grow, but the continuous commitment to innovation by South Korean firms has been critical in helping it both create and sustain its prosperity. Today, South Korea has overcome debilitating poverty in many aspects of its economy, including governance, which has markedly improved since the 1960s. The economic freedoms ignited by this growth in prosperity are giving way for political freedoms previously unthinkable in the country.

————

The growth and development of these countries stunned so many that, during the 1997 Asian financial crisis, the once-celebrated "East Asian Miracle" was said to be "no more than a mirage," with suggestions that the chickens had finally come home to roost.[22] Recovery would be questionable as there were suggestions that their growth had been built on a tenuous foundation without the proper systems and structures to support robust economic development.[23] But they did recover, and have since thrived. The level of learning, innovation, and development of markets in these nations—and their resilience in the face of economic setback—points to growth built on a strong foundation. It is hopeful.

Although these nations got some things wrong—as does every nation—they got the innovation piece of the puzzle right.

Market-creating innovations are not the only way for a country to develop. Taiwan, for example, initially focused on developing simple products such as textiles and processed foods for the eight million people on the small island, but, very soon after, it targeted other markets outside its borders.[24] And just as innovation played a critical role in the development of Japan and South Korea, it also played a critical role in the development of Taiwan, which eventually achieved prosperity.

There is, of course, more work to be done to better understand the specific circumstances in which different economies develop. However, what we have learned is that prioritizing investments in market-creating innovations, even in difficult circumstances, provides poor countries a viable path to prosperity.

NOTES

1.   William K. Tabb, *The Postwar Japanese System: Cultural Economy and Economic Transformation* (Oxford: Oxford University Press, 1995), 14.

2.   That stereotype has long since washed away. In fact, it did so rather swiftly. When Marty McFly, the main character in the 1985 hit movie *Back to the Future*, finds himself accidentally launched back in time to 1955, his partner laments that a key circuit in the car they're trying to repair broke because it's labeled "Made in Japan." McFly doesn't understand the reference. "What are you talking about? All the best stuff is made in Japan."

3.   Sony Corporation 50th Anniversary Project Team, *Genryu: Sony 50th Anniversary* (Tokyo: Sony Corporation, 1996).

4.   Jeffrey Alexander, *Japan's Motorcycle Wars: An Industry History* (Vancouver: UBC Press, 2009), 36.

5.   Toyota, "Resumption of automobile exports and Toyota in Okinawa," 75 Years of Toyota, accessed March 30, 2018, http://www.toyota-global .com/company/history_of_toyota/75years/text/taking_on_the_automotive _business/chapter2/section9/item2.html.

6.   At the outset, Toyota's exports to other Asian and Oceanic countries also surpassed exports to North America, even though those markets were significantly poorer than the North American market. From 1956 to 1967, for instance, Toyota exported twice as many vehicles to Asia and Oceanic countries (186,815) as it did to North America. These numbers highlight President Toyoda's commitment to a strategy of first targeting local and regional nonconsumption before going after global nonconsumption. Toyota began exporting its Corona model, the precursor to the Corolla, to North America in the 1960s and watched sales of the affordable car grow rapidly. By 1971, Toyota was exporting more than four hundred thousand cars to North America annually, and by 1980 almost eight hundred thousand.

Toyota, "Exports to the United States," 75 Years of Toyota, accessed March 30, 2018, http://www.toyota-global.com/company/history_of_toyota /75years/text/entering_the_automotive_business/chapter1/section5 /item5.html.

7. Yukiyasu Togo and William Wartman, *Against All Odds: The Story of the Toyota Motor Corporation and the Family that Created It* (New York: St. Martin's Press, 1993), 194.

8. Ibid.

9. Alexander, *Japan's Motorcycle Wars*, 36.

10. Toyota, "Toyopet Crown: America's First Japanese Car," Toyota, December 16, 2016, http://blog.toyota.co.uk/toyopet-crown-americas-first-japanese-car.
   "After Toyopet trauma, Corona got Toyota up to speed in U.S.," *Automotive News*, October 29, 2007, http://www.autonews.com/article/20071029/ANA03/710290307/after-toyopet-trauma-corona-got-toyota-up-to-speed-in-u.s.

11. David Henderson, research fellow at Stanford University's Hoover Institution and professor of economics at the Naval Postgraduate School in California, has written about the Japanese government's influence in Japan's rise. He writes in one of his pieces, "Many people believe that Japan's outstanding growth is due in large part to MITI. They believe that MITI has decided what industries the Japanese should invest in, and that MITI persuaded other Japanese government agencies to use their coercive power to get companies to go along. But the evidence goes against this view. Between 1953 and 1955 MITI did persuade the government's Japanese Development Bank to lend money to four industries—electric power, ships, coal, and steel. Some 83 percent of JDB financing over that period went to those four industries. But even with hindsight, what has not been established is whether those were good investments . . . Moreover, had MITI succeeded in preventing Sony from developing the transistor radio, and in coercively limiting the auto industry, two of Japan's most successful industries would probably have been much less successful."
   David Henderson, "Japan and the Myth of MITI," *The Concise Encyclopedia of Economics*, accessed April 9, 2018, http://www.econlib.org/library/Enc1/JapanandtheMythofMITI.html.

12. Alexander, *Japan's Motorcycle Wars: An Industry History*, 34.

13. Ibid., 91.

14. In the 1930s, the Japanese yen was a much stronger currency than it was in the 1950s. For instance, 2,000 yen in 1935 equated to approximately 352,109 Japanese yen ($920) in 1952.
   Source: http://www.historicalstatistics.org/Currencyconverter.html.

15. Bryan Mezue, Clayton Christensen, and Derek van Bever, "The Power of Market Creation," *Foreign Affairs*, December 15, 2014, https:// www.foreignaffairs.com/articles/africa/2014-12-15/power-market -creation.

16. Ezra Vogel, *The Four Little Dragons* (Boston: Harvard University Press, 1993), 42.

17. While it is true that South Korea invested significantly in "heavy" industries, such as steel and shipbuilding, the country's investment in heavy industries by itself does not account for South Korea's economic transformation from less than $200 in per capita income in the 1950s to more than $27,000 today. Korea's economic transformation represents a 13,400 percent increase in per capita income. Surely, the heavy industries helped, but it is difficult to make the case that they are the causes of such a significant economic transformation, followed by social and political transformation, that has happened in South Korea. Take the shipbuilding industry for example: according to an OECD report, numerically speaking, the industry now represents just under 2 percent of South Korean GDP and around 10 percent of the country's exports (the steel industry is around 2 percent as well). From an employment standpoint, the shipbuilding industry accounts for about 0.65 percent of South Korea's total employment. There is no doubt that the industry is important to the South Korean economy, but it is not enough to explain South Korea's transformation from less than $200 in per capita income to more than $27,000 in just over fifty years.

Council Working Party on Shipbuilding, "Peer Review of the Korean Shipbuilding Industry and Related Government Policies," *OECD* (January 2015): 7–9, http://www.oecd.org/officialdocuments/publicdisplay documentpdf/?cote=c/wp6(2014)10/final&doclanguage=en.

18. Kia, "History of Kia," accessed March 30, 2018, http://www.kia.com /worldwide/about_kia/company/history_of_kia.do.

19. "From Fish Trader to Smartphone Maker," *New York Times*, December 14, 2013, https://archive.nytimes.com/www.nytimes.com/interactive /2013/12/15/technology/samsung-timeline.html#/#time298_8340.

20. Ahn Choong-yong, "Iron and steel helped Korea's industrial takeoff," *The Korea Times*, July 19, 2010, http://www.koreatimes.co.kr/www /news/biz/2016/05/291_69759.html.

21. Bryan Mezue, Clayton Christensen, and Derek van Bever, "The Power of Market Creation."

22. Arno Tausch and Peter Herrmann, *The West, Europe, and the Muslim World* (New York: Nova Publishers, 2006), 123.

23. Gary Dymski and James Crotty, "Can the Global Neoliberal Regime Survive Victory in Asia? The Political Economy of the Asian Crisis," Political Economy Research Institute, September 1, 2000.

24. For a short piece on the idea that not all exports are created equal, see: Efosa Ojomo, "Assessing exports through the lens of innovation," Christensen Institute, June 5, 2018, https://www.christenseninstitute .org/blog/assessing-exports-through-the-lens-of-innovation/.

Chapter 7

Mexico's Efficiency Problem

Mexico has been one of the losers of the 20th century. We tried many different alternatives to development and unfortunately we have 40 percent of the population poor [that number is now approximately 44 percent]; we have a per capita income that is extremely low. It is the same per capita income we had twenty-five years ago, so we must change things.[1]

—VICENTE FOX, PRESIDENT OF MEXICO, APRIL 2001

The Idea in Brief

A little over a decade ago, American business headlines were dominated by tales of woe—American manufacturing jobs were moving to Mexico. Thousands of American jobs would be lost. But from the other side of the border, things looked very, very promising. US and international automobile companies invested roughly $24 billion in the Mexican manufacturing market, according to the Center for Automotive Research. That had the potential to create thousands and thousands of jobs and, in turn, to spur ailing local economies anywhere a factory was built. Hope in Mexico was palpable.

But Mexico today is not prosperous. In 2014 alone, an extra two million Mexicans were added to those living below the national poverty line. What's gone wrong?

When you look at Mexico's economy not through the lens of investment dollars, but through the lens of innovation, a pattern becomes clear. Many companies in the country—domestic and international—have invested heavily in *efficiency* innovations. But in what should be a vibrant economy, flush with resources, there is a disappointing lack of market-creating innovations. And as Mexico painfully illustrates, an overreliance on efficiency innovations can only take an economy so far.

––––––

Bursting with enthusiasm about a project he'd been given the chance to work on, Javier Lozano called his mother back home in Mexico to discuss an assignment he'd started as part of his master of business administration degree (MBA) at the Massachusetts Institute of Technology (MIT). Lozano was interested in learning everything he could about innovation in the health-care arena and had cross-registered at the Harvard School of Public Health. He had begun helping a professor think about how to use technology to help diabetics in Zanzibar suffering from health complications in their feet. To Lozano, the discovery that the then–newly introduced iPhone could potentially work with a device to monitor blood sugar, the crucial measure of health for type 2 diabetes, seemed like something from the future. His own mother was battling diabetes back home in Mexico, so he was eager to share what he was learning in school.

"I was just so excited about the ways technology could help people with diabetes, I wanted to share it with my mom," he recalls. For years, his mom had quietly dealt with her type 2 diabetes diagnosis without, Lozano admits, much interest or support from her family. But this assignment had made him realize he had a perfect primary source of information right at his fingertips. "I started peppering her with questions," he recalls now. "Did you know about *this*? Did you know about *that*? Did you know about all these different devices?" The answer to each query was no. Not only did his mother not know about any of the devices that might help her better monitor and control her diabetes, she told Lozano how deeply disheartened she felt with her own health struggle. "For the first time she started sharing with me how she felt—and she felt very lonely," Lozano recalls. "As a family we didn't understand what she was going through and worse, we kept blaming her for her own disease. We thought she was just eating too much sugar and that she didn't really want to get better." More worrying, Lozano's mother said she was simply exhausted with the fight to feel better. "She didn't want to get care anymore," Lozano recalls, his voice choked with emotion—even if this meant that she could die from diabetes.

Lozano was shocked. How had it gotten this bad? His family in Mexico had access to private health care—an advantage not shared by the majority of the millions of Mexicans dealing with the disease on a daily basis. If it was this difficult for his mother, it must be many times worse for the ten to fourteen million people believed to be living with diabetes in Mexico. "That was my 'aha!' moment," Lozano says. "Diabetes is a catastrophe in Mexico." Most people cannot afford quality health care, leaving those who can't manage their diabetes with a litany of terrible health problems. In Mexico, uncontrolled diabetes is the leading cause of death, amputations, blindness, and in Lozano's home state of Nuevo León it is the leading cause of suicide.

Those problems were not ones Lozano was content to ignore. And so he began to plan his assault on the diabetes epidemic in Mexico. He initially imagined starting a nonprofit that would help poor people get access to diabetes care—a cost, he roughed out, of $1,000 a person a year. Asking patients to chip in $200 a year seemed possible, but to come up with the remaining $800 per person he would need a steady stream of donations and reliable backers who would have to support his mission year after year. Having spent some of his teenage years working for a nonprofit helping indigenous communities gain better access to tools and technology to create more sustainable farms, Lozano found that the thought of having to raise that money, consistently, was overwhelming. Such projects, he knew from his own experience, are very difficult to scale and depend on the whims and priorities of donors. "You can hope to be the passion project of a couple of people," he said, "including the individual donors or people running the organizations, but it's almost impossible to find a sustainable funding source, year after year."

So Lozano started to think about the challenge entirely differently—through the lenses of nonconsumption and Jobs to Be Done, theories he learned in his days at MIT and ones he quickly put to use in Mexico. There were not that many active diabetes patients using the existing health-care options. Like his mother, they were often doing almost nothing to manage the disease, not because they didn't care about their health, but because their options for improving their situation felt overwhelming. Lozano saw immense opportunity in that nonconsumption.

After completing his MBA in 2011, Lozano founded Clinicas del Azúcar, which directly translates to "sugar clinics." If patients couldn't afford private insurance or $1,000 a year for diabetes care, Lozano realized he'd have to make a business model that worked with what they could afford. Lozano set out to create what he calls the McDonald's of diabetes care—a one-stop shop to deal with all issues related to caring for diabetes. For an annual membership of roughly $250, diabetes patients and their supporters can visit any clinic location and quickly run through various "stations" that address each challenge of tracking and managing their diabetes. Lozano says he considers the Job to Be Done of *each individual station* to select the best technology and human resource to provide the care for that moment with patients.

The service is not pampering, but it's effective in every way. As of this writing, the Clinicas del Azúcar are now the largest private care provider of diabetes care in Mexico, with twelve clinics and on a path to reach two hundred in the next five years. Lozano's mother was, he reports, patient number five at his first clinic: a statistic that annoys her to this day because she wanted to be patient number one, but too many people were ahead of her in line the day the clinic opened. She has been a model patient in every way.

Two years ago, when Lozano and his team were trying to improve the Clinicas' support for patients outside of their routine visits, they realized that calls from well-meaning doctors and nurses about how a patient was doing were often answered with what the patients thought the doctor wanted to hear, not what was actually true. "Mexicans don't like to hurt anyone's feelings," Lozano says. Borrowing a page from research that suggests complications from childbirth were dramatically reduced when the pregnant mother had a peer companion to guide her through the process, Lozano decided to set up a call center staffed not by medical professionals, but by other diabetes patients. He asked his mom if she'd like to run the center. Now she works just three doors down from his office, and he sees her on a daily basis—and she's thriving. "On Sundays, we always have a big family gathering for lunch. These days, my mom can't stop talking about what she learned and the patients she talked to each week," Lozano reports. But it's a welcome change from the tenor of the phone call he had with his mother back when he was still at MIT. "I love that enthusiasm."

Lozano and Clinicas del Azúcar are still in the early stages of the journey to creating a scalable business from an unresolved Job to Be Done, and there's work to be done to ensure that it's an enduring success story. As of this writing, the clinics have treated more than thirty thousand patients, 95 percent of whom say it's their first time receiving access to specialized care. The clinics have also created hundreds of jobs, enabling people to help others and make a living. Lozano has created a new market that serves people who were deemed too poor—a market that many doctors and experts initially dismissed as impossible when Lozano approached them with his idea. When that kind of new market is created, emulators and competitors follow, a process that triggers vastly more development. Besides Lozano's company, to date roughly ten more companies have begun to spring up throughout the country, following the model of Clinicas del Azúcar. That may be the most obvious sign that he's hit on something important. Imagine what could happen if he is able to successfully scale his business not only across Mexico, but also across Latin America.

Lozano's success should inspire entrepreneurs across the country—look at what is possible when you target nonconsumption with an innovative business model. But there are far too few stories of market-creating innovations like Clinicas del Azúcar in Mexico. In a country rife with nonconsumption, the question then becomes *Why not?*

Mexico's Efficiency Innovation Conundrum

Mexico is not a poor country. When compared with some African countries, such as Senegal and Lesotho, or some Asian countries, such as Nepal and Bangladesh, or even countries in the Americas, such as Honduras and Guatemala, Mexico is faring quite well, with several of the key ingredients to be prosperous.

First, from a geographic standpoint, Mexico's proximity to the United States, the richest country in the world, puts it in an advantageous position. Mexican companies can trade relatively easily with American firms and sell to rich American consumers because of their proximity to the border.

Second, Mexico has had a free trade deal with the US and Canada since 1994 (though, as of this writing, NAFTA's future is unclear under the current US administration). This free trade deal essentially allows all three countries to trade goods relatively freely among themselves. In addition to NAFTA, Mexico has signed twelve free trade agreements with forty-four other countries, including many in the European Union. It remains one of the countries most open to trade in the world.

Third, according to reports by the World Trade Organization (WTO) and the OECD, Mexico has levels of labor productivity similar to those of most major economic powers.[2] Mexicans also consistently rank as the hardest-working people, when measured by the number of hours worked.[3] South Koreans come in second.

Fourth, Mexico's industrial and manufacturing sector is quite advanced. The country's main industries are aerospace, electronics, petrochemicals, and consumer durables. In essence, Mexico is not simply making and selling simple toys, T-shirts, and basic raw materials to its rich neighbors; the country is making and exporting cars, computers, and complex aerospace components.[4]

Finally, Mexico has maintained a relatively stable macroeconomic environment and has kept interest rates and inflation low over the past couple of decades.[5] These factors are conscientiously monitored and meticulously managed by economists, finance ministers, and investors.[6]

But somehow, even with all these factors, widespread prosperity still evades Mexico.[7] It might be tempting to blame Mexico's underdevelopment on other factors, such as corruption or the ease of doing business in the country. But the World Bank's Ease of Doing Business rankings tell us Mexico is faring relatively well there as well. It ranks 49th out of 190 countries, higher than Italy, Chile, Luxembourg, Belgium, Greece, Turkey, and China. And although Mexico isn't excelling on every metric, it is doing quite well on a couple of submetrics. For example, on "Getting Credit," the country ranks sixth; on "Resolving Insolvency," it ranks thirty-first; and on "Enforcing Contracts," Mexico ranks forty-first. And thus, the puzzle remains.[8]

But if we look at Mexico through the lens of the types of innovations prevalent in the country, we start to see things differently. Mexico is a magnet for *efficiency innovations*. Many companies in Mexico—domestic and international—have pinned their hopes and dreams on investing primarily in efficiency innovations. Those innovations by themselves, as we described in Chapter 2, do not often lead to vibrant economic development. Although efficiency innovations are valuable—they release cash flows to investors, make organizations more efficient in their operations, and provide tax payments to the local economy for a time—they do not, on their own, create large enough markets that can pull in and pay for other important components necessary for the long-term development of a society. As a result, they mostly only support the creation of what we described as *global jobs*, which can be easily moved elsewhere.

For example, Fiat Chrysler Automobiles announced in January 2018 that it decided to shift the production of Ram heavy-duty pickup trucks from Mexico to Michigan in 2020. Fiat Chrysler said it would create 2,500 jobs at a factory in Warren, Michigan, near Detroit, and invest $1 billion in the facility. Until that move, Fiat Chrysler was the third-largest producer of automobiles in Mexico. The existing plant in Mexico will be "repurposed to produce future commercial vehicles" for sale in global markets, but what, if any, future vehicles will be produced there remains unclear. Just like that, Fiat Chrysler moved thousands of *global jobs* out of the Mexican economy.

The Risk of Overrelying on Efficiency

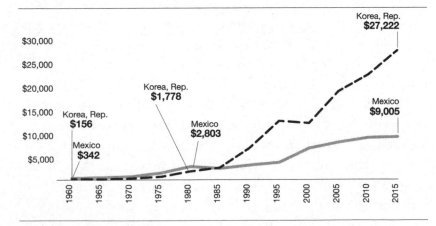

Figure 6: South Korea and Mexico, GDP per capita from 1960 to 2015
Source: The World Bank

In 1960, from a macro and GDP per capita standpoint, Mexico was more than twice as rich as South Korea. Twenty years later, Mexico was still 58 percent richer than South Korea.[9] But today, South Korea is more than three times richer than Mexico.[10] Even more sobering is the fact is that there are more people living in poverty in Mexico today—approximately fifty-four million—than there are people living in South Korea (about fifty-one million).[11]

The most obvious example of the proliferation of efficiency innovations in Mexico is the popularity of the *maquiladoras. Maquiladoras* are manufacturing operations where factories import components from other countries, typically tariff-free, to manufacture a product and export it to other markets. There's nothing wrong with *maquiladoras*, but they play a very specific role in the economy.[12]

For example, one of the visibly positive outcomes of the *maquiladora* program, which began in the mid-1960s, is that it got a boon after the United States, Canada, and Mexico signed the North American Free Trade Agreement (NAFTA) in 1994.[13] Maquiladora employment grew; exports boomed; and foreign direct investment

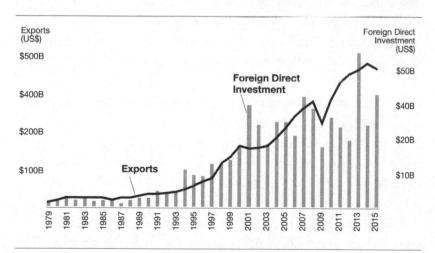

Figure 7: Growth in Exports and FDI in Mexico (in billions of US $), 1979 to 2015

in Mexico ballooned. The prospect of further industrializing Mexico with higher-value-added manufacturing was tantalizing to investors and policy makers. Audi, Ford, General Motors, Nissan, and Honda are just a few of the auto manufacturers with operations in the region.[14] Electronics manufacturers, such as Sharp, LG, Philips, and Sony invested heavily as well. Attracting global brands like this is the hope of most countries. On the surface, these are all good economic indicators. However, these investments have not brought about the kind of prosperity many hoped for and envisioned.[15] We have identified some key reasons why this is the case.

An efficiency innovation–based strategy—which enables companies to squeeze as much as possible from existing and newly acquired assets—typically sells its products into the "consumption economy," those who can already afford existing products on the market. Because these innovations are not targeted at nonconsumption, they typically do not create new markets. Companies struggle for market share with their competitors, because the market size can only increase as the population in the consumption economy grows. Because the potential market of those who can afford the product can only grow so fast, managers eventually start focusing instead on increasing their margins for each product sold by cutting costs. Outsourcing is one of the most tangible examples of efficiency innovations.[16] For example, when Ford made the decision in 2008 to set up the Cuautitlán Stamping and Assembly Plant, the primary purpose of the plant was to "regain profitability" for the struggling automaker—the average Mexican worker made approximately a sixth of what an American worker made, which helped Ford save on labor costs. By 2010, the manufacturing facility in Mexico was producing Ford Fiestas and selling most of them to consumers in the United States.

Since Ford began manufacturing the Fiesta in Mexico in 2010 however, consumers have not benefitted from the cost savings. The price of a Fiesta has actually increased by 19 percent. The profits generated from increasing prices and decreasing manufacturing costs have gone primarily to Ford and its shareholders, as the company has not fundamentally changed the cost structure of its business model. With the exception of integrating cheaper manufacturing, everything else typically stays the same. In fact, in order to boost sales, investments in other components in the organization's business model, such as advertising, marketing, and sales, might actually go up. Mexico will see little to none of those investments; it is the country where the bulk of the products are being sold that will reap the rewards, and in this case that's the United States.

SELLING PRICE OF A FORD FIESTA

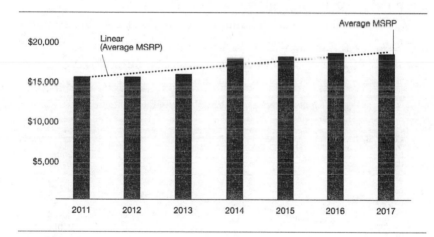

Figure 8: Manufacturer's Suggested Retail Price (MSRP) of Ford Fiesta, 2011 to 2017
Source: *U.S. News & World Report*

Another reason an overreliance on efficiency innovations has not brought sustained and widespread prosperity to Mexico is because these investments are often too easily moved elsewhere, especially as lower wages emerge in other regions or as mounting political pressure in other countries to curb outsourcing prevails.

The footloose nature of efficiency innovations does not enable them to create vibrant markets that can pull in other components of a thriving economy, such as good schools, good roads, or a good health-care system, which can all be sustained by the local economy. In rare circumstances where these investments lead to investing in other supporting infrastructures, the infrastructures are typically connected to one particular industry.

Consider Carrier's decision to halt the transfer of hundreds of jobs to Mexico or Ford's decision not to build a plant in the country after those companies faced pressure from the US government. Such decisions are more easily made when company executives don't have to worry about the impact on local markets and can focus only on improving supply chain or labor cost efficiencies.

When an economy is dependent on wages of citizens remaining low, it is not being driven by thriving and vibrant markets that can enable the development of new products. Since 1990, average

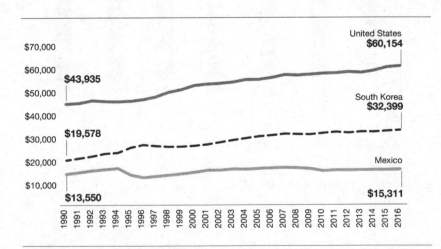

AVERAGE ANNUAL WAGES BY COUNTRY

Figure 9: Average annual wages, in 2016 constant prices at 2016 USD PPPs

annual wages in Mexico have increased by just 13 percent. In that same period, wages in the United States and South Korea have increased by approximately 37 percent and 65 percent respectively— even when starting from a much higher base.

Finally, the proliferation of efficiency innovations in Mexico is not creating prosperity because efficiency innovations are typically targeted at growth that has little or nothing to do with markets in the country, and this can be hard to manage. For example, Mexico is one of the world's largest oil-producing nations and has historically exported tens of billions of dollars' worth of crude oil to the United States. However, the drop in crude oil prices has drastically reduced the value of Mexico's crude oil exports, from approximately $37 billion in 2012 to $7.6 billion in 2016.[17] Because a significant part of its economy ultimately depends on something it has little control over (the fluctuation of oil prices and demand from other nations) Mexico struggles to have control over a critical component of its own economic growth.

A similar phenomenon is also playing out in Russia.

From an export standpoint, Russia's economy is very different from Mexico's. In fact, they appear to be polar opposites. For instance, Mexico's largest exports are vehicles and automobile parts (approximately 24 percent) and electrical machinery (approximately 21 percent); Russia's are crude petroleum (26 percent), refined petroleum (16 percent), and several other commodities. Mexico's exports suggest a more industrialized and thus more economically advanced country, while Russia's suggest an overly resource-dependent country without much industry. Upon closer observation, however, the phenomena that drive both economies are identical: *efficiency innovations.*

As we described in Chapter 2, resource extraction industries are notorious for fueling investments in efficiency innovations. Managers in these industries seek to squeeze out as many resource costs as they can. Although this can be a good thing from the company's perspective, it does not often lead to vibrant economic development, except when the nation's population is very small, like in Qatar. And even then, jobs have to be created from other sectors in the economy as the industry does not create enough jobs to keep people meaningfully employed.

At the core of Russia's economy, much like Mexico's, is an overreliance on efficiency innovations. Consider, for instance, how the movement in oil prices impacts the Russian economy. From 1998 to 2008, while oil prices increased from approximately $18 to $103, in 2017 dollars,[18] Russia's economy averaged a growth rate of 7 percent. However, that kind of growth, fueled in large part by the increase in commodity prices, doesn't necessarily translate to an increase in jobs or a notable development impact on Russia. And because the growth is often unpredictable, it can create shock waves when the commodity prices drop, something we saw happen in Russia a few years ago. As oil prices cooled down, Russia's economy contracted by 2.8 percent in 2015 and another 0.2 percent in 2016.

On the surface, efficiency innovations seem to hold a lot of promise in poor countries because they are typically characterized by manufacturing, industrialization, and, sometimes, heavy industries. But instead of realizing the promise of prosperity, an overreliance on efficiency innovations often promotes short-term, fragile investments that leave societies in a precarious position.

Through a Different Lens

Mexico's population is approximately 127 million and it has a GDP of more than $1.1 trillion; Latin America is home to over 600 million people and has a GDP of more than $5.5 trillion. When many people analyze the potential of these regions, they note the GDPs, per capita incomes, levels of education, infrastructure, or poverty rate—which do not provide a lot of hope. But we see something different. We see nonconsumption and its enormous potential. In these regions, we are looking for the daily struggles that hundreds of millions of people face, and *there* we see opportunity.

Mexico and many other nations that are not yet prosperous have the ability to become thriving nations. But for prosperity to come about, especially in countries as populated as Mexico, we have to think about how to create new markets that serve the vast nonconsumption. And we do see some hopeful signs.

Michael Chu, managing director of the IGNIA Fund and senior lecturer at Harvard Business School, sits in an office two doors down from mine.[19] When I spoke with him about some of our ideas, he introduced me to a company called Opticas Ver De Verdad (Opticas), which is targeting Mexico's nonconsumption of vision care. Opticas was founded in 2011 with a business model designed to provide affordable prescription lenses and eye-care services for the average Mexican. Approximately 43 percent of Mexicans have a visual deficiency for which they need corrective eyeglasses. Many of the existing solutions on the market, which on average cost $75, are too expensive for most people. And so too many Mexicans simply go without glasses and live without good sight.

Instead of analyzing the potential in Mexico through the lens of poverty, Opticas is analyzing it through the lens of *struggle*. How might a new pair of glasses impact the life of an electrician, or a plumber, or a nurse? How might affordable glasses affect the life of a brilliant twelve-year-old girl who is unable to see clearly what she reads, and as a result is doing poorly in school?

As opposed to building a business that targets the wealthiest Mexicans, who can afford high-end brands such as Ray-Bans, Opticas is focusing on solving that struggle. The company has developed a simple business model that allows it to provide prescription lenses for around $17. Its margins might be low, but its volumes have the potential to be very high (at one point, Ford Motor Company made just two dollars on each Model T car the company sold— but also sold millions of them). And Opticas's fiercest competitor for this market on nonconsumers would be *nothing*: people who would rather suffer poor eyesight and do nothing than try to find the money (and time) to acquire prescription glasses they can't afford. Opticas opens stores in convenient locations, offers customers free eye exams, and provides inexpensive prescriptions. This can be life-changing for people who had previously resigned themselves to living with poor eyesight. Now anyone can walk into a store, get tested quickly, and purchase prescription lenses.

Since opening its first store, Opticas has performed more than 250,000 eye tests and has sold over 150,000 pairs of glasses—meaning 150,000 people who previously were not buying any prescriptions glasses have now come into the market. The company is slowly making the nonconsumption of "sight" a thing of the past in Mexico. And Mexicans are responding to the opportunity very well. As of this writing, Opticas is planning to operate over 330 stores across the country by 2020.

Bread and Development

Emerging markets are peppered with ample opportunities to create new markets that can yield significant returns if you know where to look for them. But the creation of new markets typically requires patience as the nonconsumers are found, understood, and then served. Once a market is created, however, it is difficult to destroy. Markets fundamentally change the way people live their lives, and when you are responsible for creating a market, the rewards can be abundant. The Servitje family, who owns 37 percent of Grupo Bimbo, can attest to that fact. Today, they are worth more than $4 billion.[20]

The name Grupo Bimbo might not be familiar to you, but it's the source of some of the world's most beloved baked goods, including Thomas' English Muffins, Sara Lee, Entenmann's, and Canada Bread, just to name a few of the brands this Mexican bakery giant owns and manages. Today, Grupo Bimbo is the largest bakery in the world. The company grosses more than $14 billion annually, operates 165 plants in 22 countries, and employs more than 128,000 people globally.[21] With a market capitalization of over $11 billion, Bimbo also owns more than one hundred brands and sells its products in Ecuador, Colombia, and Peru, as well as in the United States, the United Kingdom, and China. It is truly a global company. But in 1945, when the founders of Bimbo started the company, they didn't set their sights on exporting American favorites to their wealthier neighbors to the north. Instead, they envisioned ways to make bread and distribute it to the average person in Mexico City. In other words, they were focused on creating a new market for fresh bread in Mexico.

It's easy to assess Bimbo's success today and not appreciate the company's humble beginnings. In 1945, Mexico, like many other countries at the time, was very poor—much poorer than it is today. Life expectancy was around forty-five years and more than half the country lived in rural areas and engaged in agriculture—typically a sign of poverty. But it was in these circumstances that the founders of Bimbo saw immense opportunity to create a market for the average Mexican for whom fresh bread was a luxury.

Although Bimbo sells more than ten thousand different products today, the company started by baking and selling small loaves of white and rye bread. Bimbo focused on targeting average Mexicans who, in 1945, mostly had access only to moldy bread wrapped in opaque packaging. Capitalizing on this opportunity to differentiate itself, Bimbo's first product innovation was wrapping its bread in cellophane bags—so customers could see that they were buying mold-free bread before they brought it home. As we described earlier, innovation is not only about high-tech solutions; it is the change in the processes by which an organization transforms labor, capital, materials, and information into products and services of greater value. That doesn't necessarily involve cutting-edge technology. In this case, making fresh bread and packaging it in transparent bags was the relevant innovation necessary to help Bimbo create and grow this market. But even more important than finding a way to sell mold-free bread or better packaging was Bimbo's decision to target the average Mexican—who simply wanted the experience of providing good, fresh food for their families.

If Bimbo had decided to serve only those who could afford expensive bread, it might not have made some of the investments necessary to create and grow a market in Mexico. For instance, in order to guarantee a predictable supply of quality flour for its factories, Bimbo built and acquired several flour mills. With a milling capacity of two thousand tons per day, Bimbo had become the number two flour mill in the country by 1997. Integrating milling into its operations was not an option for Bimbo, just as integrating steelmaking and mining into his company's operations was not an option for Henry Ford. These things simply had to be done in order to create and serve the markets these companies were targeting.

Although the up-front investment was high, Bimbo's mills quickly transitioned from a cost center to a profit center as the company began selling excess output to outside customers. Bimbo also needed to integrate the actual farming and cultivation of wheat. In the 1980s, more than 60 percent of the wheat Bimbo used was imported. In order to reduce its dependence on foreign wheat, Bimbo decided to invest in Mexican farmers. The company provided capital to Mexican farmers to purchase quality seed stock and then purchased the harvest from the farmers.

As the company grew, scaling human capital to manage the growth also became a problem. Bimbo executives realized they needed to supplement the education their new hires were receiving from the traditional Mexican schooling system. And so they created a structured two-year management program where employees learned both technical skills and the intricacies of the Bimbo business.

In order to grow and sustain a successful bread market that caters to the average Mexican, Grupo Bimbo has directly supported many markets and industries, including agriculture, milling, financial services, education, distribution and logistics, packaging, and several others. Indirectly, it has enabled the flourishing of the markets that its thousands of employees support, including their housing, education, health care, transportation, and leisure. And these are not simply markets that can move from one country to another when wages increase. These are vibrant markets deeply rooted in the local economy.

These markets are vibrant largely because they integrate many components in Grupo Bimbo's value chain, including sales and distribution, marketing, advertising, and so on. And these markets are sustainable because they are connected directly to the local population. If Grupo Bimbo's impact is still not impressive enough, consider this: Grupo Bimbo pays its lowest-ranking staff more than three times the Mexican minimum wage.[22] And the company has still been able to keep its prices 15–25 percent lower than those of its competitors. Grupo Bimbo has become so much more than a bread company.

Investors, development practitioners, and policy makers should see Grupo Bimbo as a symbol of what is possible. But the gap in years and scale between Bimbo and the smaller, hopeful success stories of companies like Clinicas del Azúcar or Opticas is still far too wide. We recognize that these companies, by themselves, cannot single-handedly make a nation as large as Mexico prosperous. But the principles guiding them—developing products and services for the average Mexican and pulling in the necessary resources to succeed—can.

Hitching its future to the prospect of continued export and trade with the US and other superpowers—trade based primarily on efficiency innovations—is not a long-term strategy for stable prosperity. In 2018, *Bloomberg Businessweek* estimated the enormous potential hit to Mexico should the political hot potato of NAFTA disappear. "The greatest job loss could come from U.S. companies shutting down their Mexican factories and moving them to another country, like Ford did last year when it canceled plans to build a car plant in the city of San Luis Potosi, and built it in China instead. The $1.6 billion investment would have directly employed almost 3,000 people and would have provided indirect jobs to about 10,000 more."[23] Oxford Economics, a global forecasting and quantitative analysis think tank, estimated that, should the NAFTA agreement collapse, Mexico's gross domestic product would lose 4 percentage points by 2022 and fall into a technical recession by mid-2019—taking *decades* to recover.

For years, international scholars and media pundits have pointed to Mexico as the next potential superpower—but it's always stuck there. Potential. We believe that Mexico does, indeed, have the potential to become one of the world's great success stories in creating prosperity, and the efforts of Clinicas del Azúcar and Opticas give us hope that the country can break the cycle of *almost*, but never fully, getting there. But that is not going to happen until the country recognizes that different types of innovations impact its economy differently. It's not going to get there by relying on efficiency innovations alone.

NOTES

1.   "Vicente Fox," PBS interview Commanding Heights, interview conducted April 4, 2001, http://www.pbs.org/wgbh/commandingheights /shared/minitext/int_vicentefox.html.

2.   From the OECD website: "GDP per hour worked is a measure of labour productivity. It measures how efficiently labour input is combined with other factors of production and used in the production process. Labour input is defined as total hours worked of all persons engaged in production. Labour productivity only partially reflects the productivity of labour in terms of the personal capacities of workers or the intensity of their effort."
   "GDP per hour worked: OECD Data," OECD, accessed April 10, 2018, https://data.oecd.org/lprdty/gdp-per-hour-worked.htm.

3.   David Johnson, "These Are the Most Productive Countries in the World," *Time*, January 4, 2017, http://time.com/4621185/worker-productivity -countries/.

4.   In 2015, according to the Observatory of Economic Complexity, Mexico's five largest exports were cars, $31.4 billion; vehicle parts, $26.2 billion; delivery trucks, $23.4 billion; computers, $21.2 billion; and telephones, $15.7 billion. More than 80 percent of Mexico's exports end up in the United States. See Mexico's profile on the Atlas for Economic Complexity site here: https://atlas.media.mit.edu/en/profile/country/mex/.

5.   Mexico has maintained an average inflation rate of 3.9 percent since 2006. Real interest rates in 2015 hovered around 0.9 percent; Iceland, the United States, and Switzerland had real interest rates of 1.6 percent, 2.2 percent, and 3.3 percent respectively.

6.   FDI in Mexico in 1993 was approximately $4.3 billion; twenty years later, in 2013, it had increased more than eleven times, reaching approximately $47.5 billion. This increase in FDI is due in part to Mexico's relatively stable macroeconomic environment.

7.   The fact that Mexico doesn't simply export toys and T-shirts is important. Research by Harvard University's Ricardo Hausmann and MIT's César A. Hidalgo has helped us understand that the complexity of a country's economy (how sophisticated the products it makes are) is highly correlated with its development level. More *capable* countries that can produce more sophisticated products tend to be richer.

César A. Hidalgo and Ricardo Hausmann, "The building blocks of economic complexity," *Proceedings of the National Academy of Sciences* 106, no. 26 (June 2009).

8.   "Economy Rankings," Doing Business, The World Bank, accessed April 2, 2018, http://www.doingbusiness.org/rankings.

9.   For a more in-depth economic history of Mexico pre-1960, read Section 2 of "Catch-up Growth Followed by Stagnation: Mexico, 1950–2010," written by Timothy J. Kehoe and Felipe Meza, https://www.minneapolis fed.org/research/wp/wp693.pdf.

10.   From a business standpoint, even though Mexico has more than twice the population of Korea and enjoys the benefits we mentioned above, the country has just nine companies on a Forbes list of the one thousand biggest public companies, compared with South Korea's thirty-one. Also, South Korea's credit rating is currently AA2, the third highest, according to Moody's Investors, and AA- according to Fitch. Mexico's is A3 with a negative outlook according to Moody's, and it is BBB+ according to Fitch. By most measures, South Korea is outperforming Mexico economically.

11.   Anahi Rama and Anna Yukhananov, "Mexican government says poverty rate rose to 46.2 percent in 2014," *Reuters*, July 23, 2015, http://www .reuters.com/article/us-mexico-poverty-idUSKCN0PX2B320150723.

12.   Gordon Hanson, of the University of California in San Diego and the National Bureau of Economic Research, has written extensively about Mexico and the role of *maquiladoras* in their economy. His 2002 paper, "The Role of Maquiladoras in Mexico's Export Boom," for instance, highlights some of the risks and rewards associated with this component of the Mexican economy.

Gordon H. Hanson, "The Role of Maquiladoras in Mexico's Export Boom," University of California, San Diego, accessed April 30, 2018, https://migration.ucdavis.edu/rs/more.php?id=8.

13.   The five years before NAFTA, employment in *maquiladoras* grew by 47 percent, but in the five years following the enactment of NAFTA, employment increased 86 percent. Additionally, in the mid-1980s, *maquiladoras* employed approximately 180,000 people; by 2000, the system employed more than one million and generated approximately 50 percent of Mexico's exports. Hanson, "The Role of Maquiladoras in Mexico's Export Boom."

14.   Gary Hufbauer, formerly of the Council of Foreign Relations and professor at Georgetown University, notes that "the transformation of the

auto industry in Mexico, as a result of NAFTA, was nothing short of dramatic. It was, in fact, the biggest transformation of any industry in all three of our countries [the United States, Canada, and Mexico]." Prior to NAFTA, auto manufacturing in Mexico was a very protected industry where cars could cost two to three times the cost of production in the United States. NAFTA, which promoted efficiency innovations in the region, reduced the cost of production dramatically. Sonari Glinton, "How NAFTA Drove the Auto Industry South," NPR, December 8, 2013, http://www.npr.org/templates/story/story.php?storyId=249626017.

15. We focus on exports here because, while they are not the entirety of Mexico's economy, they are a microcosm of it. Exports account for more than 35 percent of the Mexican GDP, the fourth highest among the world's top twenty most populous countries and the highest of any country with a population of more than one hundred million people.

16. More broadly, Mexico exports three out of every four cars it manufactures, most of which go to the United States. Sara Miller Llana, "Mexico prepares for (Ford) Fiesta," *The Christian Science Monitor*, June 2, 2008, http://www.csmonitor.com/World/Americas/2008/0602/p06s02-woam.html.

17. In 2015, about 9 percent of the crude oil imported by the United States came from Mexico. Earnings from crude oil sales represent a significant portion of Mexican exports and the Mexican economy, providing almost $20 billion annually.

"U.S. energy trade with Mexico: U.S. export value more than twice import value in 2016," Today in Energy, U.S. Energy Information Administration, February 9, 2017, https://www.eia.gov/todayinenergy/detail.php?id=29892).

18. Tim McMahon, "Historical Crude Oil Prices (Table)," InflationData.com, August 27, 2017, https://inflationdata.com/Inflation/Inflation_Rate/Historical_Oil_Prices_Table.asp.

19. IGNIA Fund is a venture capital firm in Mexico dedicated to investing in innovative companies delivering high-impact goods and services to low-income populations. The company has raised funds twice. In 2008, IGNIA raised $102 million from Omidyar Network, JPMorgan, International Finance Corporation, and the Inter-American Development Bank. In 2015, it raised a subsequent fund worth $90 million through Mexican publicly traded certificates known as CKDs. IGNIA was also the first venture capital fund in Mexico to raise capital from Mexican pension funds, signaling investors' "confidence in IGNIA's track record, as well as the accelerated economic growth found at the base of the socio-economic pyramid in Mexico."

20. "Daniel Servitje Montull & family," *Forbes*, accessed April 30, 2018, https://www.forbes.com/profile/daniel-servitje-montull/.

21. Some might look at Grupo Bimbo and suggest that the company put many Mexican bakeries out of business and that, in effect, it was bad for the Mexican economy. While that is true, it misses the significant impact Grupo Bimbo has had and is having on the Mexican economy. Grupo Bimbo can be likened to the Ford Motor Company, specifically during the era of the Model T. Before the Model T, there were more than one thousand automobile manufacturers in the United States. Many of them were making custom cars for wealthy individuals. When Ford introduced the affordable Model T, almost all went out of business save a few. But it would be hard to argue that Ford was not good for the American economy as a result. Consider how he impacted steel production, glass manufacturing, R&D for engines and automobiles, regulation, agriculture, road construction, gas stations, auto-repair shops, iron ore mining, paint production, higher wages, and many other aspects of the American economy. Although bread is no Model T, Grupo Bimbo has also positively impacted the Mexican economy, even though smaller and perhaps less efficient bakeries have been put out of business. The company has improved agriculture, distribution and supply chain, and education, and has also increased wages.

22. In fact, Grupo Bimbo doesn't just pay its Mexican workers substantially more than the minimum wage in Mexico; it pays everybody, including its American, European, Latin American, and Asian workers, more. On average, Grupo Bimbo pays its lowest-ranked staff about twice the minimum wage in the countries where it conducts business. "Grupo Bimbo Annual Reports," Grupo Bimbo, https://www.grupobimbo.com/en/investors/financial-information/annual-information.

23. Andrea Navarro, "This Mexican Town Paid the Price for Trump's Attacks on Ford," *Bloomberg*, February 1, 2017, https://www.bloomberg.com/news/articles/2017-02-01/when-trump-s-taunts-cowed-ford-this-mexico-town-paid-the-price.

Overcoming the Barriers

Chapter 8

Good Laws Are Not Enough

Liberalizing states will have to actively create the institutional structures within which market economies operate and redefine the particular rights, entitlements, and responsibilities that underlie economic activity.

—WILLIAM ROY, *SOCIALIZING CAPITAL: THE RISE OF THE LARGE INDUSTRIAL CORPORATION IN AMERICA*

The Idea in Brief

The lack of "rule of law" and "institutions"[1] is a plague that affects poor countries. These countries can't hope to make progress until they fix their institutions—which often means they should adopt Western-style systems, conventional wisdom suggests. "If only we had X or Y institution in place, people could finally build and sustain businesses." To that end, billions of dollars are invested annually by many organizations to help poor countries improve their institutions. Institutions are pushed onto these countries with the best of intentions, but could there be a reason why so many "pushed" institutions in emerging economies end up being ineffective, or, worse, corrupt? We cannot fix problems with the law, systems, and institutions by simply adding another law, system, or institution. Effective institutions are not just about rules and regulations. Ultimately, institutions are about culture—how people in a region solve problems and make progress. At their core, institutions reflect what people value. And that, it turns out, has to be homegrown. Innovation can play a critical role in this process.

———

In the spring of 1990, two dozen of the Western world's leading constitutional scholars, lawyers, and judges gathered in Prague for what seemed like a once-in-a-lifetime opportunity: to help guide the drafting of a country's new constitution. In the months after the downfall of the former Soviet Union, Czechoslovakia (as well as virtually every other former Soviet Bloc country) began the process of redefining its values, in a post–Soviet Union world, through the process of creating a new constitution. The Western scholars who were invited to guide and advise on this process couldn't get there fast enough. As the *New York Times* put it, a constitutional convention is hard to resist. "I rescheduled three classes to come to this," Harvard Law School professor Laurence Tribe told the *Times*. "I haven't ever rescheduled a class for a Supreme Court case."

Among the legal luminaries: Lloyd Cutler, former counsel to US president Jimmy Carter; retired Senator Charles Mathias Jr.; Charles Fried, the former solicitor general under US president Reagan; former Canadian prime minister Pierre Trudeau; and Martin Garbus, at the time one of the US's leading human rights lawyers. The invited delegates, from eight different countries, spent a week debating and discussing the merits of various approaches to crafting a constitution that would divide power between the Czech and Slovak regions of the country. It was an exciting endeavor, one that led to large and small debates at the conference, on the bus between venues, and in the hallways for days. As University of Virginia law professor Dick Howard put it at the time, "For somebody who couldn't be there in 1787 [when the US created its constitution], this is the nearest thing to it."

Two years later, with the benefit of the constitutional dream team's advice and months and months of work by leading Czechoslovakian politicians and scholars, a new constitution was finally drafted and adopted as part of the peaceful breakup of the country into two new ones: the Czech Republic and Slovakia.

Similar rituals happened throughout the former Communist bloc countries, including Romania, Hungary, the former Yugoslavia, and Bulgaria, to name a few. Western constitutional scholars jumped at the chance to guide these newly formed democracies on how to get their institutional values right from the start. Good economic and political institutions protect secure property rights, democratic pluralism, open markets, consumers, and so on. Alternatively, bad economic and political institutions protect oligarchies, single-party systems, crony capitalism, nepotism, dysfunctional judiciaries, rampant corruption, and so on. In general, poor countries are overwhelmed with bad institutions, while prosperous countries are filled with good ones, or at least much better ones. Conventional wisdom suggests that countries that want to tackle poverty must first establish rule of law, fix their institutions, and adopt Western-style systems before they can make progress toward prosperity.

But that is often not how the march to healthy institutions plays out in reality. On the surface, it seems logical that establishing the right institutions —what Nobel laureate Douglass North describes as "the rules of the game in a society or, more formally, the humanly devised constraints that shape human interaction,"[2]—is important to building economic prosperity. Seen this way, institutions might logically be *pushed* onto a society, perhaps by a government or a very influential NGO, to help pave the way for getting this right.

Though the former Czechoslovakia has made enormous strides since that constitutional convention, the new constitution didn't magically create an ideal country. For example, corruption is still prevalent in varying degrees throughout the Czech Republic.[3] More than two-thirds of businesses consider corruption to be widespread in national and local public procurement, for example, according to a 2014 European Commission report. That's not to say that the Czech Republic is a wholly bad or morally bankrupt country. It is an *evolving* country, with evolving institutions.

One of the distinct features of an economy with vast nonconsumption is the lack of infrastructural and institutional competency. Harvard Business School professors Tarun Khanna and Krishna Palepu call these "institutional voids." To that end, in the world of economic development, there is intense focus on creating good institutions in poor countries as a necessary precondition of healthy economic growth. From 2006 to 2011, more than $50 billion in World Bank–sponsored projects had some focus on institutional reforms.[4] Examples of institutions that have been pushed range from Western lawyers rewriting Eastern Europe's laws as a condition for disbursing foreign aid, to the British initiating private property rights in parts of Kenya in the hopes of increasing transparency and certainty. However, without understanding the complex local social structures in which these societies have evolved over time, many of the *pushed* institutions fail to deliver on their promise of efficiency and transparency. Instead, they unintentionally often breed confusion and corruption.

The problem is, the institutions of a society *reflect* its values rather than create them. So building strong institutions—ones that will shape and hold a country's values for generations—is not as simple as "export what works elsewhere, add water, and stir."[5]

That's because there's a fundamental mismatch between the efforts to "import" institutional underpinnings—such as court systems, forms of governance, financial systems like stock markets and banking practices, and law enforcement systems—for a poor country and the reality of how institutions and values are formed in any country, says Lant Pritchett, a senior fellow at Harvard's Kennedy School of Government and longtime economist with the World Bank. Outside experts "tend to focus on the rules because it's their comparative advantage," explains Pritchett. "We tend to bring experts in to create rules that work elsewhere, but make no sense in a different context." There may be, say, two hundred pages of legislation about health care in Denmark, for example. But those pages do not explain what motivates a Danish doctor or why funding a nationalized health system is a priority in that country. That, Pritchett says, "is a normative story."

Pritchett is right. Institutions are not something that can be pushed in by virtue of good intentions, even with all the expertise in the world. Institutions are not absolutes. They morph and evolve in context. A society's institutions are typically a reflection of the culture and values of the people of that society—values that dictate how problems are solved and how people choose to work and live together. And even when the intentions are to help spur an economy's growth, effective institutions cannot simply be pushed in. They require pull.

There is growing evidence that pushing institutions isn't having the desired effects on creating and sustaining well-functioning systems in many poor countries. By some estimates, as much as 70 percent of reforms have had "muted results."[6] In effect, if the fundamental dynamics of a society—what people value and how they choose to make progress—have not changed, newly imposed institutions are doomed to fail.

How Not to Fix Problems

In a recent World Bank paper titled "How (Not) to Fix Problems That Matter," development specialists Kate Bridges and Michael Woolcock go into detail about this phenomenon. Using Malawi as a case study, they profile several learnings from the country over the past few decades. There was heavy emphasis on institutional reform in Malawi: the number of projects focused on institutional reform in some manner (171) far outweigh those focused on the next four development areas—industry and trade; agriculture, fishing, and forestry; health and social services; and education—combined (151). On its own, perhaps that wouldn't be such a problem. However, what the paper goes on to illustrate is that not only do many programs focused primarily on institutional reform eventually fail, but also that we keep doing the same thing over and over again. And failing, over and over again.[7]

Part of the problem, Bridges and Woolcock say, is that we often don't study and understand the full complexity of the problem, and as a result fail to "deinstitutionalize the status quo." In Malawi, for example, the newly created anticorruption bureau was largely a "wholesale transfer of structures and laws from countries with very different contexts (specifically Hong Kong SAR, China, and Botswana)."[8] In focusing on adopting "best practices" that seem to work in other parts of the world we often fail to understand the contextual complexities specific to a particular region. As a consequence, we measure success on how much a system resembles another system that works versus on whether it actually solves a particular problem.

Unfortunately, this model of solving problems is not likely to yield positive long-term results in either institutional reform or the more important issue of economic development.[9] For that, we have to get to the root of a society's values and culture. And to do that, we have to understand how culture is formed.

Solving Problems, Together

"Culture," much like "innovation" or "institutions," is a word we hear on a day-to-day basis, and many of us associate it with different things. In the case of a company, it's common to describe culture as the visible elements of a working environment: casual Fridays, free sodas in the cafeteria, or whether you can bring your dog into the office. But as MIT's Edgar Schein—one of the world's leading scholars on organizational culture—explains, those things don't define a culture. They're just artifacts of it. Schein has one of the most useful definitions of culture that we've seen:

> Culture is a way of working together toward common goals that have been followed so frequently and so successfully that people don't even think about trying to do things another way. If a culture has formed, people will autonomously do what they need to do to be successful.[10]

Those autonomous instincts are formed neither overnight nor with the implementation of a new law or system. Rather, they are the result of *shared learning*—of people working together to solve problems and figuring out what works.

The same is true in forming culture in a society. In each instance of a problem or task arising, those responsible reached a decision together on what to do and how to do it in order to succeed. If that decision and its associated action resulted in a successful outcome—a "good enough" decision to navigate a dispute, for example—then the next time those in that society face a similar type of challenge, they return to the same decision and same way of solving the problem. If, on the other hand, it failed and the dispute was not resolved, those people trying to solve the problem would be hesitant to take that approach again. Every time they tackle a problem, they aren't just solving the problem itself; in solving it, they are learning what matters. They are creating or dismantling culture.

An *institution* is really a reflection of the *culture*, or a pattern of behavior that has been codified. When one observes the culture of a country and tries to push an institution that does not align with the culture, it will be very difficult to sustain.

The importance of culture and norms in dictating and perhaps even predicting the strength of institutions cannot be overstated. Katrin Kuhlmann, who founded the law and development center at the New Markets Lab and also teaches at both Harvard and Georgetown law schools, experienced this when working on a project in Kenya to help investors and entrepreneurs navigate the complexities of laws and regulations there. She quickly saw that approaches that might work in one country could send the wrong signal elsewhere. In Nairobi, for example, a number of entrepreneurs indicated that "overcontracting" might imply a distrust among business partners. "This project highlighted that the legal system surrounding the market is so much more intricate than a single transaction," Kuhlmann says. "As is always the case with our work, we have to understand how laws—both in letter and in practice—impact different aspects of human behavior." In effect, what might seem simple and obvious—creating a legal framework and enforcing contracts—turns out to be more nuanced. Kuhlmann's experience is not unusual.

Democratizing Risk

Still, even with most institutional reform projects failing, it is understandable why trying to change a poor country's institutions feels so urgent. In many poor countries, the government is often the only game in town and wields significant influence on the economy. In addition, think about the well-functioning institutions in the United States, the United Kingdom, Japan, or the many other prosperous nations in the world. Prosperity and good institutions seem to go hand in hand. Consider, for instance, the legal systems in the US or the UK, where citizens can generally depend on the enforcement of contracts and the rule of law. This, in turn, creates trust not only among citizens, but also between citizens and the State. Conversely, Angola, Ecuador, and Bangladesh might be seen, broadly speaking, to have institutions that prevent their economies from flourishing because their institutions have not been able to engender that trust. How likely, for instance, are you to trust the legal system in Angola? Who would choose to invest millions of dollars in a country in which they couldn't trust the government or other private sector players in the same way they would if they operated in Japan, or Singapore, or Germany?[11] Fixing institutions is very important.

But willing economies to have better institutions and ensuring that they do actually have them are two different things. We have found that the most successful institutions grow out of culture, not the other way around. History is full of examples.

We now consider the institutions of Europe to be among the

most sophisticated and valued in the world: look no further than the complex negotiations going on as we write this book to extricate the United Kingdom from the binding obligations of the European Union. As difficult as those negations may be, what's not in question is that both sides value the process and will honor the ultimate agreement. Europe, however, did not get there overnight; it has taken hundreds and hundreds of years of trial and error, and of success and failure, to build such a culture.

The development of domestic institutions in Venice helped it become one of the world's capitals of trade as far back as 800 AD. "Long-distance trade enriched a large group of merchants and these merchants used their new-found muscle to push for constraints on the executive i.e., for the end of a de facto hereditary Doge (the Venetian head of state) in 1032 and for the establishment of a parliament or Great Council in 1172,"[12] according to economists Diego Puga and Daniel Trefler. This period in Venice, from the 1000s to around 1297, saw the rise of many modern-day institutions, one of which was the Colleganza.

The Colleganza was essentially a joint stock company created to finance long-distance expeditions. Considering the significant risks associated with long-distance travel at the time, the Colleganza was an innovative way to distribute and democratize the risk across a larger number of people than ever before. More important, however, it also democratized the rewards by creating wealth for many Venetians for whom investing in such trade expeditions had been historically impossible. "The Colleganza was so innovative because they limited liability for each partnership and to the joint stock of the partners," journalist Max Nisen writes about the institution. "It was incredibly important to the history of the city [Venice] because it allowed poorer merchants to gain access to international trade by taking on risk as traveling partners."[13] All of a sudden, poorer merchants could now partake in investing in profitable long-distance trade, an activity that was historically reserved for the rich.

As we noted earlier, market-creating innovations make historically expensive, complex, and out-of-reach products and services
accessible to a new class of consumers who could not afford them,
thereby creating a new market for the democratized solutions.
Because the poor in most societies, and certainly in Venice at the
time, "outpopulate" the rich, when a new solution is able to pull
the poor into consumption of a particular product or service, that
new solution can have a vast impact on society. The Colleganza provided a mechanism that brought many poorer merchants, who had
neither the capital nor the collateral, into the investing class. As a
result, this innovation increased economic mobility, international
trade, wealth, and, ultimately, political power.

Take, for example, the impact the Colleganza had on the shipbuilding industry. Many people were employed in supplying parts
to build ships, in designing the ships, in selling or leasing the
ships, in staffing the ships for these trade expeditions, and many
other components that contributed productively to the economy.
And that's just one of the industries that was affected. As demand
for tradeable goods increased, farmers and traders were pressured
to innovate to meet those demands. The impact of creating new
jobs, especially for people in impoverished cities, is immense.
Overnight, a jobless person is transformed into a productive con-
tributor to that society. As Schein notes, the rewards and punishment systems in organizations and societies matter as we look to
improve economies. If there are no jobs that reward people, they
will find other means of getting rewards, many of which will not
be productive for society.

As more and more wealth was created for many more Venetians
and the city became one of the richest in Europe, the political structures in Venice began to change as well. Historically, the office of
the doge was held by someone from one of three elite families,
wielding absolute power over the city.[14] Once wealth began to be
democratized, the balance of power began to shift, and a growing

number of wealthy merchants were capable of challenging the doge. And they did. Some of the institutional reforms pushed by this new and growing merchant class included: banning doges from appointing their successors; enacting and enforcing a system of elections; ensuring the office consulted with judges and abided by the judicial decisions; and establishing a parliament known as the Great Council.[15] These institutions then gave rise to other institutions, which reinforced the role of business, innovation, and investment in societal development.[16]

By the early fourteenth century, financial innovations in Venice included the forerunners of limited-liability joint-stock companies; markets for debt, equity, and mortgage instruments; bankruptcy laws that distinguished illiquidity from insolvency; double-entry accounting methods; business education (including the use of algebra for currency conversions); deposit banking; and a reliable medium of exchange (the Venetian ducat).[17] While all these innovations connect to the "demands of long-distance trade," we believe they more accurately reflect the "democratization" of long-distance trade.

That is the kind of impact market-creating innovations can have on a society.

Cart Before the Horse

By contrast, consider the failure of many well-intended institutional reform programs in the world today. In his book on institutional reform and development, Harvard University's Matt Andrews lists several notable failures. For example, in 2003, many international experts hoped that in just seven years, institutional reform would transform Afghanistan into a new South Korea. That theory led to pouring billions upon billions of dollars into the country to first change the prevailing institutions in government, which many hoped would lead to change in the country. Time has passed; billions have been spent; and new laws, regulations, and "institutions" have been pushed, but Afghanistan is still cited as one of the most corrupt countries in the world. But perhaps Afghanistan is too extreme; the country is not only very poor, but is also actively at war and has the Taliban. So Andrews cites another example: the country of Georgia. He explains that the government went through the arduous efforts of streamlining taxes and cutting regulations to "catalyze private industry and create jobs." The hope was that the small country would become a "Caucasian Singapore." The reforms seemed to work, and Georgia leapt up in the World Bank's Ease of Doing Business rankings. Unfortunately, this did not spur domestic innovation in the way many hoped. Andrews concludes, "Government regulations may no longer burden entrepreneurs, but reforms have not led to a government that effectively catalyzes employment-generation production either."[18]

Another example is in India, where the Karnataka Project, undertaken by the Indian Ministry of Rural Development, designed to register and computerize land records in about six hundred districts in the country, was implemented. Much like the institutional reform projects in Georgia, there was some success with the project (it reduced the time it took to register property from thirty days to thirty minutes), but there's little evidence of any progress in reducing underlying conflict over land ownership in the region. In addition, the computerization of records, which was supposed to lead to easier transfer of land between parties so as to spur economic activity, didn't quite materialize.[19]

The major difference between these, and many other well-intended institutional reform projects, and the Venice example is an insight central to this book. No matter how well-intentioned an institutional reform, if it is not connected to innovations that create or connect to markets that serve as many people in a region as possible, it will be difficult to sustain. When we put the cart before the horse, neither the cart nor the horse moves.

What Would Be More Effective Instead?

We have learned three important lessons as we've studied institutions and innovation. The first is that *innovations, especially those that create new markets, typically precede the development and sustenance of good institutions*; the second is that *institutions must be built with the local context in mind* because, if they do not solve local problems, they are almost always rendered useless by those for whom they are designed; and third, *innovation serves as the glue that keeps institutions together.*

Vibrant Markets Typically Precede Good Institutions

One of the most common pushbacks we get when discussing our ideas with people who work in regions with less-developed institutions is that innovating in poor countries is not just hard, it's impossible. And so we find ourselves with a classic *chicken-or-the-egg* problem: Which should we focus on first in order to foster innovations and thereby create economic prosperity? Many people are adamant that institutions must come first.[20] "How can one innovate in an environment without good political and economic institutions?" is their common refrain. We certainly understand that point of view.

But there are several problems with that argument, chief of which is that good institutions are not only very expensive to create and maintain, but often don't work when placed in a society without the relevant markets to absorb what they have to offer. How does a poor country such as Mali, with roughly fifteen million people and a GDP per capita of approximately $900, pay for a legal system modeled after France's, a country with sixty-six million people and a GDP per capita of around $44,000? In addition, the French system has had hundreds of years to evolve so that it makes sense in the context of France's increasing prosperity. How can Mali simply adopt a system that is expensive and fails to solve many of the problems that present-day Malians face? Schein's theory of culture predicts that it is going to be incredibly difficult.

His theory also predicts that there is a better way. It may be counterintuitive and even uncomfortable, but we believe that if we begin by helping people make progress in their local economies, then change in their culture and institutions will follow. History has born this out, time and again.[21]

Innovation as a Glue

Just as it is one thing to have a child and quite another to raise a successful and productive member of society, it is one thing to create institutions and quite another to sustain them.

As we have noted, prosperity is a process, not an event. Institutions are the same. They are not marked by buildings or places; they are marked primarily by processes. The lesson from Venice helps us see the pivotal role of innovation not only in creating institutions, but also in sustaining them.

As quickly as many of the prosperity-supporting institutions in Venice were built, they were destroyed by a group of very wealthy and influential merchants who sought to curb competition. Several wealthy merchants began wielding their influence to change existing laws. For instance, they sought to make "parliamentary participation hereditary and erect barriers to participation in the most lucrative aspects of long-distance trade."[22] Over time, fewer merchants were able to participate in long-distance trade. This killed the market in Venice, ultimately causing the city to become less prosperous. While the rest of Europe grew in the seventeenth and eighteenth centuries, Venice continued to decline in population and wealth.

The institutions in Venice were developed, but they did not last, because some wealthy merchants reversed the laws. Why did the merchants reverse the laws if the laws were good for Venice? The laws might have been good for Venice, but they were not good for the merchants who were focused on feathering their own nests and not others'. So in order to maintain their profits and position in society, they changed the laws to benefit themselves. Institutions reflect a culture, they don't cause it. So when the culture in Venice was allowed to change—the way merchants were allowed to solve their problems—so did the institutions. And in the long run, Venice paid the price, falling behind its peers in economic development.

This behavior, by the way, is not anomalous—it is the norm in many societies. History tells us that those who can use the law to their advantage almost always do. But when the law is manipulated to serve one side over others, the playing field is no longer level. Just look at the United States, where total lobbying spending in 2017 topped $3.4 billion.[23] But there are almost always long-term consequences for these actions.

What might have happened if the wealthy merchants in Venice had new and exciting opportunities (new innovations) to increase their wealth and status in society? We believe they may not have been as quick to change the laws for their profit. Innovation, therefore, can serve as a great equalizer. The more that innovators democratize solutions for the masses, thereby creating opportunity and potential for growth and wealth creation, the more institutions can remain strong.[24]

From Gray Market to Formal Economy

Why would hundreds of millions of people in lower-income countries and emerging markets remain in the "informal economies"— the gray- or black-market economies—even when they know it is illegal to do so? It is because, in their particular context, it makes little sense for them to insert themselves into the formal economy. Their common experiences have informed the ways they solve the problems of running their businesses. Some of their common experiences are related to cost, difficulty, and lack of benefits they get when they, or people they know, have tried registering businesses in the past. And not until this experience becomes easier for companies. When that happens, the shift can be profound.

When Matias Recchia returned to his native Argentina in 2013 after years of studying and working abroad, he looked forward to settling down in a new apartment and making it feel like home. An alumnus of Harvard Business School and McKinsey & Company, Recchia had spent years navigating the complexity of building the largest online gaming company in Latin America. But what should have been a simple process by contrast—planning his own apartment move—turned out to be one of the more challenging experiences of his adult life. "The experience was terrible for me," he recalls. "Finding a moving company in Argentina is extremely painful by itself. But then add on top of it the experience of needing to find a plumber and electrician and painter . . . it was just awful." Not only was there no price transparency—he had no idea what these tradesmen would charge in advance—but they also wouldn't stick to whatever rough agreement they'd made initially, and they would simply never show up on time.

Recchia spent hours in frustration, trying to track people down, grumbling about an unjustified bill he'd just been presented, and lamenting to friends about how one-sided the system felt. Nearly every contractor Recchia hired operated in the "informal" sector of the economy of Argentina; they built their one- or two-person businesses mostly by word of mouth, they priced each job in what seemed to be a total random guess, and they did not bother to encumber themselves with formalities, such as reporting earnings, paying taxes, abiding by health and safety regulations, or allowing themselves to be held responsible for inferior work. Even though there were laws on the books that explained the requirements in starting and running businesses, these business owners didn't see the need to obey them. This was not just an Argentinian problem. In other Latin American countries, as much as 70 percent of labor was operating in the informal economy. In South Asia and sub-Saharan Africa, the percentage that operated in the informal economy hovered around 90 percent.[25]

But in his struggle to manage what should have been simple home repairs, Recchia recognized a Job to Be Done, not just for himself, but for many other people, too. All this pain caused half of the 120 million households in Latin America that needed home improvement services not to pursue them.[26]

As it turned out, disgruntled homeowners were not the only ones seeking progress with their struggle. As Recchia began to share the idea of creating a formal marketplace for buyers and sellers of contractor services with service providers, he realized that the pain ran deep on both sides. "There were very good reasons that these people didn't want to participate in the 'formal' economy," Recchia says now. "Their lives were very difficult. It was very hard to get new customers. They lived hand-to-mouth, day-by-day. Because they were not part of the formal economy, they could never access financing to actually build or grow a real business. They were relegated to simply trying to make as much as they could, whenever they could, and hoping for the best." What was the reward for these contractors, Recchia recognized, if they abided by the rules of the formal economy and stood behind their work? "There was absolutely no benefit to being an honest guy who showed up on time, did his best work, and charged a fair price." What was rewarded, instead, was focusing on making as much as possible in whatever way worked best for the individual contractor. If a contractor was likely to finish a job at, say, three p.m. on a given day, he was probably unable to get to another job that same day because of Argentina's notoriously difficult traffic, especially in the capital city of Buenos Aires. So he would simply charge the first customer as much as he possibly could to make his day worthwhile. That neither led to good word of mouth, nor did it, understandably, lead to more business opportunities. It was a vicious cycle, one in which tradesmen could never realistically hope to create a better life for their families. They simply hoped to work enough to survive. "If you were born poor in some of these countries," Recchia recognizes, "there was simply no way for you to move up the social chain. People didn't even try. It became a self-fulfilling prophecy." And no amount of laws, rules, and regulations seemed to be able to change that.

But four years after his own frustrating experience, Recchia is hoping he will be more successful. He and partner Andrés Bernasconi started IguanaFix, an online service connecting consumers with reliable, transparent contractors. In its first three years alone, IguanaFix generated some $25 million and directly employed 140 people. But perhaps more significantly, IguanaFix has attracted more than twenty-five thousand contractors in four countries (Argentina, Mexico, Brazil, and Uruguay) into the formal economy, with thousands more on a waiting list. Not only are these contractors now reporting earnings and paying taxes (both of which are part of the service that IguanaFix both requires and provides), but some of them are also beginning to expand and build their own businesses in ways they couldn't have imagined before.

This leap into the formal, tax-paying, rule-abiding economy has not been one born of a sudden sense of civic responsibility or crushing penalties for not abiding by the established rules of business. After all, what incentive does a hand-to-mouth contractor have for reporting his income? *So the government might take some of it away in taxes?* "Most of our service providers don't see the direct benefit of paying taxes; and the fear of penalties is not enough of an incentive," Recchia says. "It was extremely hard to get people to break the habits that they've been used to for generations." But IguanaFix has succeeded at something many governments and large development organizations have been trying to do for decades: bringing people into the formal economy. How? Through Recchia's understanding of the struggle of both customers and contractors, and his creation of a new market that has now made it profitable to be more honest and transparent. "By joining the formal market, service providers can access corporate customers, get access to health and work insurance, open their first bank account and access financing. We emphasize the positive consequences of joining the formal economy. We do not force them to do it nor highlight the negative consequences of not doing so."

IguanaFix's contractors have come to understand that by joining the formal economy, they will be able to have more control of their work schedules, their lives, and their wallets. As more innovative companies like IguanaFix start to make clear to the market that participating formally in the economy is actually good for everyone, the stronger and more successful the formal economy will become. As management expert Peter Drucker once reminded us, *procedures are not instruments of morality; they are exclusively instruments of economy. They never decide what should be done, only how it might be done more expeditiously.*

IguanaFix is creating a new market that is enabling tens of thousands of home improvement service providers—electricians, plumbers, carpenters, and so on—to *pull* into their lives the legal, economic, and political institutions that several Latin American governments have, for a very long time, been trying to *push* onto their citizens.

There is no one company or one innovation—not even one as hopeful as IguanaFix or one as established as Mexico's Bimbo—that can, single-handedly, change a country's underlying culture and respect for institutions. It's a cumulative process. But understanding what can *create* and *sustain* healthy institutions is a key question to answer on the road to prosperity.

NOTES

1. The late American political scientist Samuel Huntington defines institutions as "stable, valued, recurring patterns of behavior." Institutions can be political, economic, or social in nature. They can also be formal (systems set up by the governing bodies) or informal and represent customs in a region (how a society celebrates weddings or childbirth). Some examples are a country's legal system, government or public organizations, and financial systems.

2. This definition, as highlighted by Daron Acemoglu and James Robinson, MIT and Harvard economists respectively, has three important features. First, they are "humanly devised." Second, they are "the rules of the game," effectively setting constraints on human behavior. Third, their major effect will be through incentives.

Daron Acemoglu and James Robinson, "The role of institutions in growth and development," *World Bank Working Paper* 1, no. 1 (January 2008).

3. In one corruption case, an aide to former prime minister Mirek Topolánek had been charged for demanding a multimillion-dollar bribe from a foreign company in return for a government defense procurement contract (Reuters, February 2016). After a lengthy trial, including a conviction that was overturned but ultimately reinstated by the country's Supreme Court, the aide was handed a five-year jail sentence (Radio Praha, May 2017).

4. Kate Bridges and Michael Woolcock, "How (not) to fix problems that matter: Assessing and responding to Malawi's history of institutional reform," *World Bank Policy Research Working Paper* 1, no. 8289 (December 2017).

5. Shaking off the ways of getting things done prevalent under Communist-ruled Czechoslovakia was not solved by writing a new constitution in the country—nor was that the solution in any of the other hopeful renewed democracies in the post-Soviet era. In January 2018, more than fifty thousand people marched, in heavy snow, to the parliament building in Bucharest, Romania, chanting, "Thieves," and holding signs that read, "Demisia," which means "Resign" in Romanian. They were protesting the lack of law enforcement and the prevalence of corruption in their country. The situation is not much better for Hungary, as the coun-

try slid down in the Transparency International corruption rankings in 2018. So far down, in fact, that Hungary, which is a member of the EU, now has a worse corruption ranking than Montenegro, a small country that has not been allowed to join the EU partly because it is deemed too corrupt. Andrea Shalal, "Hungary slides deeper down corruption index, watchdog says," *Reuters*, February 21, 2018, https://www.reuters.com /article/us-global-corruption/hungary-slides-deeper-down-corruption -index-watchdog-says-idUSKCN1G52E6.

6.   Matt Andrews, an associate professor at the Center for International Development, wrote an article in the *Guardian* that highlighted this point. In the piece, Andrews writes, "Billions of dollars are spent each year on institutional reforms in development, aimed ostensibly at improving the functionality of governments in developing countries. However, evaluations by the multilateral and bilateral organisations sponsoring such reforms show that success is often limited. These evaluations reveal that as many as 70% of reforms seem to have muted results. They produce new laws that are not implemented, or new budgets that are not executed, or new units and agencies that go unstaffed and unfunded. In short, new forms may emerge but they frequently lack functionality: what you see is not what you get."
    Matt Andrews, "Why institutional reforms in the developing world aren't working," *Guardian*, March 8, 2013, https://www.theguardian.com /global-development-professionals-network/2013/mar/08/institutional -reform-international-development.

7.   Kate Bridges and Michael Woolcock, "How (not) to fix problems that matter: Assessing and responding to Malawi's history of institutional reform," 4.

8.   Bridges and Woolcock note that, of all the projects they analyzed, 92 percent of them were regulative (i.e., activities focused on strengthening laws and regulatory bodies), 3 percent were normative (i.e., activities that tried to understand cultural practices and professional norms), and 5 percent were cultural cognitive (i.e., activities education or guidance toward compliance with international standards). Their analysis shows that solutions that are overwhelmingly regulative without appreciating the cultural cognitive or normative nature of the environments in which they are implemented are often part of the problem.
    Kate Bridges and Michael Woolcock, "How (not) to fix problems that matter: Assessing and responding to Malawi's history of institutional reform," 12–17.

9.   When the 2017 World Bank Ease of Doing Business rankings came

out, Nigeria celebrated its progress. The country moved up the rankings by twenty-four points and is now the 145th "easiest country to do business with" out of the 190 countries measured. For the previous year and a half, the country had been pushing regulations and institutional reform to help it move up the rankings. When the country's efforts were rewarded by an increase in its rankings, understandably there was excitement. But how does Nigeria moving up in the rankings affect average Nigerians for whom daily life is about making progress as they interface with the local police, the local judiciary, and the local systems in place? The response to that question could be that "the reforms will have long-term effects." But in 2016, the Nigerian economy contracted and, as a result, shed tens of thousands of jobs. The everyday culture of how Nigerians made progress and solved their problems would remain unaffected even as the country moved up in the "rankings." Change will come when there is a strong imperative from within the country to make the institutions reflect a new reality of doing business in Nigeria.

10. Edgar Schein, *Organizational Structure and Leadership* (San Francisco: Jossey-Bass Publishers, 1988).

11. This is one of the many reasons Sudanese entrepreneur Mo Ibrahim struggled to raise money to fund the building of his telecommunications company across Africa. The question of effective governance is so powerful for Ibrahim that he has, in the years since his success, created the Mo Ibrahim Foundation. The foundation publishes the Ibrahim Index of African Governance, an index that rates African governments on several metrics including safety and rule of law, public management, human rights, and others. See http://mo.ibrahim.foundation/iiag/.

12. Diego Puga and Daniel Trefler, "International Trade and Institutional Change: Medieval Venice's Response to Globalization," *Quarterly Journal of Economics* 129, no. 2 (May 2014): 753–821, http://www.nber.org/papers/w18288.

13. Max Nisen, "How Globalization Created and Destroyed the City of Venice," *Business Insider*, September 8, 2012, http://www.businessinsider.com/the-economic-history-of-venice-2012-8.

14. Ibid.

15. Diego Puga and Daniel Trefler, "International Trade and Institutional Change: Medieval Venice's Response to Globalization," 753–821.

16. A similar occurrence of increasing incomes leading to institutional change was observed in the Netherlands, another early developer.

In a seminal paper, "The Rise of Europe: Atlantic Trade, Institutional Change, and Economic Growth," Acemoglu et al. write, "Critical was the Dutch merchants' improving economic fortunes, partly from Atlantic trade, which were used to field a powerful army against the Habsburg Empire . . . Overall, both the British and Dutch evidence, therefore, appears favorable to our hypothesis that Atlantic trade enriched a group of merchants who then played a critical role in the emergence of new political institutions constraining the power of the crown."

Daron Acemoglu, Simon Johnson, and James Robinson, "The Rise of Europe: Atlantic Trade, Institutional Change, and Economic Growth," *American Economic Review* 95, no. 3 (June 2005): 546–579.

17. Diego Puga and Daniel Trefler, "International Trade and Institutional Change: Medieval Venice's Response to Globalization," 753–821.

18. Matt Andrews, *The Limits of Institutional Reform in Development: Changing Rules for Realistic Solutions* (Cambridge: Cambridge University Press, 2013), 1–3.

19. Matthew McCartney, *Economic Growth and Development: A Comparative Introduction* (London: Palgrave Macmillan, 2015), 219.

20. The late William Baumol of Princeton wrote extensively about innovation, entrepreneurship, and economic growth. Baumol was of the view that the conditions on the ground are what most affects the kinds of innovations that entrepreneurs pursue. Baumol writes, "How the entrepreneur acts at a given time and place depends heavily on the rules of the game—the reward structure in the economy—that happen to prevail." Although we generally agree with Baumol, that the rules of the game matter, the important question we ask is "How do the rules of the game get formed? How do they get changed?" When you observe circumstances where the rules have changed, you will see that innovations, especially those that have created new markets, have been major drivers.

William J. Baumol, "Entrepreneurship: Productive, Unproductive, and Destructive," *Journal of Political Economy* 98, no. 5 (October 1990), http://www.jstor.org/stable/2937617?seq=1#page_scan_tab_contents.

21. Although it began happening more than 150 years ago, this pattern of getting prosperity before getting institutions that can actually work for the average citizen is what we observe in the United States. As America was beginning to industrialize, many of the institutions in the country, much like in many poor countries today, worked for the rich. This is because the rich had markets that could fund their own "institutions," but average Americans did not. Hard as it may be to believe, trains and industrial accidents regularly killed or maimed many Americans who had

little to no recourse. But as more and more Americans began developing markets for average citizens, these markets pulled in good institutions. And thus a virtuous cycle was created. Hardly ever does the enforcement of institutions, without markets, lead to the development of good institutions that are sustainable.

22. Diego Puga and Daniel Trefler, "International Trade and Institutional Change: Medieval Venice's Response to Globalization," 753–821.

23. "Lobbying: Overview," OpenSecrets.org, Center for Responsive Politics, accessed March 5, 2018, https://www.opensecrets.org/lobby/.

24. What about countries like China, or Chile, or South Korea, that were able to develop institutions that fueled economic growth? These countries coupled the development of their institutions with intense investments in innovations that created markets. These markets ultimately paid for the creation and sustenance of the institutions. And even then, it wasn't that straightforward. Oxford professor Matthew McCartney notes that in the 1980s, fast-growing East Asian countries had corruption scores similar to those of many "developing countries" today. South Korea, for instance, had the same measure of institutional quality as Côte d'Ivoire. He concludes that the implication of this is that "improving institutions was an outcome not a cause, of rapid growth in East Asia."

Matthew McCartney, *Economic Growth and Development: A Comparative Introduction*, 217.

25. "New Study Reveals the Complexity of the Informal Sector," The World Bank, July 20, 2016, http://www.worldbank.org/en/news/feature/2016/07/20/new-study-reveals-the-complexity-of-the-informal-sector.

26. Frank V. Cespedes, Thomas R. Eisenmann, Maria Fernanda Miguel, and Laura Urdapilleta, "IguanaFix," Harvard Business School Case Study, November 10, 2016, 2.

Chapter 9

Corruption Is Not the Problem; It's a Solution

In our theory, whatever law enforcement strategy the society chooses, private individuals will seek to subvert its workings to benefit themselves.

—EDWARD L. GLAESER AND ANDREI SHLEIFER,
"THE RISE OF THE REGULATORY STATE"[1]

The Idea in Brief

Corruption. Ask investors why they choose not to invest in certain regions or ask citizens of those regions why their countries are not developing, and corruption is almost always at the top of the list. A recent International Monetary Fund estimate put the annual cost of bribery alone at about $1.5 to $2 trillion. The overall economic and social costs of corruption are likely much larger, since bribes constitute only one of the possible forms of corruption. The problem of corruption is so corrosive and widespread that hundreds of millions of dollars are spent annually trying to eradicate corruption around the world—and yet corruption is still stubbornly pervasive.

In this chapter, we examine the problem of corruption differently. Instead of asking, *How can we eliminate corruption?* we ask, *Why does corruption persist in the first place?* The answer, we believe, lies not solely in some fundamental moral failings, but rather in understanding why many people choose to "hire" corruption. History has shown that successful economies develop in spite of widespread corruption. Seen through a new set of lenses, we may understand corruption better, and, we hope, begin to find new ways to mitigate it. In today's most prosperous countries, proper enforcement of laws against corruption followed investments in innovations that either created new markets or grew and connected to existing ones. If we get the sequence right, we can begin to stoke progress in even the most corrupt countries.

————

When I was a missionary in South Korea, we were visited monthly by a man who was selling "safety" insurance. If you paid him (and it was not a small amount of money from our perspective), he would guarantee that your home would not be robbed. If you didn't buy that insurance, somebody picked your house clean. Making sure that our modest possessions were not taken away from us was important for our survival, so we paid. It's only in hindsight that I see that we were all willing participants in a form of low-grade corruption—the kind that establishes a power balance in a local community, makes lives easier (or harder, for those unwilling to participate), and keeps the economic wheels of daily life greased. Corruption was a matter of survival. On both sides.

Seeing how easily this happened—not just to us but to others around us—made me wonder whether corruption is just a moral issue. I know that the Koreans I met were good people. But if corruption is mostly a moral issue, why did these good people participate in it so easily?

And they're far from an anomaly. Today, more than two-thirds of the countries measured by Transparency International, the international NGO committed to combating corruption, score lower than 50, out of a possible 100, on the annual Corruption Perceptions Index. A score of 0 is very corrupt, 100 is very clean. The average score, across the world, is 43. According to the organization, six billion of the total 7.6 billion people in the world live in countries with "corrupt" governments. That's a lot of us. It's hard to estimate the chilling effect corruption—or the threat of corruption—has on impoverished countries, especially when the mere *perception* of corruption impedes investments that can help those countries create wealth and prosperity, but we know that the impact is enormous.

In most of today's prosperous countries, proper enforcement of laws against corruption followed investments in innovations that either created new markets or grew and connected to existing ones. If we get the sequence right, we can begin to stoke progress in even the most corrupt countries in the world today. History has proved that out, time and again.

Fighting corruption often feels like playing a game of Whac-A-Mole, where a player uses a hammer to hit toy moles that appear at random from different holes on the playing surface. You hit one and another mole pops up in another hole. You expend so much energy hitting and hitting and hitting that you eventually throw up your hands in despair.

This has made us wonder if we are focused too much on the *symptoms* of corruption, instead of seeking to truly understand its *causes*. To get to the bottom of this, we must ask two important questions: First, why is overt corruption so much more pervasive in poorer countries than in rich ones? And second, how did many of today's prosperous countries became less overtly corrupt. As we will see, answering these questions will provide a framework that can help reduce the prevalence of corruption in many of the world's poorest countries.

Understanding Corruption

Corruption is not a recent phenomenon. Many of today's prosperous countries were once very corrupt; in fact, some were as corrupt as many poor countries today. But corruption is not a permanent phenomenon, either. Or at least, it doesn't have to be. Although we know there are still individual cases of corruption in even the most admired countries in the world (and America is no exception), it is no longer a pervasive part of these cultures. So what caused the change?

You might quickly list off what seem to be the obvious answers: good leadership and governance from the top, a change in the moral values of a society, or the right institutions being put in place. But we don't believe those fundamentally change the prevalence of tolerance for corruption in a society. This is important to recognize because so many anticorruption programs are directed almost exclusively at governance and operate on a foundation of instilling a sense of right and wrong. If this were the key to fighting corruption, why have these very worthy efforts, overall, had relatively little sustained impact on winning the war on corruption?

According to the most recent Corruption Perceptions Index report published by Transparency International, "the majority of countries are making little or no progress in ending corruption."[2] So even with intense international focus—and a flood of resources to combat the problem, including initiatives to inculcate a fundamental sense of integrity in children—progress has been very slow.

We believe that people born into poor societies are not somehow missing the fundamental moral fiber of those of us fortunate enough to be born into more prosperous circumstances. Nor are they simply ignorant that there is a better way. Corruption *is* the better way, a *workaround*, a utility in a place where there are few better options. Corruption is being hired for a Job to Be Done, or, more specifically, to help people make *progress* in a particular circumstance. This is an important insight. Once we understand why people turn to corruption, we can begin to see different approaches to solving the problem.

Why Do People *Hire* Corruption?

So to begin the process of building trust and transparency, we have to understand why people hire corruption to solve their problems in the first place. We have uncovered three powerful reasons.

First, the vast majority of individuals in society want to make progress. From the poor person looking for employment to the wealthy person looking to gain more status, most of us want to improve our financial, social, and emotional well-being. It is why we go to school, go on vacation, and also go to places of worship. It is also why we save money, buy homes, start businesses, and run for office. Each of those things, in one way or another, helps us feel like we are making progress in life. When society offers us few legitimate options to make progress, corruption becomes more attractive.

Second, every individual, just like every company, has a cost structure. In business, a company's cost structure refers to the combination of the fixed and variable costs it incurs in order to run its business. It defines how much the company must spend to design, make, sell, and support a product. For example, when a company spends $100 to create and deliver a product to a customer, in order to make a profit, it must sell the product for more than $100.

Similarly, individuals also have a cost structure—how much money they spend to maintain a particular lifestyle. This includes things such as rent or mortgage payments, school fees, hospital bills, food, and so on, and, just like companies, individuals must also have revenues (income from their work or investments) that surpass their costs. Understanding this simple revenue-cost relationship can help predict circumstances where the likelihood of corruption will be high and the efficacy of anticorruption interventions. In essence, if anticorruption programs don't fundamentally affect the revenue-cost equation, they are unlikely to be sustainable.

For illustration, consider this simple example. If a police officer in India earns 20,000 rupees a month (approximately $295) but has a cost structure that demands he spend $400 a month, he is going to be susceptible to corruption, regardless of what the laws dictate.[3] As a result, one can predictably expect the average police officer to demand bribes, especially in a society where law enforcement and prosecution of corruption crime is not prevalent. It's not that he's inherently a bad person—in fact, personally I believe that people are inherently good—but the circumstances of his life dictate that he make difficult choices to survive.

The third reason people hire corruption is that most individuals—regardless of income level—will seek to subvert the prevailing law enforcement strategies in order to make progress or benefit themselves, according to Harvard academics Edward Glaeser and Andrei Shleifer, who studied the rise in regulations in the United States at the turn of the twentieth century. Human beings are hardwired to make the best decision for themselves in the *circumstances*. When we are confronted with a law that limits our ability to do something we want to do, most of us instinctively make a mental calculation. Do I need to obey this law, or can I get away with disobeying it? And which way will I be better off?

The reasoning behind this insight is quite straightforward: to live according to the laws established by the state requires effort, and so the average rational person will juxtapose the benefits of obeying the law with the consequences of disobedience. If the scale tips toward disobedience, then it is actually *irrational* for the individual to obey the law, no matter how "good for society" it might seem. Consider the fact that so many of us, all over the world, flout the speed limit when there are no police officers in sight. Twenty years ago, having a "fuzz buster" (a portable police radar detector) was almost a status symbol in America. These days, the community-based GPS smartphone application Waze allows us to warn each other when a police car is lurking behind the bushes up ahead. We have developed a social network–enabled product that is dependent on many of us agreeing we should help one another avoid getting caught in speed traps. We want to make progress—get to where we are going quickly—and willingly ignore the law that informs us of the legal speed limit because we believe we're ultimately better off making that choice. While the circumstances may differ, the calculation process rarely ever does.

But societies evolve. The path, however, from a society steeped in corruption to one where trust and transparency thrive typically follows a predefined and often predictable pattern, with three phases: "overt and unpredictable corruption," followed by "covert and predictable corruption," ultimately transitioning to what we will call a "transparent" society.

Just because a particular country is categorized as being in phase one doesn't mean it doesn't have some components of phase two. Instead of thinking of these three phases as distinct absolutes, think of them as three points on a spectrum. Our assumption is that we all want to end up as close to phase three as possible, a society where trust and transparency are valued. History tells us that the path from corruption to transparency in many of the world's most admired countries has followed a relatively predictable path through these phases. Understanding how these phases evolve is essential in our quest to create the transparency required for healthy economies.

Phase 1: Overt and Unpredictable

The first phase is what we call Overt and Unpredictable Corruption, and this is where many poor countries find themselves. In these countries, contracts are difficult to enforce, government institutions are hard to trust, and corruption scandals are commonplace. Travel to any of these countries and pick up a newspaper, and you will likely see a headline on the front page about gross mismanagement of funds by business and political elites. Many of the countries in this phase get a low score in Transparency International's Corruption Perceptions Index.

It is very difficult for capital to be deployed in this kind of environment. Investors understandably shy away from this kind of unpredictability and opacity. For example, imagine doing business in Venezuela, where at the time of this writing the government can no longer fund the social programs that provide for the basic needs for many of its people.[4]

Although the situation in Venezuela might seem hopeless, it is important to note that many prosperous and advanced nations have come from similar circumstances. In the late 1940s, for instance,

Taiwan was quite corrupt and unpredictable. Mayors and local public officials handed out favors to their cronies and lined their own pockets in the process, and many forms of corruption, such as bribery, embezzlement, nepotism, and even organized crime, went unchecked.⁵ Taiwan, however, has since become a very successful and productive economy, and ranks 29th out of 180 in the Corruption Perceptions Index.

In this first phase of a society's evolution, especially when the country is poor, a corruption-fighting strategy focused primarily on instituting new laws does not, in reality, do enough to curb corruption. In fact, it is likely to make things worse as a premium is placed on finding ways to work around laws that get in people's way of making progress. In addition, many poor countries are unable to properly enforce the law. It just so happens that law enforcement is costly—financially, socially, and politically. This is not to say that corruption goes without notice. Protests against corruption are massive and frequent all over the world. This fervor has led to a proliferation of anticorruption candidates throwing their hats in the ring for key political positions. Sometimes they actually win. Russia's Vladimir Putin and Venezuela's Hugo Chávez (now deceased), for instance, came to power promising to eradicate corruption. Let's just say that those campaigns didn't pan out as voters might have hoped.

Even in the rare case of a genuinely good leader with a powerful will to transform a country—take for example Nelson Mandela's influence on South Africa in the years he led the country—corruption does not magically disappear with good intentions from the top. When Mandela was elected as president of post-apartheid South Africa in 1994, he was, without question, one of the most universally admired leaders in world. Twenty-seven years of political imprisonment had not dampened his will to make South Africa a better place. If anything, they had made it stronger. We still think of Mandela today as the embodiment of great leadership. "Although he professed to be an ordinary man who became a leader only because of extraordinary circumstances," the dean of Harvard Business School Nitin Nohria said at the time of Mandela's death, "he exemplified the characteristics of leadership we value most highly: integrity, morality, compassion, and humility."

But even during the most hopeful years of his tenure, South Africa was, and has since remained, mired in corruption. In fact, in the years since Mandela stepped down, corruption has only gotten worse. Jacob Zuma, who became president after Mandela's initial successor was pushed from office, was dubbed South Africa's "Teflon president" for his ability to brush off an extraordinary number of corruption allegations and scandals in his eight years in office.

How did South Africa, so hungry for change during Mandela's leadership, slide so far and so quickly away from the hope that he represented? By most accounts, South Africa possesses most of the institutional features necessary to combat corruption: a much-admired constitution, an independent judiciary, and a robust media. In most indices of corruption, including those produced by Transparency International, South Africa is still only ranked somewhere in the middle—a ranking that has actually deteriorated year after year.

South Africa's struggle is not unique. Five years after Liberia's Ellen Johnson Sirleaf became Africa's first democratically elected female president, Sirleaf was awarded the one of the highest international honors, the Nobel Peace Prize, for her leadership in securing peace in Liberia. She had spent years focusing on building—or rebuilding—the nation's democratic institutions and strengthening the position of women. But even with such international acclaim, Sirleaf's leadership was not able to fully transform Liberia, where Transparency International reported that 69 percent of people admitted to paying a bribe in 2016 for access to basic services like health care and education. Sirleaf eventually left office with the country still facing what she had dubbed "public enemy number one" when she took office more than a decade ago. "We have not fully met the anti-corruption pledge that we made in 2006," Sirleaf told lawmakers in her final state of the nation address. "It is not because of the lack of political will to do so, but because of the intractability of dependency and dishonesty cultivated from years of deprivation and poor governance."

Corruption is not primarily about the lack of good leadership. Although that's certainly part of it, the causal factors are far more fundamental. Corruption is about "hiring" the most expedient solution for what seems to be, in the moment, the greatest good of the options available to us.

Phase 2: Covert and Predictable

The second phase in the corruption spectrum is Covert and Predictable Corruption. In this phase, corruption is more or less an open secret—think of the film *Casablanca*, in which police captain Louis Renault professes to be "shocked—shocked!" to find that there is gambling in Rick's thriving, illicit nightclub, an establishment that routinely greases Renault's palms. People are aware that there is corruption, but it's baked into the system. Because development is happening in parallel, corruption is seen as a necessary cost of doing business.

The transition from unpredictable to predictable corruption can be very expensive—economically and politically—and primarily requires the creation of new markets, not laws. Most people who engage in corruption know they *should not* do what they are doing. New laws only help solve a problem when there is confusion about what to do and when governments have the capability to enforce the laws.

Consider China. By some estimates, corruption could be costing the Chinese government as much as $86 billion annually.[6] That's more than the GDP of sixty-one countries. Since 2000, between $1 trillion and $4 trillion is estimated to have left the country, and some of those funds have been linked to government officials, including President Xi Jinping's brother-in-law. According to one report, the net worth of the 153 Communist Chinese Parliamentarians topped $650 billion in 2017, up about a third from the previous year.[7] That's larger than the GDPs of Finland and Norway combined.

Note that China and many other poor countries have tried to eradicate corruption primarily by using laws, but with limited success. Paradoxically, the more laws these countries enact to fight corruption, the more corruption has seemed to spread. China, for instance, has "more than 1,200 laws, rules, and directives against corruption." But what good is a law if the law-providing body has neither the muscle, the money, nor the will to enforce the law?

At the same time, it is hard to argue with China's recent development and the influx of foreign direct investment (FDI) over the past four decades. In 1970, China's GDP per capita was approximately $112; today it is about $8,200. Back then, life expectancy was fifty-nine years; today it is about seventy-six years. The country has grown at an annual average rate of more than 10 percent and has accounted for approximately 40 percent of the world's global growth during this period.[8, 9]

It's notable, however, that even as China experiences this growth, the country still ranks 77th out of 180 countries on Transparency International's Corruption ranking, below Senegal (66th), and on par with Trinidad and Tobago.[10] Corruption has not prevented development from taking root. Perhaps most telling of all is China's meteoric increase of FDI over the past four decades. In 1980, FDI into China was around $400 million. In 2016, FDI totaled more than $170 billion, a 42,400 percent increase. In fact, from 2006 to 2016, more than $2.3 trillion of FDI flowed into China.[11] Did the foreign investors who poured trillions of dollars into China not know that corruption was widespread in the country? Why didn't they wait for China to eradicate corruption before investing? It is primarily because the type of corruption in China differs from that of other countries in the first phase. It's covert, but predictable.

And thus, can be included in the calculation of the "cost of doing business" in China.

Even though development is happening in China (as we mentioned earlier, the country has lifted close to one billion people out of poverty over the past few decades), we would all agree that it is not yet a transparent society, and that there is still progress to be made. For prosperity to become sustainable in the long term, a nation must transition to the third phase.

Phase 3: Transparency

In 2017, total lobbying in the United States totaled more than $3.3 billion.[12] Lobbyists are employed to influence governments in order to enact laws that are favorable to their causes, industries, or particular interests. But even with billions of dollars influencing America's government officials, the country still ranks a respectable 16th out of 180 countries in Transparency International's Corruption Perceptions Index. But even with billions of dollars influencing America's government officials, the country still ranks a respectable sixteenth out of 180 countries in Transparency International's Corruption Perceptions Index.[13]

Corruption is largely frowned upon in America, and is routinely rooted out and prosecuted to the fullest extent of the law. The 1977 Foreign Corrupt Practices Act (FCPA) serves as a deterrent to would-be corrupting American firms that operate outside the country, or international firms that operate in the United States. Walmart, Siemens, Avon, Alstom (a French industrial group), and many other companies have run afoul of FCPA, and have paid hundreds of millions of dollars in fines as a consequence.

So how are these two things consistent—we openly spend billions of dollars in influencing our governments, but we also aggressively pursue and prosecute those engaged in corruption? Beside the fact that lobbying is legal, lobbying is also fairly transparent.

Curious Americans can get data from the Senate Office of Public Records and find out who is lobbying for whom and for what cause.

In addition to the transparency, the American economy is also relatively predictable. Though America is not immune from corruption—and reasonable people may disagree on how corrupt America really is—what's different and hopeful is that corruption in America is often exposed, prosecuted, and punished. You don't have to look very hard to find headlines of corrupt politicians in America. Three of the most recent Speakers of the House of Representatives from our home state of Massachusetts have all become convicted felons on corruption charges. Former Illinois governor Rod Blagojevich was tried, convicted, and sentenced to fourteen years in prison for corruption charges when he tried to "sell" former president Barack Obama's vacated Senate seat.

But America did not always prosecute, much less convict and sentence, its Blagojevichs. So how did America evolve from a country where corruption was rife to one in which transparency has become the norm?

Boss Tweed's America

Just as it is difficult to imagine a poor United States, it's also difficult to imagine an overtly corrupt America where such incidents would not be investigated. But there was a time when corruption in America rivaled corruption in some of the poorest countries today.

Perhaps more than anyone, nineteenth-century American politician William Magear "Boss" Tweed exemplified what it meant to be overtly corrupt. Born in 1823, Tweed entered politics at an early age and was elected city alderman by the time he was twenty-eight years old. After spending several years in office, Tweed opened a law office even though he was not a lawyer. Through the office, he received payments from large corporations for his "legal services," but these payments were mostly extortions. With these funds, Tweed purchased many acres of Manhattan real estate and grew his influ-ence in New York City politics. This was just the beginning.

"The Tweed ring at its height was an engineering marvel, strong and solid, strategically deployed to control key power points: the courts, the legislature, the treasury and the ballot box," biographer Kenneth Ackerman wrote. "Its frauds had a grandeur of scale and an elegance of structure: money-laundering, profit sharing and organization."[14] During his time as the boss of Tammany Hall, Tweed (who was also a member of the United States House of Rep-resentatives) stole a sum estimated to be between $1 billion and $4 billion in today's dollars.[15]

In 1889, a cartoon titled *The Bosses of the Senate* in the satirical weekly *Puck* depicted perfectly the overtness of America's corrup-tion at the time. The cartoon shows members of the US Senate working feverishly as representatives of specific business interests, such as Steel Beam Trust, Copper Trust, Sugar Trust, and so on, watch from the balcony above. There are several entrances into the Senate chamber. One reads: "This is a Senate of the Monopolists, by the Monopolists!" The door representing the "Peoples' Entrance" is "CLOSED."[16] Corruption was so severe and widespread that Pres-ident Woodrow Wilson (1913–1921) had to address it during his presidency.

In 1913, Wilson wrote in one of his books, "There have been courts in the United States which were controlled by the private interests. There have been corrupt judges; there have been judges who acted as other men's servants and not as servants of the pub-lic. Ah, there are some shameful chapters in the story. The judicial process is the ultimate safeguard of the things that we must hold stable in this country. But suppose that that safeguard is corrupted; suppose that it does not guard my interests and yours, but guards merely the interests of a very small group of individuals. Then where is your safeguard?"[17]

Corruption was also pervasive in major infrastructure projects, like the railroads and roads, in the United States. Although the railroads in the 1800s and the roads in the 1900s were good for America, they also brought with them an unprecedented level of corruption. When the US government got into the business of railroads and extended subsidies to contractors, those subsidies were often given based on the number of miles of railroad tracks built, not on the quality or effectiveness of the tracks. Contractors built long and windy railroads, often using subpar material, as they mostly competed for "federal favors instead of railroad customers."[18]

Consider what happened with road construction after the automobile boom in the early part of the twentieth century. Thomas MacDonald, then administrator of the United States Federal Highway Administration, "visited road construction jobs where he found waste and shoddy work in abundance," Earl Swift notes in his book *The Big Roads*. "Localities often got about a dime's worth of road for every dollar they spent . . . contractors had carved the state among themselves so that each would be assured all the bridge work in a particular territory, an arrangement that cost tax payers twice in contracts that were wildly overpriced."[19]

Had Transparency International's annual rankings existed back then, America would not have been high on the list of "least corrupt" countries. But America, over time, found its safeguards and today is number 16 on the list. Was that due primarily to better laws? Better politicians being elected? Better institutions being created? Certainly all of those things helped create and support the culture of transparency we now have, but they didn't *cause* America to suddenly stop being corrupt.

As more and more Americans created more and more wealth for themselves and found better ways to make a living, their voices of dissatisfaction with corruption became louder. "Politically, the rage of victims counted for very little in 1840, not much in 1860; by 1890, it was a roaring force"[20] is how Stanford Law professor Lawrence Friedman put it. Clearly, corruption was not eradicated by 1890, but by then we see the process by which it was evolving in America. The hope for something better had begun.

And so, what we learn about America's development is that it happened *in spite of* the widespread corruption and unpredictability in the country.[21] Anticorruption in America was not triggered primarily by legislation or an increased intensity in law enforcement. It came about because the fundamental equation of how average and rich Americans could make money, make progress, and make a living for themselves and their families began to change. "American capitalism of the 1920s was less corrupt and less abusive of workers and consumers than it was in 1900,"[22] Glaeser and Shleifer concluded in their paper. We find that today's capitalism in America, while not perfect, is certainly superior to American capitalism in the 1920s.

Development often *precedes* successful anticorruption programs, not the other way around. While, over time, some people become more corrupt because that's what they've practiced all their lives, personally I don't believe most people wake up in the morning just to be corrupt.

When there are few alternatives to help people make progress, corruption often stands out as the most viable option. But when a better way presents itself, the process that leads to transparency begins. We can see this happening in countries all over the world.

Of Monarchs and Men

Consider how corruption evolved in Europe, where perhaps the most obvious forms of corruption—absolute monarchies that seized land, appropriated assets, and killed citizens at will—were common. Monarchs have been likened to robbers who are "permanently on the prowl, always probing . . . always searching for . . . something to steal."[23] Corruption permeated European society as bands of armed men, with the secret blessing of some level of nobility, would terrorize whole districts with blackmail or other draconian means of extorting money or resources. No age, gender, or place was exempted.[24] Even commoners could, with enough money, corrupt judges and juries in ways unthinkable today.[25]

Although Europe's transition from overt corruption to transparency was slower and perhaps more painful than America's, it was ultimately triggered in part by a similar engine: innovations that created new markets for many of the continent's nonconsumers, which offered viable options for the average person to make a living. The new markets also forced the hand of the governments to become more creative in how they taxed and governed their citizens.

As societies became less agrarian, wealth such as gold, silver, and other precious metals became more mobile, and governments needed to create better ways to tax their citizens. "Monarchs innovated new ways of tapping the private wealth of their citizens. Among the most significant was the creation of parliaments—fora in which they could trade concessions in public policies for the payment of public revenues," concludes Harvard professor Robert Bates in *Prosperity & Violence: The Political Economy of Development*. Governments chose seduction over bullying because, all of a sudden, citizens could move their value more easily.[26] A new type of economy had emerged—from one that plundered wealth came one that *sought its creation*.

Additionally, as monarchs continued to fight more wars and conquer more territories, they needed to borrow larger and larger sums of money. There are numerous accounts, for instance, of the English king in the seventeenth century always being short of cash. Then and today, there are few challenges worse than a government being short of cash when it is at war. And unlike today, when sovereign debt is typically viewed as safer than private debt (although this does depend on the country in question), back then it was the riskiest type of debt on the market. Sovereign debt was larger than private debt and took longer to repay, and the monarchs could renege on the debt with few consequences. So investors who typically loaned monarchs money, and whose monies were now more mobile as they were no longer tied to land, caused monarchs to create less corrupt and more transparent institutions.[27]

These institutions, at the onset, were less than ideal. But they created a fair amount of predictability for the investors in Europe. The courts, for instance, focused more on delivering judgments expeditiously than they did on delivering justice accurately. As such, investors could predictably estimate how long court cases would take, and how that might affect their business dealings. This is important because research suggests that the unpredictability in a system, even one rife with corruption, might actually be more harmful than corruption itself.[28]

As European markets grew, the court systems grew as well, in relevance. This affected the culture of the average European, and caused them to place immense value on these new transparent institutions. The new institutions worked, but it's crucial to understand *why* they worked: many of these institutions, which promoted transparency, were tied to new markets that sustained them and made them necessary.

Clearly, circumstances today are different. Not every poor country is engaged in a war and ruled by a government that is desperately in need of cash, like many European governments five hundred years ago. But the fundamental equation remains the same. There needs to be a good enough reason for people in society to want to obey the laws of the land. Think of how difficult it has been for the government of Argentina to get small contractors to declare their income in order to pay taxes. But IguanaFix, offering them something beyond moral responsibility—the ability to make progress in the struggles of their own lives—was able to change that.

Transparency Takes Root

Even in countries that look very different from the United States and countries in Europe, we see a similar pattern in the path to transparency. If anyone had told General Park Chung-hee, South Korea's dictatorial leader from 1963 to 1979, that his daughter, Park Geun-hye, would someday become president of the country, he surely wouldn't have been surprised. But if that person had gone on to tell the general that his daughter would be *impeached* by South Korea's Parliament and be charged with corruption, he might have been stunned.

But that is exactly what has happened in South Korea. In late 2016, President Park Geun-hye, General Park's daughter, was removed from office for alleged bribery, abuse of power, and other crimes related to corruption. In March 2017, the Constitutional Court of Korea unanimously upheld the parliament's decision, and in April 2018, the former president was sentenced to twenty-four years in prison.[29]

To appreciate just how significant that is, consider the fact that South Korea was ruled by General Park until his assassination in 1979. Under his dictatorship, the scale of economic development achieved by the Korean government was enviable, but the scale of corruption was equally indisputable. The government handed out favors to several large corporations, and those corporations in turn gave kickbacks to government officials. This propped up the system, and as long as the economy was growing, the corruption seemed relatively minuscule. But it was not minuscule at all.

"Measures of institutional quality based on bureaucracy, rule of law, expropriation risk and contract repudiation by governments in successful East Asian countries in the mid-1980s were only slightly better than in many poor-performing countries" is how economist Mushtaq Khan describes corruption and institutional development in the region. "Fast-growing Indonesia scored the same as Burma or Ghana, and South Korea, Malaysia, and Thailand the same as Cote d'Ivoire. The corruption index created by Transparency International showed that the rapidly growing East Asian countries had corruption scores in the 1980s that were little different from those of other developing countries."[30] Yet South Korea today is well on its way to a more transparent society.

As societies invest more in innovation, which creates prosperity for their citizens, their corruption-fighting systems will slowly improve and the prospect of impeaching a corrupt head of state will become not only possible, but probable. Many of today's corrupt countries have the potential to become more transparent, too, but in order to get there, we will have to get the sequence right.

What, Then, Must We Do?

So what *can* we do to reduce corruption? With our understanding that people are trying to make progress in their lives when they "hire" corruption, we make two suggestions. First: What if we stopped focusing all our effort on *fighting* corruption? Without simultaneously providing a *substitute* for what people can hire, corruption will be incredibly difficult to minimize. Like that game of Whac-A-Mole, as soon as one effort to tamp it down succeeds, another form of corruption will spring up.

The *circumstance* in which a particular state finds itself should determine which institution or law enforcement mechanism it employs, suggest Harvard's Glaeser and Shleifer. Their model proposes that "when the administrative capacity of the government is severely limited, and both its judges and regulators are vulnerable to intimidation and corruption, it might be better to accept the existing market failures and externalities than to deal with them through either the administrative or the judicial process. For if a country does attempt to correct market failures, justice will be subverted, and resources will be wasted on subversion without successfully controlling market failures."[31] In other words, if a country does not have the capacity to enforce the laws on the books, it will matter very little how many new laws, institutions, or public mandates are created to combat corruption or impose transparency.

Instead of earnest poor-country governments continuing to aggressively fight corruption with the very limited resources they have, what would happen if they instead focused on enabling the creation of new markets that help citizens solve their everyday problems? Once enough markets are created, people have an interest in those markets succeeding. Governments will begin to generate more revenue to improve their courts, law enforcement, and legislative systems. In addition, markets begin to provide jobs that give people a viable alternative to accumulating wealth through corrupt means. Asking people to fire corruption without giving them anything else to hire is not very realistic, and, as the data show, often doesn't work.

Integrating and Internalizing Your Organization's Operations

Second, we must focus on what we *can* control, by integrating and internalizing our operations in order to reduce opportunities for corruption to occur. Organizations understand the importance of vertical or horizontal integration in order to control costs and build predictability into their operations. This is one of the reasons many large companies in emerging markets vertically and horizontally integrate operations that might seem unnecessary in more prosperous countries. As we described earlier, for example, Tolaram— makers of Indomie noodles—supplies its own electricity and built a distribution and retail network to guarantee stable and predictable supply.

The more components of an organization's business model that it brings in-house, the more opportunity the organization has to reduce corruption. In a sense, it's like an organization has a fresh slate upon which it can create new rules that define the reward and punishment system within the organization. This is exactly what Roshan, the leading telecommunications provider in Afghanistan, did in order to reduce corruption.

With a score of 15/100, Afghanistan ranks 177th out of 180 in Transparency International's Corruption Perceptions Index. A recently released Transparency International report suggests that the country is unlikely to meet its commitments to curbing corruption, in spite of efforts throughout the country to do just that. But Roshan understood that to overcome the culture of corruption that has been cultivated in the country for a long time, it had to do something different.

Many people might forget what it was like to make phone calls in Afghanistan two decades ago, but, thankfully, Philip Auerswald reminds us in his book *The Coming Prosperity*. He quotes Karim Khoja, founder of Roshan, who remarked that, "unless you were very rich, if you wanted to make a phone call you had to walk seven hundred kilometers [435 miles] to the nearest country. There was one cellular phone company which was charging $500 for the handset and $12 per minute for international calls, or $3 for local calls. You had to bribe their salespeople even to see you."[32] Today, Roshan serves approximately six million people and has earned a reputation for operating ethically, with a 1,200-person workforce that consists almost exclusively of Aghanis. But achieving this has not been easy. In 2009, Roshan was spending upward of $1,500 per local Afghani employee, training them on both the technicalities of the business and on ethics.

Roshan didn't simply stop at ethical training, however, in the hopes that people would always appeal to their better natures. The company understood it had to integrate further. And so, Roshan set up a government relations department that handles corruption allegations and reports. Whenever employees were asked to pay bribes, they were instructed to report it to this department, which would, in turn, report these incidences to Afghanistan's ministers, donor organizations, and members of the media. Today, the company is perceived as a beacon of hope and a community asset in Afghanistan.

Afghanistan still ranks poorly on many corruption metrics, but the case of Roshan shows that it is possible to avert corruption even in the most difficult business environments. If transparency can begin to take root in present-day Afghanistan, we are hopeful that it can work in other countries as well.

From Pirate to Paying Subscriber

Corruption for most people, especially in poor countries, is simply a means to an end. If they had an alternative, most people would not choose to hire corruption to make progress. And short of enforcing morality—often an expensive and difficult strategy with mixed results—we cannot think of a better strategy for curbing corruption than the subsequent creation of new markets.

Consider what happened in the music industry in America at the turn of this century—where, in relatively rapid succession, a culture of piracy and illegal music sharing gave way to one in which customers opted to pay for streaming music instead.

If you're old enough to remember the golden age of the "mixtape," you will remember that after the innovation of a dual-cassette recorder, copying music was easy. So easy that once you bought a tape, it was easy for you to make copies for yourself and your friends. And many of us did. Mixtapes for parties. Mixtapes to share with girlfriends or boyfriends. Mixtapes for road trips. With our homemade mixtapes, we could create just the right musical montage, to play whenever we wanted it. Music industry executives spent years lobbying Congress for stricter copyright protections, and millions of dollars in awareness campaigns designed to deter people from "stealing" music this way. But none of that made a dent in the practice of making copies. Essayist Geoffrey O'Brien called the personal mixtape "the most widely practiced American art form." Put another way, it was the art of stealing from the artists we loved. All of a sudden, America had become a nation of thieves who stole music. And few people outside the music industry seemed to care.

In fact, things only got worse for the music industry with the invention of Napster, a pioneering peer-to-peer file-sharing technology that made the practice of home taping seem quaint by comparison. Suddenly, people all around the world could share their music—all of it, anytime, with anyone. And they did, indiscriminately. The situation got so big and unwieldy that practically everyone in the music industry took Napster to court. And the music industry won. Napster had to shut down its operations, eventually declaring bankruptcy. Although the music industry might have won the battle, it lost the war to stop music-loving Americans from illegally sharing music. Illegal sharing just went further underground.

In an extraordinary confessional book titled *How Music Got Free*, journalist Stephen Witt chronicles his own exhilarating foray into the world of music piracy—and his eventual change of heart. He did not stop stealing music because he had a moral revelation. Rather, after years of reveling in the furtive online music piracy industry, Witt finally decided to throw in the towel in 2014 because *it was simply not worth the trouble*. "Piracy was becoming too expensive and time-consuming—after a certain point, it was cheaper to subscribe to Spotify and Netflix," Witt writes. "Individual ownership of 'private' digital property was disappearing; in the new paradigm, digital goods were corporate property, with users paying for limited access. Using Spotify for the first time, I immediately understood that the corporations had won—its scope and convenience made torrenting music seem antique. For the first time, a legal business was offering a product that was superior to what was available underground."

The music industry might have been able to knock down music pirates here and there, but until it truly understood why people were "hiring" those alternative solutions, it was never going to prevail. It was playing its own game of Whac-A-Mole. The same is true throughout society. We might win cases against corrupt politicians and corrupt practices, but until we truly understand why people hire corruption, we will continue to spend our hard-earned resources fighting this problem. We aren't suggesting that the world turn a blind eye to corruption, waiting for market-creating innovations to eventually push it aside. We understand that this process will take time. But we must aggressively complement our existing efforts with market-creating innovations if we are to have a fighting chance against corruption.

———

Were the agents in South Korea demanding that I pay "safety insurance" forty years ago corrupt? By our definition, they were. What about the police officers in impoverished countries who take bribes? Absolutely. Are these people engaging in corruption because they are somehow morally bankrupt individuals? I don't think so. For each of these people, corruption is a solution to a struggle, and often the most cost-effective way for them to make progress in their societies—and to support their families. And as we see, time and again, simply enacting new laws—or even harsher penalties—isn't going to make them change their behavior. It just drives the corruption underground.

We are not saying that corruption can be completely eradicated from any society, but we believe it can be significantly mitigated. And this matters to a society's potential for growth because limiting corruption makes room for predictability, which ultimately improves trust and transparency. And just like prosperity, achieving transparency is a process.

When we examine widely held beliefs that establishing solid institutions and abolishing corruption are preconditions of an economy's development, we find again and again that innovation, especially market-creating innovations, can be a critical catalyst for change. Market-creating innovations have the ability to *pull in* what's needed, regardless of the existence of sound institutions or the state of corruption. Those will follow, as will, we believe, the most visible piece of the development puzzle: infrastructure.

NOTES

1. Edward L. Glaeser and Andrei Shleifer, "The Rise of the Regulatory State," *Journal of Economic Literature* 41, no. 2 (June 2003): 401–425.

2. "Corruption Perceptions Index 2017," Transparency International, February 21, 2018, https://www.transparency.org/news/feature/corruption _perceptions_index_2017.

3. "The monthly remuneration received by each of its officers and employees including the system of compensation as provided in its regulations," Maharashtra State Anti Corruption Bureau, accessed April 6, 2018, http://acbmaharashtra.gov.in/.

4. The drop in oil prices, which accounts for as much as 95 percent of the Venezuelan government's revenues, has not helped. It has caused revenues to dwindle from about $80 billion in 2013 to around $22 billion in 2016. Not only can the government no longer fund some basic needs, but the government has also gotten more creative in "fund-raising." For instance, some in the government have targeted food aid distribution programs, asking for bribes before containers of food can be cleared from the country's ports.
    The Associated Press, "US Lawmakers Call for Action on Venezuela Food Corruption," NBC News, January 23, 2017, http://www.nbcnews.com/news /latino/us-lawmakers-call-action-venezuela-food-corruption-n710906.

5. Christian Goebel, "Taiwan's Fight Against Corruption," *Journal of Democracy* 27, no. 1 (January 2016): 128, https://www.researchgate.net /publication/291821592_Taiwan's_Fight_Against_Corruption.

6. Minxin Pei, "Corruption Threatens China's Future," *Carnegie Endowment for International Peace Policy Brief* 55, October 2017, http://carnegie endowment.org/publications/index.cfm?fa=view&id=19628.

7. Sul-Lee Wee, "China's Parliament Is a Growing Billionaires' Club," *New York Times*, March 1, 2018, https://nyti.ms/2t7KA4z.

8. Howard French, *China's Second Continent: How a Million Migrants Are Building a New Empire in Africa* (New York: Alfred A. Knopf, 2014).

9. Jeff Desjardins, "These countries are leading the way on growth," *World Economic Forum*, October 30, 2017, https://www.weforum.org /agenda/2017/10/these-countries-are-leading-the-way-on-growth.

10. "Corruption Perceptions Index 2017," Transparency International, February 21, 2018.

11. "Foreign direct investment, net inflows (BoP, current US$)," The World Bank, accessed April 6, 2018, https://data.worldbank.org/indicator /BX.KLT.DINV.CD.WD?locations=CN.

12. "Lobbying: Overview," OpenSecrets.org, Center for Responsive Politics, accessed March 5, 2018, https://www.opensecrets.org/lobby/.

13. The Congressional Research Institute, an independently financed think tank focused on improving governance in the United States so it better represents Americans, has done extensive research on the effects of transparency in governments, particularly the US Congress. One of their core theses is that increasing transparency can actually "degrade the quality of a democracy." Their research shows that, as the legislative process becomes more transparent to the citizens, including lobbyists, those lobbyists can begin to influence legislators to vote in ways that don't represent the needs and wants of the American people. What this means is that, even a transparent society is not one devoid of corruption. And as such, we must continually look for ways to help people find a substitute to this economic cancer. Read more here: http://congressionalresearch .org/index.html.

14. Pete Hamill, "'Boss Tweed': The Fellowship of the Ring," *New York Times*, March 27, 2005, https://nyti.ms/2jLJRNi.

15. Faith Jaycox's book *The Progressive Era* provides an account of some of Tammany Hall's (New York City's Democratic Party machinery) corrupt practices. The organization was involved in "police corruption, including widespread shakedowns, voter intimidation and election fraud, collaboration with rent-raking landlords and strikebreaking employers, and maltreatment of new immigrants." When a case was brought against it by some reformers in New York City, the governor refused to fund an investigation into the organization. The investigation was funded by the Chamber of Commerce and other "Good Government Clubs," as they were known at the time. These clubs sprang up all over the United States in response to the government's growing corruption. These Good Government Clubs were funded by concerned citizens who wanted better representation from their governments.
　Faith Jaycox, *The Progressive Era* (New York: Facts on File, 2005), 80.

16. Jack Beatty, *Age of Betrayal* (New York: Vintage Books, 2008), xvi.

17. President Woodrow Wilson was a prolific writer, even before he

became president. He wrote often about the state of government in the United States and on corruption. In August 1879, the influential journal *International Review* published one of Wilson's essays, which he wrote while an undergraduate student at Princeton. In it, the future president wrote, "Both State and National legislatures are looked upon with nervous suspicion, and we hail an adjournment of Congress as a temporary immunity from danger." Wilson later goes on to write in a speech titled "Government and Business": "What is it that is wrong with the business of this country? In the first place, certain monopolies, or virtual monopolies, have been established in ways which have been unrighteous and have been maintained in ways that were unrighteous; and have been used and intended for monopolistic purposes."

Woodrow Wilson, *The New Freedom: A Call for the Emancipation of the Generous Energies of a People* (New York: Doubleday, Page & Company, 1913), 240.

18. Larry Schweikart, *The Entrepreneurial Adventure: A History of Business in the United States* (Fort Worth: Harcourt College Publishers, 2000), 153–154.

19. Earl Swift, *The Big Roads: The Untold Story of the Engineers, Visionaries, and Trailblazers Who Created the American Superhighways* (Boston: Houghton Mifflin Harcourt, 2011).

20. Lawrence Friedman, *A History of American Law*, 3rd revised ed. (New York: Simon & Schuster, 2005).

21. During the time when Isaac Singer released his sewing machine, innovators were more likely to be sued for their innovations than to sell their products. Lawsuits were so commonplace that Singer and a group of other innovators created the first-ever "Patent Pool." The notion that, somehow, America's business environment was predictable and law and order was respected is not quite true.

In addition, during the time of the railroad construction, there was widespread speculation and dealings with members of Congress. Many members of Congress took advantage of this opportunity to line their pockets by granting favors to the highest bidders.

22. Edward L. Glaeser and Andrei Shleifer, "The Rise of the Regulatory State," 419.

23. Ralph V. Turner and Richard Heiser, *The Reign of Richard Lionheart: Ruler of the Angevin Empire, 1189–1199* (London: Routledge, 2000), 12.

24. Sir John Fortescue and Charles Plummer, *The Governance of En-*

gland: The Difference between an Absolute and a Limited Monarchy (Oxford: Clarendon Press, 1885): 24.

25. Deirdre McCloskey, *Bourgeois Dignity: Why Economics Can't Explain the Modern World* (Chicago: University of Chicago Press, 2010), 317.

26. Harvard University professor Robert Bates provides a brilliant summary about the evolution of institutional development in Europe in his short book *Prosperity & Violence*. He peels the covers and goes behind the scenes to show us how Europe's courts and parliaments were developed. In both cases, the connection between growing and thriving markets and the ability for the State to generate more revenue by developing these new institutions is apparent.

Robert Bates, *Prosperity & Violence* (New York: W.W. Norton & Co., Inc., 2010), 41, 52.

27. Ibid.

28. In their paper, "Predictable Corruption and Firm Investment," economist Krislert Samphantharak and political scientist Edmund Malesky write that predictability of bribes is at least as important for a firm's investment decisions as the amount of bribes firms pay, provided the amount is not prohibitively expensive.

Krislert Samphantharak and Edmund J. Malesky, "Predictable Corruption and Firm Investment: Evidence from a Natural Experiment and Survey of Cambodian Entrepreneurs," *Quarterly Journal of Political Science* 3 (March 31, 2008): 227–267.

J. Edgar Campos also comes to the same conclusion that, in terms of how corruption impacts investments, predictability matters. He explains this in his paper "The Impact of Corruption on Investment: Predictability Matters."

29. Choe Sang-Hun, "Park Geun-hye, South Korea's Ousted President, Gets 24 Years in Prison," *New York Times*, April 6, 2018, https://nyti .ms/2Heh68v.

30. Mushtaq H. Khan, "State Failure in Developing Countries and Institutional Reform Strategies," *Annual World Bank Conference on Development Economics—Europe 2003*, http://eprints.soas.ac.uk/3683/1/State _Failure.pdf.

Matthew McCartney, *Economic Growth and Development: A Comparative Introduction* (London: Palgrave Macmillan, 2015), 217.

31. Edward L. Glaeser and Andrei Shleifer, "The Rise of the Regulatory State," 420.

32. Philip Auerswald, *The Coming Prosperity: How Entrepreneurs Are Transforming the Global Economy* (Oxford: Oxford University Press, 2012), 58.

Karim Khoja, "Connecting a Nation: Roshan Brings Communications Services to Afghanistan," *Innovations* 4, no. 1 (Winter 2009): 33-50, https://www.mitpressjournals.org/doi/pdf/10.1162/itgg.2009.4.1.33.

Chapter 10

If You Build It, They May Not Come

Between the ocean and the mountain [in Cape Town], there's the unfinished highway. It is an odd-looking landmark in a beautiful city: sections of elevated road left suspended in mid-air when construction stopped in the 1970s. Four decades later, the hulking slabs of concrete still end in precipitous drops.

—THE ECONOMIST[1]

The Idea in Brief

Children sitting on dirt floors in one-room schools without desks. Patients lining the corridors of hospitals and clinics, desperate for help. Women walking long distances on unpaved roads to fetch water. Nonexistent sewage treatment facilities. Unpassable roads. Dysfunctional rail. Inefficient ports. Poor infrastructure is one of the most visible signs of poverty and is one of the primary reasons poor countries cannot escape their cycle of poverty, according to a United Nations Conference on Trade and Development (UNCTAD) report.[2] If poor countries could just improve their infrastructures, the thinking goes, investment will flow in, and prosperity will follow.

Although it's true that investors and entrepreneurs, development workers, and multinational corporations alike are frustrated by the lack of reliable infrastructure in many low-income countries across the globe, assuming that prosperity will follow after investments in infrastructure misses one critical question: *What sustains successful infrastructure development?* Is it as easy as a government or well-meaning development agency earmarking millions or billions of dollars for construction? In this chapter, we will explore the relationship between market-creating innovations and infrastructure. We find that without a serious commitment to fostering innovations that create new markets or support existing ones, many infrastructure projects are vulnerable to failure.

————

When Mo Ibrahim first conceived of setting up a mobile phone company across the continent of Africa, he and his colleagues had to find creative ways of coping with the poor physical infrastructure that they faced, country by country. Challenges that even a lifetime of experience in the UK's telecom industry had not prepared him for. "Building a mobile phone company in Europe requires doing deals with existing telecom companies, filling out forms, and making calls," Ibrahim recalls of the process, which seemed quaint in comparison to what he was about to face. "In Africa we had to literally build the network, tower by tower."

Initially, Ibrahim and his team focused on a handful of countries that had inexpensive or free network licenses available, including Uganda, Malawi, the Democratic Republic of Congo, Congo-Brazzaville, Gabon, and Sierra Leone. The pent-up demand was almost overwhelming; they couldn't get set up fast enough. When setting up operations in Gabon, for example, customers actually knocked down the door of one of the Celtel offices trying to get in. That's how badly people wanted to make phone calls. But that demand just served to put more pressure on Ibrahim's need to actually set up the infrastructure required to get the business up and running, a herculean task. Doing business in a place like the Democratic Republic of Congo was initially a nightmare, because it had no good roads—and sometimes not even any bad roads. Ibrahim's team had to use helicopters to move its base stations and take heavy equipment up a hill or into the middle of nowhere. They had to figure out how to get power to those spots.

Celtel's teams had to supply their own electricity and water. They had to fuel their generators and replenish them frequently. And there was one challenge that his extensive experience in the telecom industry had not prepared him for: making sure they didn't make enemies of any of the local warring groups, in whose territory Celtel needed to set up towers. Ibrahim's critics warned him that he would never be able to work in territories dominated by local warlords. But that, it turned out, was an unfounded fear. Not only did these groups welcome Celtel towers in their territory, they actually protected them. They quickly recognized that those towers facilitated better communication during times of conflict. It helped *them* solve a struggle.

And so, tower by tower, Ibrahim and his team were able to build the infrastructure he needed to get his company off the ground. It was, at first, imperfect and spotty. But as the company's customer base grew, so did its ability to create—or partner with local governments to create—the sophisticated infrastructure needed to fully support the network. Today, Africa's mobile telecommunication infrastructure supports approximately one billion subscribers. Not only was Ibrahim's company wildly successful, but his investments in infrastructures also ignited further investments and catalyzed a flurry of entrepreneurs to consider Africa's telecommunications industry. A nonexistent industry with no infrastructure twenty years ago, the industry today attracts billions of dollars in investments and now adds more than $200 billion in economic value to the continent.

Although many would see the lack of fundamental infrastructure in struggling economies as an insurmountable obstacle—or an essential fix before companies can begin to plant themselves and grow in emerging markets—others recognize that infrastructure is pulled into a market, in dribs and drabs, often in "good enough" solutions where it's really needed. Just ask the many African telecommunications subscribers how much cell service has improved in the past twenty years. It might not be perfect today, but it is vastly better than it was twenty, ten, and even five years ago. Interestingly, we observed a similar phenomenon happen in America 150 years ago. Successful infrastructure projects grow up with companies and improve as economies develop. Good infrastructure will come when there are markets that can absorb the cost of building and maintaining it.

The Push for Infrastructure That Never Quite Delivers

The notion that infrastructure must be pushed onto societies, by poor-country governments before any meaningful development can happen, has not been a time-honored path to prosperity. In fact, the idea that large-scale infrastructure investments are a precondition for economic development is a relatively new theory, which began to take root in the 1950s. Even the word "infrastructure" was not commonly used until several influential papers were written to promote it as a precursor to economic development.[3] After that, it became synonymous with a promise for "progress," but often linked to the changing vicissitudes of political winds.

If you ever visit Cape Town, South Africa, you'll be struck by the sight of an elevated highway running right over the center of the city because it literally drops off, midair, without so much as a guardrail to prevent a car from going off the edge. This road to nowhere has been sitting there, unfinished, for more than forty years. It was planned originally, in part, as a means of helping some of the Cape Town region's poorer residents travel more quickly to higher-paying jobs out of their local neighborhoods. Except, it turns out, there weren't really a lot of higher-paying jobs just waiting for people to find a way to get to. So when funding ran out and priorities changed—and all those higher-paying jobs available to the most impoverished and uneducated residents failed to materialize—the bridge became a glaring symbol of good intentions gone wrong. It's been used as a backdrop for edgy commercial and modeling shots, or the occasional movie or television show, but for little else, in the past four decades.

Pushing infrastructure into a low- and middle-income economy before there are enough markets to use the infrastructure can result in big, beautiful—and ultimately failed—infrastructure projects costing billions and billions of dollars, visible and painful reminders of what once seemed possible.

By contrast, as we described when we wrote about Isaac Singer, there's still a Singer railway station in Scotland—built originally in 1907 as a way for Singer sewing machines to get from the factory in Scotland into the market more efficiently. The first major railroad in the United States, the Baltimore and Ohio Company, was built by a consortium of investors and entrepreneurs in Baltimore and Ohio for the primary purpose of improving access to markets. American engineer, businessman, and politician T. Coleman du Pont of the influential du Pont family was responsible for building the DuPont Highway, a one-hundred-mile highway in Delaware, which he later donated to the state. Today, we know it as US Route 113 and US Route 13. During the automobile mania in the United States, Goodyear tire company's president, Frank Seiberling, pledged $300,000 for the building of roads in the country. He did not consult his board, later saying it was "a movement upon which [Goodyear] will expect to realize dividends."[4] People who wanted to sell tires were very happy to build roads.

The construction of many successful infrastructure projects—then and now—often starts out because entrepreneurs are trying to solve a problem more efficiently. It was the proliferation of motorcycles and motorized vehicles in Japan that led to the paving of roads, or at least that made it sustainable. In 1949, there were fewer than two thousand kilometers of paved highways and barely 370,000 registered motorized vehicles in the country. Ten years later, the number of registered motor vehicles surpassed five million, while the length of paved highways had more than quadrupled. But transportation is not the only sector where we see this phenomenon. It is present in others, such as electricity, education, health care, communications, and so on. Even today, companies around the world are often leading infrastructure efforts that are essential to scale their businesses. As we described earlier, Tolaram, the billion-dollar noodle company, provides its own electricity and water treatment and is actively developing what will become one of the largest ports in Africa. POSCO, the Korean steel company, one of the largest in the world, created POSTECH, a school to train technical managers and technicians. When Ford decided to democratize the car, he had to build and run a few railroads as well.

As expensive as many of these infrastructure projects might seem, when we figure out how to properly communicate the opportunity, capital will follow. When infrastructure projects are connected to market-creating innovations, they become more viable and are able to attract the necessary capital for construction and maintenance. When the same infrastructure projects are viewed in isolation, they hardly ever seem profitable, and as a result, it becomes difficult for them to attract capital.

My colleague and fellow Harvard Business School professor Joseph Bower detailed a similar phenomenon in his book *Managing the Resource Allocation Process: A Study of Corporate Planning and Investment*. In the book Bower explains how many good ideas languished within corporations because middle managers were unable to communicate the value of the projects in relation to how the organization made money. As such, the higher-level executives never even got a chance to consider many potentially bankable projects because the middle managers deemed them unprofitable and never brought them to their attention. Infrastructure projects, especially in poor countries, are similar. Many investors may never seriously consider funding a new road, technical college, port, or hospital because those projects are often seen purely through the lens of being necessary and unprofitable investments. If seen through the lens of the market they are helping either create or grow, many of these infrastructure projects would become more interesting for both governments and companies.

It might be tempting to think this is a "poor-country" or "emerging-market" phenomenon. It isn't. It is an "innovation typically precedes infrastructure" phenomenon—rich and poor countries alike. In late 2017, for example, Facebook and Microsoft built a significant digital infrastructure called MAREA. It is a four-thousand-mile transatlantic subsea cable between Virginia, USA, and Bilbao, Spain. According to Microsoft, this is the highest-capacity cable ever to cross the Atlantic Ocean. And just like railways helped us move goods and services in the 1800s, the Internet infrastructure is helping us move digital information today. MAREA, however, wasn't funded by Virginia or Bilbao. It was funded by Microsoft and Facebook.

Right now poor countries are trying to replicate many of the infrastructures that have grown up and matured for over hundreds of years in rich countries. And, worse, these countries are often trying to replicate different infrastructures without connecting them to the needs of organizations, and, more specifically, market-creating innovations. Unfortunately, and as we can see from one failed infrastructure project to another across many countries, that is not a sustainable strategy.

Afghanistan, where the US government has spent more than $1 billion on education infrastructure in the country with little to show for it, offers an example. In 2011, according to the education ministry, there were 1,100 schools in operation. By 2015, most of the schools were empty buildings with neither students nor teachers.[5] In Tanzania, a $200 million project to build a paper and pulp factory designed to support the country's commitment to universal primary education (the country would need to print a lot of books for students) went bust after the planners realized it was too large and technically complex for Tanzanians, at the time, to manage. It was an unfortunate white elephant project for which Tanzanians paid the bill for the following twenty years.[6] A similar thing happened with health care in Kabul when the US government funded a state-of-the-art primary care clinic. At one point, the clinic saw thousands of patients a month, but it was closed in 2013 because it lacked the funds to remain sustainable and solvent. The situation is similar in Zimbabwe's Parirenyatwa Hospital. Once a thriving hospital that cared for thousands of Zimbabweans, the hospital is now an abandoned space with a "disquieting sense of abnormality," by one account.[7]

Why do these projects start out with such hope and promise but almost always fail to deliver?

Categorizing Infrastructure

Infrastructure is often defined as *the basic physical and organizational structures and facilities **needed** for the operation of a society or enterprise.*[8] This definition leads us to make the case that infrastructure development must be pursued at all costs in order for development to happen.[9] By this definition, we see all infrastructure through the same lens—as essential for the operations of a society or enterprise. But when you understand the role of infrastructure more accurately, you can see that when infrastructure is pushed into a local economy before it's ready, it rarely succeeds.

In order to truly understand why many infrastructure projects don't deliver on their promises, we must first define and categorize infrastructures properly. Categorizations matter. It's a fundamental part of how our brains make sense of information. When we learn something new, we put it into a category of "like" or "not like" something else in our brains. It's how we understand relative meaning. In academia, properly categorizing problems, solutions, and ideas is key to improving our knowledge of how the world works. If we don't categorize things properly, then we can never truly make sense of the problems we are trying to solve. We can never quite properly diagnose faults in our analysis—meaning we'll never be able to solve the underlying problem. Infrastructure is no different.

It's important, then, that we understand that infrastructure is broken into two categories: hard and soft. Hard infrastructures are things such as roads, bridges, and the energy and communications systems of a region. Soft infrastructures are things like the financial, health-care, and education systems.

With this categorization in mind, we see a different, perhaps more helpful, definition of infrastructure as *the most efficient mechanism through which a society stores or distributes value*. For example, roads are the most efficient medium we have developed to distribute or transport cars, trucks, and motorcycles; schools are the most efficient medium to distribute knowledge (so far); hospitals and clinics are the most efficient medium we have to distribute health care (compared to a time when most doctors made house calls); the Internet is the most efficient medium to distribute information; ports are the most efficient medium we have developed to temporarily store transported goods. This definition thoroughly simplifies the concept of infrastructure.

Infrastructure	Category	Value	Store or Distribute
Schools	Soft	Knowledge	Distribute
Financial system	Soft	Credit	Both
Ports	Hard	Goods	Store
Electricity	Hard	Power	Both
Sewer systems	Hard	Sewage	Distribute
Roads and bridges	Hard	Cars, trucks, motorcycles, bicycles, etc.	Both
Water works	Hard	Water	Both

Figure 10: Some examples of infrastructures and the value they either store or transport, or both

Understanding the functional purpose of infrastructure at this granular level helps us discover two important attributes of infrastructure:

1.　Ultimately, the value of an infrastructure is inextricably linked to the value it stores or distributes.

2.　The value being stored or distributed must justify—and ultimately contribute to—the cost of construction and maintenance of the infrastructure.

Let us explain what we mean.

When Schools Are Not the Same as Education

How do you determine the value of a nation's education, healthcare, or transportation infrastructure? Are these infrastructures not worth as much, or as little, as the value they provide their citizens? There is a tendency to build infrastructures without taking the time to understand the delicate connection between the infrastructure and the value it distributes or stores.

Infrastructures exist to serve a purpose. By themselves, they do not create value—they distribute or store it.[10] For example, unfortunately many poor countries are building schools that are not distributing real value to students. And so, while we might celebrate the fact that their education infrastructure is "improving," the real value—that is, the quality of education being distributed to students—is low. "More kids are in school now than ever before. International attention to improving enrollment and targets such as the [UN's] second Millennium Development Goals have had much to do with that improvement," observes Harvard Kennedy School's Lant Pritchett, who has written extensively on the topic. "But while there have been many schooling goals, there has been no international education goal, and schooling—to make one thing clear—*is not the same as education.*"[11] In essence, school is not synonymous with education.

What Pritchett describes plays out in the value of education many students in poor countries get. For instance, even though the rate of primary school enrollment in most low-income countries is now almost at the level of that in high-income countries, the quality of education couldn't be more different.[12] International assessments of literacy and numeracy show that the average student in a low-income country performs worse than 95 percent of the students in high-income countries. In addition, students who are at the top quarter of their classes in low-income countries would end up at the bottom quarter in high-income countries.[13]

The situation does not seem to be drastically different for those who go through the entire schooling system in many poor countries. The value many seem to be getting even from the higher-education infrastructure also seems to be quite low. In Ghana, for instance, many educated graduates who cannot find jobs have created an organization called the Unemployed Graduates Association. (The association rebranded itself in late 2017 to the more optimistically named Association of Graduates in Skills Development.) Tunisia has a similar organization as well, the Union for Unemployed Graduates. In Nigeria, South Africa, and Kenya, unemployment among graduates continues to soar, and students are now considering self-employment as their most viable option to make ends meet.[14]

Although these nations might boast rising primary, secondary, and tertiary education enrollment rates, the value these schools are distributing to students is low. The same thing goes for other forms of infrastructures—from health care to transportation, and the many other infrastructures we develop. These infrastructures are only worth the value they can distribute to citizens. If they cannot efficiently, profitably, and sustainably distribute value to citizens, they are not likely to last.

Who Bears the Costs?

Ribbon-cutting ceremonies that highlight new and flashy infra-structures are ubiquitous in many countries, rich and poor. They are a chance for politicians to highlight (or take credit for) the work they are doing to serve the people. However, many infrastructure projects that are pushed onto poor communities do not store or dis-tribute enough value to justify the construction and maintenance of the infrastructure. Those ribbon-cutting ceremonies are quickly forgotten as once-promising infrastructure efforts languish with-out generating enough revenue to be maintained.

If the value of what is being stored or distributed in a particular infrastructure is unable to fund (often by way of taxes—directly or indirectly—or by the fees charged by the infrastructure suppliers) the infrastructure's development and maintenance, then the infra-structure project will most likely fail. If that continues to happen, unfortunately, poor countries will continue to borrow money to fund large-scale infrastructure projects and may never get out of their debt cycle. In March 2018, the International Monetary Fund (IMF) released a report that 40 percent of low-income countries are now in a debt crisis or are highly susceptible to one.

Consider the example of the recently commissioned Mombasa–Nairobi Standard Gauge Railway, which opened in May 2017. A recent article in *The Economist* notes that the $3.2 billion railway "may never make money." The new rail line was supposed to trans-port roughly 40 percent of the cargo from the Mombasa port, but in its first month transported just 2 percent. Unfortunately, the economics of the investment don't seem to be adding up. A 2013 World Bank study estimated that the "new railway would be feasi-ble only if it were able to move at least 20m tonnes of cargo a year, just about everything that goes through the [Mombasa] port. At best, the new line will transport half of that."[15] Already, there is some evidence that the rail line will not be sustainable, and if not maintained properly, it may not last very long. But Kenya's debt to the Chinese who financed and built the railway will last, and, with interest, will increase. It seems the issue isn't the absence of rail (infrastructure) per se, but the absence of value (innovations) to move across the rail.

There are many more examples of hospitals, schools, and other infrastructure projects that are not moving or storing enough value to remain economically viable. In Brazil, there are almost too many failed infrastructure projects to count. For example, a $32 million cable car project meant to transport residents to the hilltop favela in Rio de Janeiro has not functioned since 2012. There were not enough riders to justify the maintenance of the cable car system. There are several others in and around the country, including the $3.4 billion network of concrete canals in the northeastern part of the country, the dozens of new wind farms, and several stadia and rail projects. It almost is as if infrastructure projects just can't survive the Brazilian climate.[16]

With our understanding of what infrastructure is and how it relates to the value it stores or distributes, how can we more sustainably invest in viable infrastructure projects?

Infrastructure Development

Infrastructure development not only is expensive—economically, politically, and socially—but also often underdelivers on its promise of economic impact in both rich and poor countries. For instance, Danish economist Bent Flyvbjerg, who has done extensive research on megaprojects (projects that cost over a billion dollars) and risk, notes that nine out of ten megaprojects are late, are over budget, and underdeliver on their economic projections. And most of the issues and studies that Flyvbjerg cites aren't in the poorest countries in the world, which lack the institutional capacity, technical prowess, and managerial oversight to manage these big projects; they are in the wealthiest.[17]

This makes pushing infrastructures all the more difficult in poor countries. By definition, poor countries do not have the funds to invest in infrastructure, nor are poor-country governments able to attract the investments they need to build and maintain their nonexistent infrastructures. In light of the high costs of infrastructure and the severe lack of investments pouring into poor countries, what hope is there for the development of their infrastructures? There is little hope when infrastructures are thought of in the conventional manner—essentially as a necessary precondition for development, which must be funded almost exclusively by the government or well-meaning agencies or NGOs. However, when the development of infrastructures is pulled into society by innovations that create new markets, the investments become more viable. All of a sudden, the high cost of infrastructure development becomes more manageable and the costs are often internalized by the new markets created (taxes, charged fees to use the newly built infrastructure, or companies making long-term investments and pulling them into their business model).

In India we see how Aravind Eye Care System, now the world's largest and most productive eye hospital, pulls in the infrastructure it needs in order to provide health care for millions of people in India. The hospital has treated more than thirty-two million patients and performed over four million eye surgeries. But Aravind does not recruit trained nurses; instead it internalizes the training costs for nurses and other medical professionals. The hospital recruits smart people, trains them, and then offers them jobs at the prestigious organization. "They don't come from nursing school; we provide the training for them," R.D. Thulasiraj, one of the organization's leaders, noted about the training of nurses. "It is like getting a prestigious degree and training all in one."[18]

Aravind is able to internalize the cost of this education infrastructure it provides largely because it has created a vast new market for eye surgeries in India and must ensure quality of care delivered to its patients. And because there are few schools that can train health-care workers up to the level necessary for Aravind, the company has to internalize the cost of education into its business model. Most of Aravind's patients are very low income in India, but the organization has developed such a unique and sustainable business model that numerous case studies have been written about it. Aravind's business model not only involves the extensive training of its medical personnel so they are optimized for work at the hospital, but also includes manufacture of intraocular lenses (IOLs) and several other activities. IOLs are an integral part of the eye surgeries the hospital performs. Before building their manufacturing plant, Aravind imported IOLs from the United States at a cost of roughly $30. After Aravind finished their plant, IOLs cost about a quarter of the US imports.[19]

If Dr. Govindappa Venkataswamy, Aravind's founder, had waited for the Indian government to build India's medical education infrastructure before he built the hospital, then the world's largest and most productive eye hospital would not exist today.

But Isn't It the Government's Job?

It may be an uncomfortable thought that we're somehow letting governments off the hook for developing, funding, and managing infrastructure. Isn't that a critical part of what the government is supposed to do for a society?

Indeed, infrastructure development has certainly evolved to become the government's responsibility, and we are not absolving governments of their duties. But once again, the *sequencing matters*. History is full of examples of creative entrepreneurs and innovators finding a faster path to creating the infrastructure their businesses need long before the government is willing—or able—to step in.

In America, as we discussed earlier, it was individual entrepreneurs and private companies who built most of the early roads, rails, and canals. At the time, the government could not afford it, so many of these companies issued stocks and bonds in order to fund the construction of these infrastructures. In New England, for example, private companies invested more than $6 million, which helped construct thousands of miles of highway. New York and Pennsylvania followed suit, handing out charters to hundreds of private corporations that invested tens of millions of dollars for the construction of thousands of miles of roads.[20]

Over time, the government became more involved not only in developing and managing infrastructures, but also in setting standards. For example, as different companies built and managed railroads in the United States, they used whatever *track gauge*—spacing between rails on a railway track—was most convenient for them, from standard gauge to minimum, narrow, and broad gauge. Naturally, this limited the efficiency of a growing rail network in the country, as either trains would need to be fitted to maneuver different gauges or customers and cargo would need to transfer trains depending on the gauge network in their journey. In 1863, the federal government passed the *Pacific Railway Act of 1863*, which mandated every new federal railroad to be built using "standard gauge." While the act didn't impact private railroads directly, it certainly did indirectly. After the Civil War, trade between the North and South began to grow, and the different gauges in the country (especially in the South) significantly hampered commerce. Since a majority of gauges in the country at the time were standard gauge, Southern railroads decided to convert to standard gauge in 1886.

Today, considering the size, scale, and importance of most infrastructures—especially from a national security standpoint—governments are tasked with managing and funding them. However, different countries should have different infrastructure strategies depending on the needs of their citizens, industries, and the markets they hope to create.

Creating and maintaining infrastructures is often too expensive for poor-country governments to fund and manage by themselves, especially when there is little to no foundation of market-creating innovations. If, according to the American Society of Civil Engineers, the United States—the richest country in the world—gets a grade of "D+" for the state of its infrastructure, and needs more than $4.5 trillion to get its infrastructure to a grade of "B," then how can the governments of Honduras, Togo, or Liberia even begin to consider developing their infrastructures?[21]

Most early entrepreneurs who invested millions of dollars to build infrastructures did so not because it was profitable by itself, but because building roads, rails, canals, and better communications infrastructures helped improve their other business interests.[22] This is the same thing we see with many organizations working in poor countries today—companies that understand the need to create markets and the process of building a successful business in low- and middle-income countries invest in their own infrastructures because it's essential for their business. Companies in the manufacturing sector fund their own education programs because it's essential for their business. They don't rely on the knowledge the graduates get from local universities. This is not atypical.

"If you build it, he will come." It's one of the most famous Hollywood movie lines of the past few decades. In the 1989 movie *Field of Dreams*, struggling Iowan farmer Ray Kinsella, played by actor Kevin Costner, is instructed by a mysterious voice to build a baseball field in the middle of his corn crop. That, it turns out, will solve all his problems. But for governments in poor countries, we believe the reverse advice may be even more powerful. If they come, then you build it.

If They Come, We Will Build It . . .

When economic development stakeholders, including entrepreneurs, development practitioners, and policy makers, work to develop markets that require infrastructure, the infrastructures have a much better chance of not only surviving, but also thriving. Just as initial innovations are often of poor quality, those that have identified a promising market opportunity typically get better and better. The same is true for infrastructure: infrastructure that is pulled in for a pressing market-creating innovation is often just "good enough" to survive. It may start off just good enough, but it'll almost always improve as long as there's a good reason (typically a vibrant market) for it to get better. When governments step in to play a supporting role, they can improve rapidly—helping those infrastructures serve a much wider population.

It might be tempting to compare the infrastructure investment that companies in poor countries must make to get to a "good enough" solution with those of companies in rich countries, and conclude that the investment is just too much. But the context matters. In many lower-income countries, if companies cannot rely on their suppliers, they are better off vertically integrating—owning or managing parts of their business they ordinarily would outsource to suppliers, such as distribution, electricity, education, and so on. The process of vertical integration when suppliers are unreliable ultimately helps companies reduce cost. It is almost always a necessary step in the market-creation phase of a company. The up-front costs will be high, but over time, the benefits are clear. Often, a necessary infrastructure investment that started out as a cost center for companies ends up becoming a profit center. Many of the companies we have mentioned are clear examples of this as they begin to "sell" the infrastructure they develop to other companies that need it.

There's no question that it's difficult to build and then maintain infrastructures. It would be *easier* to rely on governments to take the lead and remove that worry and responsibility from private enterprise. But history tells us that that doesn't often happen.

When you create a new market, the profits from the market help pay for the infrastructures pulled into the economy. This is how many major infrastructure projects in the United States were developed. By themselves, many of the infrastructures—the roads, the rails, the canals, and so on—were not profitable. But once the infrastructures were pulled into an American economy that was creating a lot of value that needed to be stored or transported, the infrastructures then became viable. The infrastructure-innovation equation has not changed. Pulling it into the economy is likely to be far more powerful in the long run.

The Value Matters

Ultimately, we must do the hard work of first creating the *value* that we intend to store or distribute on a particular infrastructure. If we don't, we fall victim to the doctrine of "infrastructure first" and can find ourselves in a very difficult situation—one where, if successful, we may have just built a house without anyone able to afford to live in it.

Building that house, however, is enticing, and we understand the allure all too well. Efosa's organization, Poverty Stops Here, raised tens of thousands of dollars and built five wells before he understood the equation wasn't working. The completed wells, or shall we say the water infrastructure, created a sense of accomplishment. How could that not be a good thing? But the wells were not connected to an organization that was able to create lasting value from them. And as such, all but one of them eventually broke and were left unrepaired.

Economies around the world have more in common than we might initially think. We're just at different stages of development. When I read about Tolaram, for instance, the company reminds me of Ford Motor Company during its early days. When I travel to India and I learn about companies like Zoho, which funds training programs for its IT staff, I think about POSCO and how the company created POSTECH. Sustainable infrastructure development is possible, and it can happen in a more predictable manner. But first we have to get the equation right.

NOTES

1. "Plans for a weirdly unfinished highway in Cape Town," *The Economist*, April 12, 2017, https://www.economist.com/news/middle-east
-and-africa/21720649-road-nowhere-may-finally-reach-end-plans-weirdly
-unfinished-highway.

2. Chiponda Chimbelu, "Poor infrastructure is key obstacle to development in Africa," *Deutsche Welle*, July 26, 2011, http://p.dw.com/p/122ya.

3. Yale University professor William Rankin explains in "Infrastructure and the international governance of economic development" that in the 1950s, "debates about development aid shifted attention from an economic definition of infrastructure towards one framed more in terms of general prerequisites." He goes on to further write that "early development theory is often portrayed as infrastructure-centric; if there is a single theory that stands for the economic thought on development in the 1950s, it is the 'big push', where a huge infusion of lumpy infrastructure capital is seen as necessary for overcoming the vicious circle of low productivity, low savings rate and low investment thought to exist in underdeveloped countries . . . Only in the context of international debate about economic development after the Second World War did the term infrastructure become a label for the technical-political systems required for growth and modernity . . . But nowhere in these earlier uses of infrastructure can one find the idea that large-scale engineering systems, especially those of transportation and communication, together constitute a supportive base for other kinds of economic activity. It is only in the 1950s discussion about international financing for economic development that infrastructure becomes recognizable as a concept relating engineering to larger socioeconomic concerns."

This has significant implications for economic development, especially in poor countries. If infrastructures are now considered prerequisites for development, then technically there can be no development without first developing one's infrastructures. And because the prevailing model is "the government must provide the infrastructure," poor countries find themselves on an economic development treadmill, running as fast as they can but not going anywhere.

4. Earl Swift, *The Big Roads: The Untold Story of the Engineers, Visionaries, and Trailblazers Who Created the American Superhighways* (Boston: Houghton Mifflin Harcourt, 2011), 33.

5. Andrew Degrandpre and Alex Horton, "Ghost schools and goats: 16 years of U.S. taxpayer waste in Afghanistan," *Chicago Tribune*, August 21, 2017, http://www.chicagotribune.com/news/nationworld/ct-us -afghanistan-spending-20170821-story.html.

6. The story of the Mufindi Pulp and Paper Project is profiled in Robert Calderisi's book *The Trouble with Africa: Why Foreign Aid Isn't Working*. In it, Calderisi explains that Tanzania did not have the technical expertise to manage such a big project, and the World Bank staffers did not include training or capacity building into the project cost.

Robert Calderisi, *The Trouble with Africa: Why Foreign Aid Isn't Working* (New York: St. Martin's Griffin, 2006).

7. Chris McGreal, "A month ago, the hospitals were overflowing. Now they lie empty," *Guardian*, December 6, 2008, https://www.theguardian .com/world/2008/dec/06/zimbabwe-cholera-hospitals.

8. Oxford Dictionary definition of "infrastructure." Many definitions of infrastructure are not much different from this one: https://en.oxford dictionaries.com/definition/infrastructure.

9. The idea that infrastructure must come before development is understandable. In a paper by César Calderón and Luis Servén, titled "Infrastructure and Economic Development in Sub-Saharan Africa," the authors conclude that there is "robust evidence that infrastructure development—as measured by an increased volume of infrastructure stocks and an improved quality of infrastructure services—has a positive impact on long-run growth and a negative impact on income inequality." They also note that "since most African countries are lagging in terms of infrastructure quantity, quality, and universality of access, the tentative conclusion is that infrastructure development offers a double potential to speed up poverty reduction in Sub-Saharan Africa: it is associated with both higher growth and lower inequality."

Reading a paper like that can lead policy makers to make significant investments in increasing the infrastructure stock in the country. Although infrastructures are usually a good thing, we hope to show in this chapter that, if they are not connected to a market, they will be very difficult to maintain.

César Calderón and Luis Servén, "Infrastructure and Economic Development in Sub-Saharan Africa," World Bank Group, Policy Research Working Paper 4712, September 2008, https://openknowledge.world bank.org/handle/10986/6988.

10. In referring to infrastructures in England and how they contributed to the Great Divergence, economist Deirdre McCloskey put it this way:

infrastructures "changed locations, not amounts. They increased efficiency, but did not increase incomes by a factor of two or sixteen or a quality-corrected one hundred." Deirdre McCloskey, *Bourgeois Dignity: Why Economics Can't Explain the Modern World* (Chicago: University of Chicago Press, 2010), 343.

11. Pritchett goes on to note that the average adult in a poor country today is getting more years of education than the average adult in a developed country did in 1960. But it is clear that the education infrastructures in many of today's poor countries are not worth as much as those in 1960s developed countries and that these newly constructed education infrastructures are not preparing people for the future. Lant Pritchett, *The Rebirth of Education: Schooling Ain't Learning* (Washington, DC: Center for Global Development, 2013).

12. "World Development Report 2018: Learning to Realize Education's Promise," The World Bank, accessed May 3, 2018, doi:10.1596/978-1 -4648-1096-1, 5.

13. Ibid., 5–6.

14. Dayo Adesulu, "Graduate unemployment, time-bomb in Nigeria," *Vanguard*, June 4, 2015, https://www.vanguardngr.com/2015/06/graduate -unemployment-time-bomb-in-nigeria/.

15. "Did Kenya get a loan to build a railway or vice versa?," *The Economist*, March 22, 2018, https://www.economist.com/news/middle-east-and-africa /21739227-chinese-backed-nairobi-mombasa-line-may-never-make-money -did-kenya-get.

16. Simon Romero, "Grand Visions Fizzle in Brazil," *New York Times*, April 12, 2014, https://nyti.ms/2HoVtCo.

17. Bent Flyvbjerg's research on the development and evolution of megaprojects, into which category many infrastructure projects fall, is vast. Flyvbjerg lists the following indisputable and unavoidable principles, iron laws as they are called, of megaprojects. First, Flyvbjerg's research finds that nine out of ten megaprojects incur cost overruns, and many of such overruns surpass 50 percent of the original budgeted amount. These overruns are not specific to any particular geography and have stayed relatively constant over the past seventy years. For example, the Denver International Airport was 200 percent over budget. In fact, some industries have been studied so much that there are expected overruns. The rail industry is one, where the average rail project is expected to be approximately 45 percent over budget, while road construction proj-

ects are expected to be about 20 percent over budget. Second, Flyvbjerg notes that nine out of ten megaprojects are late. When many large-scale projects are proposed, their costs and schedules are inputs that are used to estimate the short- and long-term economic and societal benefits of the projects. As a result, nine out of ten megaprojects overestimate their economic and social benefits. After modeling many large-scale projects, Flyvbjerg found that a one-year delay can increase the cost of a project by up to 4.6 percent. Few projects illustrate this point more perfectly than Boston's Big Dig Central Artery/Tunnel Project, which rerouted a central highway in the city into a newly constructed tunnel. In 1982, the price tag for the Big Dig was $2.8 billion (approximately $7 billion today), but according to the *Boston Globe*, when all is said and done, the project will cost about $24 billion. The project was also nine years behind schedule. Boston's Big Dig, however, was not an anomaly. Third, and perhaps most surprising, is that cost overruns are a problem for both public and private sector projects. Flyvbjerg provides the Channel Tunnel, a thirty-one-mile rail tunnel linking the UK and France. Euro-tunnel, the private owners of the tunnel, estimated that cost overruns would likely not surpass 10 percent. Construction costs were 80 percent over budget, while financing costs were 140 percent over budget. The British economy has lost $17.8 billion from the project, with investors reaping a whopping -14.5 percent on their investment.

Bent Flyvbjerg, "What You Should Know about Megaprojects and Why: An Overview," *Project Management Journal* 45, no. 2 (April–May 2014): 6–19.

18. V. Kasturi Rangan, "The Aravind Eye Hospital, Madurai, India: In Service for Sight," Harvard Business School Case 593-098, April 1993. (Revised May 2009.)

19. Ibid.

20. Larry Schweikart, *The Entrepreneurial Adventure: A History of Business in the United States* (Fort Worth: Harcourt College Publishers, 2000), 97.

21. Jack Stewart, "America Gets a D Plus for Infrastructure, and a Big Bill to Fix it," *Wired*, March 9, 2017, https://www.wired.com/2017/03/america-gets-d-plus-infrastructure-big-bill-fix/.

22. Larry Schweikart, *The Entrepreneurial Adventure: A History of Business in the United States*, 98.

Section 4

———

What Now?

Chapter 11

From Prosperity Paradox to Prosperity Process

Most of the things worth doing in the world had been declared impossible before they were done.

— LOUIS D. BRANDEIS

The Idea in Brief

Prosperity for all? It might seem an impossibility. But consider that in my lifetime, South Korea was deemed an economic "basket case," a country so poor that many economists had written it off. Today, however, it has emerged from poverty to prosperity, and it did so "faster than the United States, Britain, and even Japan," reports the *New York Times*. While the path to prosperity will look different for different countries and will ultimately depend on their current economic circumstances, we believe that the Prosperity Paradox can become the Prosperity Process, one that is sustained by a continuous commitment to innovation.

We do not know the answers to all of the development puzzles in our world. But we hope that our book offers you a set of new lenses through which to see the world. We hope that through some of the principles, stories, and theories we've explored, you can begin to ask yourself and those around you the questions that can finally help us solve the seemingly intractable problem of global poverty.

My brother-in-law Reed Quinn has spent much of his career as a pediatric cardiothoracic surgeon in the state of Maine. From what he tells me, I believe he could spend every waking minute performing surgery and never satisfy the demand for his services. Congenital heart problems are the most common form of birth defect, occurring in about forty thousand babies in the US each year. Thousands of infants are born with heart defects so severe that they almost always require complex, high-risk operations for a chance at surviving. I can only imagine the pain a family goes through after finding this out. A successful heart surgery, however, can change the entire trajectory of a child's life.

The chance to impact as many lives as he can is what motivates Reed, and he has spent his entire career trying to find ways to do more. "We've never not operated on anybody in the state that has needed it," he told the *Portland Press Herald* a few years ago. "I don't know who pays me and who doesn't, and I really don't care." That's Reed. But in addition to serving the local population, Reed also serves children from impoverished countries around the world through the Maine Foundation for Pediatric Cardiac Surgery, an organization he founded. During his many trips to different countries, including China and Kenya, Reed has performed scores of surgeries and trained several physicians.

Until I talked to Reed about his work, I had no idea what it involved, and I'm in awe of his selfless devotion to it. Today, many children around the world owe their lives to Reed Quinn and other doctors and nurses like him. But I can't help but think of all the children who will never get the chance to meet their own "Reed Quinn." The problem feels overwhelming.

We might be tempted to throw in the towel and conclude that this problem is too complicated and too expensive to solve in poor countries around the world, far from the resources of a well-funded hospital. Fortunately, that is only partly true. There may not be enough devoted individual doctors who will spend their every waking hour helping children receive the medical care that will save their lives, but that does not mean we cannot find a better way to help people. This requires us to put on different lenses to help us develop a set of **processes** that radically scale what doctors like him do.

That is where the importance of innovation comes into focus. In Chapter 1, we defined innovation as *a change in the processes by which an organization transforms labor, capital, materials, and information into products and services of greater value.* When most organizations are initially formed, much of what gets done is attributable to the organization's *resources*—particularly its people. The addition or departure of a few key people can have a profound influence on its success. These people, many of whom are gutsy and highly skilled—such as a brilliant entrepreneur or a passionate individual doctor— are difficult to replicate.

But that's where market-creating innovations play a critical role. They help us develop the processes necessary to convert the complicated and expensive services into simpler and more affordable ones so that many more people can access them. At the outset, an organization survives because of its resources. But an organization thrives in the long term because of its **processes**.

Consider the case of Narayana Health.

The Power of Processes

Narayana Health (NH) is a chain of multispecialty hospitals in India with more than seven thousand hospital beds, seven world-class heart centers, and nineteen primary health-care facilities. Dr. Devi Prasad Shetty, who once served as personal physician to Mother Teresa, founded and built NH in India, one of the poorest countries in the world and one that is perpetually plagued with corruption and mismanagement. His dream of "curing the world's poor for less than a dollar a day" is reminiscent of Henry Ford's declaration that he "will build a car for the great multitude . . . [which] will be so low in price that no man making a good salary will be unable to own one." And in the same way Ford's vision came true, Dr. Shetty's dream is much closer to a reality today than it was in July 2000, when he started NH. Much like Ford, Dr. Shetty focused on improving the *process* by which NH delivers care. In doing so, he has democratized access to some of the most complicated and expensive surgical procedures, including, heart, brain, and spinal surgeries.

NH's obsessive focus on and commitment to developing the processes necessary to create a new market that provides quality and affordable health care for many in India are at the core of what drives the company. Affordable health care, even in rich countries, is becoming a misnomer. In the United States, for instance, we spend roughly $3.3 trillion or $10,348 per person on health care every year, effectively making health care unaffordable for many.[1] In Britain, the National Health Service is said to be "under threat" or in "crisis" and in need of a new model if it is to survive.[2] Affordable health care in poor countries is another matter altogether, as most cannot provide basic health-care services to their citizens, much less advanced tertiary care like cardiac care, neurosurgery, and other complex medical and surgical interventions. Consider heart surgeries, for example, an area that NH specializes in; in the UK and the US, open heart surgery could cost as much as $70,000 and $150,000 respectively. A majority of Indians don't make this amount in their lifetimes. As a result, when NH began operations, of the 2.4 million people who needed heart surgery every year, fewer than 5 percent got their surgeries done. In this struggle, Dr. Shetty saw an opportunity to create a new market for cardiac care. And indeed he has.

Today, NH performs open-heart surgeries for between $1,000 to $2,000, while achieving similar mortality and infection rates to those of many hospitals in the US.[3] But not only that, the hospital now offers quality health care in more than thirty specialties, including oncology, neurology, orthopedics, and gastrointestinal services, to tens of thousands of Indians annually. As a result, NH is now worth approximately $1 billion, directly employs more than fourteen thousand people, and has trained thousands of health-care workers who now work at other hospitals in India and abroad.

On the surface, what Dr. Shetty has created might seem impossible. But we see it differently. Dr. Shetty's chain of hospitals can serve as a model for how progress is possible when thinking about seemingly intractable problems in health care, or other fields. He succeeded not only because he had a vision for a better way to solve heart problems in India, but also because he created the processes within his organization that could scale what he was personally able to do.

Over time, an organization's capabilities shift primarily from its resources toward its processes, with the business model determining what it must prioritize. As people work together successfully to address recurrent tasks, processes become refined and defined. And as the business model takes shape and it becomes clear which types of activities need to be accorded highest importance, priorities coalesce. Consider how Dr. Shetty focused on building processes in his organization.

First and foremost, Dr. Shetty knew NH had to provide excellent quality care, so he developed a business model with processes that ensured a high utilization of the organization's resources—doctors, nurses, buildings, medical equipment, and so on—which are expensive. If NH could increase utilization, he thought, this would reduce the unit cost of each transaction with a patient. For example, the hospital ran their blood test machines more than five hundred times a day, while other hospitals might run theirs only several times a day. At the outset, the hospital performed nineteen open-heart surgeries and twenty-five catherization procedures a day, over 700 percent more than the average Indian hospital. Within four years of its founding, NH was performing nearly two hundred surgeries per year per surgeon, a volume and pace faster than many world-class health-care institutions.[4] This enabled NH to not only reduce its cost, but also offer the best quality. As surgeons performed more surgeries, they got better.

NH also developed such an innovative business model that its efficient processes enabled it to serve both rich and poor Indians profitably. In addition to increasing its resource utilization, from its equipment to its doctors, NH offered tiered services to patients. The organization acknowledged that wealthier patients would likely pay for extra services, such as single rooms for privacy and other special amenities. NH also charged patients for procedures depending on the patient's income level, up to a maximum amount. This way, heart surgeries cost low-income patients less than 60 percent what they cost wealthier patients who could afford the surgery. And even at this rate, wealthier patients paid roughly $2,000 per surgery while the same surgery cost about $5,500 at other Indian hospitals. NH has never turned away a patient. In 2017, the organization generated more than $280 million in revenues and made more than $12 million in profits.[5]

NH understood the value of pulling in-house a lot of infrastructure that was not readily available in India, starting with education. The hospital ran nineteen postgraduate programs for health-care workers, from cardiothoracic surgery to medical laboratory technology. The training at NH was so good that the hospital's nurses were known all across the region for both their technical and clinical excellence. This did, however, come with a downside, as the hospital's nurses were often heavily recruited by other organizations. But Rohini Paul, NH's director of nursing, did not see it that way. "Although we pay the highest salaries, we lose many of our nurses because the skills they learn here will earn them better pay abroad," observed Paul, "but this does not worry us, since there are so many more nurses waiting to join [us]."[6] And she couldn't be more right. When another organization pulls in a nurse from NH, there is a vacuum that must be filled in order to keep serving nonconsumers. This creates more opportunities for others in the country.

Training was not the only area NH integrated into its business model. As we've described throughout this book, when creating a market, organizations must incur "market development" costs that many may not see as "core" to their business model, but are in fact essential for them to scale and thrive. NH, for instance, developed an insurance product called Yeshasvini. For as little as 11 cents a month, a member of a low-income household, typically a farming cooperative, could get health insurance that would cover up to $2,200 in health-care expenses. Think about it: a premium costing 11 cents a month could cover open-heart surgery. Since its inception, the insurance product has been purchased by more than 7.5 million people. The program has been so successful that Dr. Shetty was able to pull in government support for the program. In 2016, revenue from member premiums reached $14 million, while the Karnataka state government contributed $26.5 million. But it was NH that pulled the government in, not the other way around.

NH did several other things that the typical hospital may not do, such as provide mobile cardiac diagnostic labs (large buses outfitted with medical equipment, cardiologists, and technicians) that traveled to poor communities. Like the executives at Tolaram who asked, *What is the point of your product if it is affordable but not available?* the doctors at NH also understood that there was little point in creating affordable health care if patients couldn't get to it. Although many of these investments might seem an unnecessary expense from the outside, they become absolutely necessary once organizations start focusing on creating a new market where none existed previously.

The results from NH are exemplary. Although he started with just cardiac care, Dr. Shetty gradually moved toward providing other specialties with the same rigor for cost savings, high quality, and intense efficiency. NH reduced the cost of bone marrow transplants from approximately $27,000, the national average, to just under a third, $8,900. Brain surgery would be around $1,000, while spinal surgery would be $550. This sparked a major medical tourism boom in India. In 2016 alone, NH treated more than fifteen thousand international patients from seventy-eight different countries. Consider the economic activity those patients generated in India, from their flights to the country to the food they ate. This is the process by which development occurs.

When the members of the local government in Karnataka, the state in which NH was founded, learned about its work, the government enthusiastically decided to fund twenty-nine coronary care units. NH ensured that these centers were operating up to the level necessary to provide adequate care for patients. Our belief is that governments in under-resourced countries want to do the right things, but are under significant constraints that prevent them from making good, long-term decisions. Development organizations that support market-creating innovators can serve as catalysts, speeding up the rate at which development happens.

NH isn't the only health-care organization in India working to create a new market to serve the vast nonconsumption that exists in the country. In Chapter 10, we introduced Aravind Eye Care System, one of the world's largest and most productive eye hospitals. Aravind was founded in 1976 with just eleven beds and four medical officers. Today, the hospital sees more than four million patients and performs over four hundred thousand eye surgeries annually. Although Aravind is different in the services it offers to millions of low-income Indians, fundamentally, the organization is similar to NH. Aravind has focused on creating a new market for people who historically had no access to eye care, including eye surgeries. The organization is pulling the things it needs, including training, telemedicine to reach rural areas, and even manufacturing of lenses, into its business model. Like NH, Aravind has developed a business model that serves both wealthy and low-income clients, with a commitment to provide quality eye care services to anyone in India. The eleven-bed hospital that was founded in 1976 is now a postgraduate institute for ophthalmology that trains hundreds of health-care workers and doctors in

India annually. This process of developing a business model to create a new market that provides health-care services can be applied in other countries as well.

In Chapter 7, we wrote about Javier Lozano's Clinicas del Azúcar and how that chain of "Sugar Clinics" is working to solve Mexico's diabetes crisis. Dr. Consulta, a chain of health clinics in Brazil that today employs more than 1,300 doctors and treats more than 100,000 patients monthly, is another example. Since its founding in 2011, the organization has grown at 300 percent year over year. This chain of clinics is so efficient that it can charge anywhere from $3 to $30 for diagnostics exams, such as MRIs, blood tests, and mammograms. The organization has attracted private capital from LGT Impact Ventures to fund its expansion, and now operates fifty health management clinics across São Paulo. But even with its rapid growth, Dr. Consulta still only services less than 5 percent of Brazil's population.[7] Imagine what might happen to Brazil's healthcare system when Dr. Consulta reaches five hundred clinics, or five thousand. These solutions often start out small, but as we see with NH and Aravind Eye Care System, they have enormous potential to scale. Although all these health-care solutions might look different, at their core they are illustrating similar points. Not only is there immense economic opportunity when you target nonconsumption and create a new market, but there is also significant developmental opportunity.

If we can begin to solve these problems in health care—one of the most complex sectors—imagine what we can do for food, transportation, finance, housing, and a host of other industries. As we study organizations and nations through the lens of innovation, we see clearly that the innovators who have had the biggest impact did so by creating the processes that enabled them to democratize products and services so that many more people would have access to them.

Mo Ibrahim created the processes that enabled his company to provide affordable telecommunications services to millions of people in Africa. Henry Ford improved the process by which the Ford Model T was built and sold, thereby creating an entirely new market for cars in the United States. Richard Leftley created new processes and partnerships for selling insurance in Bangladesh, India, Malawi, and several other countries to reach people who need it the most. Liang Zhaoxian saw the nonconsumption of microwave ovens in China as an opportunity and developed new processes of making, marketing, and selling microwaves in the country. Isaac Singer, George Eastman, and Amadeo Giannini each developed new processes for providing access to affordable sewing machines, photography, and banking services respectively. Their innovations radically changed those industries.

In the same way we may look at pediatric cardiac surgeries in Maine and conclude that the problem is too big to solve, we may also look at global poverty and conclude the same thing. But we *can* solve it. Our ability to develop innovations that transform complicated and expensive products and services into simple and affordable ones has significant potential to also transform the lives of billions of people in our world.

In Dr. Shetty's office, there's a quote from former US Supreme Court Justice Louis Brandeis that summarizes both the work that NH is doing and the work of many of the innovators we have profiled in this book: "Most of the things worth doing in the world had been declared impossible before they were done."

The Principles of Market-Creating Innovation

Market-creating innovations can begin to solve many of our biggest problems, and in the process they can ignite the economic engine of many countries currently struggling to prosper. By their very nature, these innovations create jobs, pull in infrastructure and institutions, and serve as a strong foundation and catalyst for future growth. As a result, they have the potential to shift the dynamics of many poor countries today.

We have written this book to emphasize the critical role innovation plays in helping us create prosperity in our world. Through our work on understanding the Prosperity Paradox, we were reminded time and again that innovation isn't simply something that happens on the fringes of society after society goes through the process of fixing itself. Instead, innovation is actually *the* process by which society fixes itself. The principles we offer here have the power to change the way we view and respond to poverty, development, and the hope for prosperity all around the world.

To recap:

1.   **EVERY NATION HAS THE POTENTIAL FOR EXTRAORDINARY GROWTH WITHIN IT.** We call this "nonconsumption," and, to us, it's a signal that opportunity lies within. Two hundred years ago we lived in a world filled with nonconsumption of all sorts of products and services that we take for granted today. From cars to financial services, there were many products that were once limited to only the rich in our society. But today our circumstances have changed. We were once impoverished, and in the same way our circumstances changed, the circumstances of many of today's impoverished nations in our world can change as well.

In the appendix, we offer several potential market-creating innovation opportunities. For example, consider that for billions of people in our world, affordable hard and sanitary flooring in their homes is a luxury. What might it look like if an entrepreneur developed a profitable and scalable business model that made, sold, installed, and serviced affordable flooring? Millions of people around the world are not consuming health care. What might happen if entrepreneurs developed a profitable and scalable model that made health care affordable and accessible? There are so many opportunities ready to be mined. But to see the opportunity, we will have to put on new lenses.

2. **MOST PRODUCTS ON THE MARKET TODAY HAVE THE PO-TENTIAL TO CREATE NEW GROWTH MARKETS WHEN WE MAKE THEM MORE AFFORDABLE.** Heart surgery for between $1,000 and $2,000? Or affordable eye surgery? What about selling health and life insurance to millions of people for whom conventional insurance products were not accessible? While many entrepreneurs who see opportunity in nonconsumption are often doubted, we hope that these stories illustrate the power, potential, and possibilities inherent in their choices.

Consider the electric car market today. Many companies—from Tesla to Ford, Hyundai, and Nissan—are developing products that compete with existing gasoline cars already on the market. They are selling these products into the consumption economy, where the competition is steep and the market is saturated. But what if they targeted nonconsumption? What if they focused their product development and sales and marketing on the majority of people in our world, for whom transportation and mobility are a daily struggle? It may not be as easy or as straightforward as developing a product for the consumption economy, but the opportunity to develop an affordable product that targets nonconsumption in this industry is vast.

3. **A MARKET-CREATING INNOVATION IS MORE THAN JUST A PRODUCT OR A SERVICE.** It is a whole system that often pulls in new infrastructures and regulations, and has the capability of creating new local jobs. One of the clearest illustrations of this point is how Mo Ibrahim's Celtel (now part of Bharti Airtel) democratized telecommunications in Africa, ultimately paving the way for the creation of an entirely new digital economy, which now supports approximately four million jobs. By 2020, the number of jobs supported by this industry is expected to top 4.5 million. The product, however, is not simply an inexpensive mobile phone—it is a whole system. It is the cell towers, which need to be installed and maintained by engineers; it is the "scratch cards" (prepaid calling min-

utes), which are sold in informal retail shops; it is the advertising, which is done by creative artists and graphic designers; it is the contracts, which are drawn up by lawyers, and the new projects financed by bankers; it is the regulations, which can now be enforced and modified to fit the needs of many in the country. In effect, it is an entire system that is built on the backs of many new local jobs.

4.   FOCUS ON PULLING AND NOT ON PUSHING. Pushing institutions, anticorruption measures, and infrastructure may temporarily solve problems, but they usually don't predictably lead to long-term change. Development and prosperity can more easily take root in many countries when we develop innovations that create markets, which in turn *pull in* necessary resources a society requires. Once a new market is created that is profitable to the stakeholders in the economy (including investors, entrepreneurs, customers, and the government), the stakeholders are often incentivized to help maintain the resources the market has *pulled in*—such as infrastructures, education, and even policies. Pull strategies ensure the ready market is waiting. This, we believe, has a significant impact on long-term and sustainable prosperity.

5.   WITH NONCONSUMPTION, SCALING BECOMES INEXPENSIVE. Once opportunity is identified in nonconsumption and a business model is conceived to make a product or service available to a large population of nonconsumers, achieving scale is relatively inexpensive. The first step, however, is recognizing an area of nonconsumption. If you chase after the consumption economy and hope to get scale that way, you might be chasing a mirage. Think about the different strategies in providing financial services to the average Kenyan. Once Safaricom, the company behind the innovative mobile money product M-PESA, realized there was a vast nonconsumption opportunity in financial services, it developed M-PESA. Scaling M-PESA came easy—in just less than a decade, more than twenty million Kenyans pulled it

into their lives. Contrast that with how much it might have cost Safaricom to replicate the conventional banking system, which largely targeted the consumption economy.

––––––––

Market-creating innovations span geographies, industries, and economic boundaries, and can catalyze new and exciting growth opportunities for many impoverished nations today. We have visited a wide variety of industries in this book—from health care to automobiles, from financial services to flooring, and from insurance to food—each providing fertile territory for market-creating innovations. Innovation really does change the world.

But for that to happen, we must be willing to challenge our assumptions and ask ourselves new questions. That is the start of opening ourselves up to a world of possibilities we never knew existed.

Reframing the Problem

Most of us associate the Wright brothers with inventing, building, and flying the first successful airplane in America. But what you may not know is that the Wright brothers were among many competitors in a fierce race in America to create a "manned flying machine." From one perspective, their odds of winning were not great: they were not the most well-known, respected, or funded. At the time others, most notably astronomer, physicist, and inventor Samuel Pierpont Langley, were considered safe bets.

Langley was a professor of mathematics and astronomy, and later became secretary of the Smithsonian Institution. Today, many aircraft facilities, including the NASA Langley Research Center and Langley Air Force Base, are named after him. In his efforts to create the first manned flying machine, Langley spent more than

$50,000 (approximately $1.4 million today) of taxpayers' money, and had the resources of the US government at his disposal. He had a clear idea of how he was going to win this race: he was convinced that if he could figure how to generate enough power, he could shoot a plane into the air, causing it to fly like an arrow flung from a bow. After much fanfare, Langley showcased his thinking with two efforts to propel his craft across the Potomac. But each time, his "aerodrome" plane crashed straight into the water. Humiliated and mocked in Congress, Langley eventually abandoned his quest.

By contrast, the Wright brothers spent roughly $1,000 on their experiments. Orville and Wilbur were humble bicycle enthusiasts, neither of whom even had a high school diploma. But they did one thing that Langley didn't: they focused on reframing the problem, which led to them to ask different questions. While Langley had concentrated on propulsion for his aerodrome to fly, the Wright brothers wanted to understand something else first. Their experience with bicycles had taught them about the importance of balance. Was balance—in relation to both lift and drag—critical in flight, too?

It turned out that this was the right question to ask. No matter how powerfully an aircraft is thrust into the air, if it isn't balanced, it won't fly. Understanding the role of balance made all the difference. Just *nine days* after Langley's final attempt landed in the icy waters of the Potomac in 1903, Wilbur and Orville Wright made and documented the first successful controlled manned flight in the Kill Devil Hills of North Carolina. The Wright brothers' flight lasted just 59 seconds over a distance of 852 feet. But that "good enough" flight helped us to finally understand many of the critical elements of flight. Langley was certainly considered a success in his day; he had several prominent buildings named after him. But in reframing the problem, the Wright brothers created an industry, and that industry, in turn, changed the world.

In my decades of teaching and advising, I have found that asking good questions is one of the most important traits in bright students and great managers. *Why do we do things this way? Why do we believe what we believe? What if we thought about things differently? What is our mission and why? Why are we in this business? Why do we do development this way?* These are simple questions. But we believe they can lead to powerful insights. To those who have been working in development and government, and to those who have been working to encourage entrepreneurship in many of the world's poor countries, your work is important now more than ever. We hope that some of the key principles that we offer here are helpful as you continue to make the world a better place.

We know this is not a perfect book. We see it as the beginning, not the culmination, of our work to more fully understanding the role innovation can play in creating and sustaining prosperity for so many in our world—and we hope you will join us in that quest. Every good theory and every good idea is made better when we understand the things it *can't* explain and the circumstances in which it is most and least relevant. We invite you to challenge and refine our thinking to help us make the theories here stronger, so that together we can get to the answers that matter most.

Dream with us for a second. The hearts of hundreds of millions of people all across the world break whenever we see images of poor children who have no easy access to food, water, education, and basic health care. These images bring out the humanity in all of us. They connect us to people we do not know and whom we will likely never meet. But unless we can convert the strong emotions these images trigger into intelligent action, our efforts will amount to putting Band-Aids on a wound that never heals. And over time, we will develop compassion fatigue. The images of sick, poor children will no longer move us to action, only despair. Or, worse, apathy.

But we can solve this problem. It is possible. We are convinced not because we are eternal optimists, but because we have done it before. The more we channel our collective passions into sustainable progress, the more we will chip away at the seemingly intractable problem of extreme poverty.

We believe in the power of innovation. And, more specifically, we believe that investing in market-creating innovations, even when the circumstances seem challenging, provides one of the best chances for us to create prosperity in many of today's poor countries. This is the solution to the Prosperity Paradox, and it can get us to the end of development in our lifetime. The stakes are too high for us not to get this right.

NOTES

1.   "National Health Expenditure Data: History," Centers for Medicare and Medicaid Services, accessed April 26, 2018, https://www.cms.gov /Research-Statistics-Data-and-Systems/Statistics-Trends-and-Reports /NationalHealthExpendData/NationalHealthAccountsHistorical.html.

2.   Kailash Chand, "The NHS is under threat. Only a new model will save it," *Guardian*, January 4, 2018, https://www.theguardian.com /healthcare-network/2018/jan/04/nhs-under-threat-new-model-of-care.

3.   Robert F. Graboyes, "High Quality and Low Price Coverage at Narayana and Health City Cayman Islands," *Inside Sources*, September 13, 2017, http://www.insidesources.com/high-quality-low-price-converge -narayana-health-city-cayman-islands/.

4.   Tarun Khanna, V. Kasturi Rangan, and Merlina Manocaran, "Narayana Hrudayalaya Heart Hospital: Cardiac Care for the Poor (A)," HBS No. 505-078 (Boston: Harvard Business School Publishing, 2011): 20.

5.   "Investor Presentations: Investor Presentation—May 2017," Narayana Health, accessed April 26, 2018, https://www.narayanahealth.org/sites /default/files/download/investor-presentations/Investor-Presentation -May-2017.pdf.

6.   Tarun Khanna, V. Kasturi Rangan, and Merlina Manocaran, "Narayana Hrudayalaya Heart Hospital: Cardiac Care for the Poor (A)," 10.

7.   Sasha Banks-Louie, "How a Small Clinic Is Having a Big Impact on Healthcare in Brazil," *Forbes*, September 26, 2017, https://www.forbes .com/sites/oracle/2017/09/26/how-a-small-clinic-is-having-a-big-impact-on -healthcare-in-brazil/#358d9e1f3ab5.

The World Through New Lenses

Entrepreneurship is the most sure way of development.

—PAUL KAGAME, PRESIDENT OF RWANDA

The innovators we profile here in this appendix—in business, in development, and in government—are seeing the world through a new set of lenses. A world in which struggle represents opportunity, development is focused on making itself unnecessary, and government rallies around entrepreneurs. The point of this appendix is not to provide a tip sheet on the hottest market opportunities (though some of these might be just that), but rather to make clear that when you begin to see the world through the lenses of nonconsumption and market-creating innovations, you can begin to assess risk and reward differently.

It's too soon to say if any of the organizations and programs we profile will be successful in the long run, but taken as a group, they offer much reason for optimism that we will find our way to a more prosperous world.

The Power of Outsiders

Every industry would do well to have outsiders—or those that are not yet experts—in it. Outsiders are able to ask simple questions that many experts, often for good reason, may not think to ask. These outsiders are not yet immersed in a pool of expertise and assumptions that sometimes leads to *cognitive capture* or *cognitive tunneling*, a phenomenon of *inattentional blindness* where observers are too focused on particular tasks and not on the environment.

Consider, for instance, the case of Malcolm McLean. Many of us have never heard of him, but we owe a lot of our ability to more efficiently trade globally to this former-truck-driver-turned-millionaire who only had a high school degree. McLean was a North Carolinian truck driver who found himself waiting for hours at a loading dock the day before Thanksgiving in 1937 when inspiration struck. As McLean was thinking about how fast he could leave the port to get home in time for Thanksgiving dinner, a time-honored tradition in the United States, he realized that the dominant shipping method at the time, break-bulk cargo, was very inefficient and quite dangerous.[1] McLean thought, surely there had to be a better way.

He asked a foreman, "Why don't you just take my whole truck and put it on the ship?" The foreman, a bit unsure of what that would even entail, laughed at McLean. At the time, every shipper **knew** that the fastest way to move products from one place to another was to build bigger and faster ships. But McLean thought the key to a more efficient transport system was not to build faster ships, but to build faster docks. Since McLean was not an expert in shipping, he wasn't taken seriously. But it was precisely because McLean was an outsider that he could *see* what the others could not.

Today it seems obvious, but it wasn't until twenty years later, after McLean bought his own shipping company and built a special boat and equipment for loading and unloading containers, that several others began to buy into his vision. McLean's innovation—*containerization*—reduced shipping costs from approximately $6 a ton to just 16 cents, and he reduced the loading and unloading time of a ship from one week to eight hours. Safety on shipping docks was also a big concern, but McLean's technology of shipping whole containers without unloading drastically reduced injuries on shipping docks.[2]

When McLean died, he not only had revolutionized global trade, but also was worth roughly $330 million. Not bad for a high school graduate from North Carolina.

Containerization, a process that seems so obvious in hindsight, was laughed at because it was not how things were done. McLean and containerization are not alone when it comes to going against conventional wisdom, especially when it has such great potential in fundamentally changing the way we do things in society.

Consider the case of the *lucky* discovery of the *Helicobacter pylori* (*H. pylori*) bacterium in the stomachs of patients with gastritis and ulcers by Drs. Barry Marshall and Robin Warren. Marshall and Warren later won the 2005 Nobel Prize in Physiology or Medicine for this discovery, but not before running a very interesting scientific experiment.

Marshall, a microbiologist, and Warren, a pathologist, had been unsuccessful in growing the *H. pylori* bacteria in the lab to show that *H. pylori* existed in the stomach. They got samples from one hundred patients, but it wasn't until they tested their thirty-fifth sample that their tests proved successful. As Dr. Marshall later recalled, "That event came about because of a *lucky* accident, in which the cultures were left in the incubator over the long Easter weekend and thus the plates were not examined until the fourth or fifth day after biopsy . . . the technologist realized in hindsight that, prior to this day, the research biopsies had been discarded after 48 hours when normal gastrointestinal or throat specimens would have been expected to be overgrown with commensal flora and thus would have been useless for any further diagnostic purpose. This rule did not apply to *H. pylori* cultures."[3]

After Drs. Marshall and Warren had successfully grown the cultures in the lab, the scientific community still did not believe that *H. pylori* was largely linked to gastritis or ulcers. Dr. Marshall later recounted in an interview with Dr. Paul Adams, "I had been arguing with the skeptics for two years and had no animal model that could prove *H. pylori* was a pathogen. If I was right, then anyone who was susceptible to the bug would develop gastritis and maybe an ulcer years later." So Dr. Marshall, who tested negative for *H. pylori*, drank a brew which contained "two culture plates of the organism." After he drank it, he began experiencing symptoms such as bloating, decreased appetite, and vomiting. An endoscopy showed he had severe active gastritis with polymorphonuclear infiltrate and epithelial damage. As Dr. Marshall notes in the interview, "Gastritis was explained."[4]

In retrospect, it might seem reasonable to conclude that members of the scientific community were being irrational. But, on the contrary, they were being very rational. Dr. Marshall was about to turn everything they believed about the survival of bacteria in the stomach upside down. Brilliant scientists had developed these rules over decades, and the notion that one of their fundamental assumptions was wrong, or perhaps not as right as they thought, could be devastating. But an outsider had the ability to see with new eyes.

Let us now take a survey of opportunities around the world, putting on our lens of market creation and nonconsumption. The potential in these examples we share here for solving many global problems, creating significant wealth, and ultimately developing more prosperous communities is inspiring.

Appliances—Portable Washing Machines in India

The global washing machine industry is about a $25 to $30 billion market, with India responsible for less than 10 percent of that market, even though the country is home to 1.3 billion people— almost 20 percent of global population.[5] Only 9 percent of households in India have a washing machine.[6] Compare that with the United Kingdom, where 97 percent of households have the product. In fact, in terms of washing machine ownership, India today lags behind the United Kingdom in the 1970s, when 65 percent of homes in the island nation had a machine. We might look at that and conclude that India is a poor country that cannot afford existing washing machines. But we might also see the vast nonconsumption opportunity instead.

Although experts estimate that by 2025 the global market for washing machines will reach $42 billion, we think it can be more.[7] Those estimates are derived by looking at the existing washing machine product as it is, estimating the growth in the "consumption economy," which we described earlier, and projecting sales. Unfortunately, there are many limitations with the existing machine.

For example, existing washing machines are complicated, power-hungry, and too expensive for most of the world's population, and they are mostly available for homes with piped water supply. In addition, purchasing a washing machine and attaching it to one's home almost always necessitates a call to the plumber, a cost that many households in India cannot bear. Existing machines also require electricity, and millions of households in India, and other emerging markets, don't have access to electricity. So, by design, most washing machines on the market exclude a majority of India's and the world's population. But what if an innovator designed, manufactured, and sold a washing machine targeted specifically at the nonconsumption market in India and in many countries like it?

A product that targets this market will have to be smaller, less bulky, easier to install and operate, and a whole lot more affordable than existing machines. The product will need to fit in a small home with few to no conveniences, and should be able to operate without access to electricity. Also, the product will need to be more easily distributed to communities that may not be on typical distribution routes for major appliance sellers. The more an innovator thinks about the circumstances in which average nonconsumers find themselves and the features this machine must have to help them get the job of conveniently washing their clothes done, it becomes clear that we are not talking about a washing machine in its existing form. We are talking about an entirely different product.

What we are writing might seem far-fetched, but one company we know of has already developed a portable washing machine that attaches to a bucket. You need only add some water and detergent, and put your clothes in the bucket. The machine does the rest. It currently retails for around $40.[8] Imagine marketing this product to all the small businesses that provide laundry services to people in their neighborhoods. Many of these people hand-wash their customers' clothes. With this product, they can wash more, charge less, and grow their businesses. The company that makes this product can either provide financing or partner with a bank to provide financing to these entrepreneurs, a move not so dissimilar from what many appliance manufacturers do in prosperous countries. It is easy to see how this can begin to help people not only grow their businesses, but also build their credit.

If a company built a business model that developed and sold this product to just 10 percent of the households in India, it would generate revenues of approximately $1 billion. This is the kind of potential that awaits innovators willing to create new markets in emerging markets.

Affordable Drugs in Nigeria

A World Economic Outlook study showed that there are currently fewer than twenty-five pharmacies in Nigeria per million people. This means that in a country with approximately 180 million people, there are fewer than five thousand licensed pharmacies. To put that into perspective, there are more Walgreen's stores (over eight thousand) in the United States than there are pharmacies in Nigeria, while Nigeria's largest pharmacy chain brand has fewer than one hundred outlets. There are approximately 67,000 pharmacies in the United States (population 325 million). This staggering statistic alone represents a significant market-creation opportunity. If the United States seems an unfair comparison to highlight Nigeria's underdeveloped pharmacy sector, then consider that Ghana, another poor West African country, has four times the number of pharmacies per capita as Nigeria. Another concern many existing pharmacies and patients face is the prevalence of counterfeit drugs in the Nigerian market, as it's often difficult for pharmacies to guarantee the quality of their supply chains.

On the face of it, these challenges seem insurmountable. So you might conclude that Nigeria must first fix the regulations in this industry before it has any chance of providing affordable and genuine medication to the tens of millions of people who fall sick every year. However, it is precisely by developing a solution that is able to provide affordable, quality drugs that Nigeria will begin to overcome these challenges, including enhancing regulations and improving the supply chain. A low-cost pharmacy business model is what is needed to pull in the necessary infrastructure that will also serve as Nigeria's infrastructure.

One of my former students, Bryan Mezue, is developing a solution (Lifestores Pharmacy) for this vast problem. After graduating, Bryan spent a year with me at the Forum for Growth and Innovation, where we explored how the theories of innovation and management can impact economic development. We coauthored an article that discusses this, "The Power of Market Creation" in *Foreign Affairs*, an article that began to identify some of the themes we discuss in this book.

Lifestores is building out a chain of low-frill, affordable pharmacies in densely populated, low-income urban areas in Nigeria. In addition to launching brand-new stores, the Lifestores team is rolling out a shared ownership platform that allows mom-and-pop stores to professionalize under a master brand. Lifestores has signed direct agreements with drug manufacturers and first-tier distributors to secure product quality and works closely with local providers such as WAVE Academy (a vocational training social enterprise also cofounded by Bryan at Harvard Business School) for customer service training. Imagine what would happen if Lifestores developed into the Walgreen's of Nigeria. Imagine the jobs that could be created, or, better yet, the lives that could be changed. This is what is possible when we invest in market-creating innovations.

Comfort—Sleep in Cambodia

I often tell people that one of the best ways to identify nonconsumption opportunities is to visit a country, find the Mormon missionaries, and simply experience life with them. They are usually in some of the poorest parts of the countries and in most circumstances, live like the average person in that society. As a result, many of their struggles can point to market-creating opportunities. Consider this opportunity in Cambodia, which was brought to our attention by a Mormon.

In parts of Cambodia, mattresses are rarely used, especially by those in the mid- to low-income earning bracket. With a GDP per capita of $1,270, most Cambodians fall into either the middle-income or low-income category. In fact, according to the World Bank, almost 30 percent of the 15.7 million Cambodians "remain near-poor, vulnerable to falling back to poverty when exposed to economic and other external shocks."[9] Most people he came across slept on bamboo mats or on the hard floor. While some people used foam mattress pads, those were bulky and very difficult to store, especially in a small single-room home.

On the surface, it might seem like an inexpensive mattress would do the trick. But considering the fact that many in Cambodia, and in other economically poor countries, live in small single-room homes, it is clear that isn't likely going to work. What if an innovator developed a low-cost, easy-to-assemble-disassemble-and-store mattress? Targeting this opportunity could create a new market of mattress purchasers who might experience better rest at night. It turns out that there might just be vast nonconsumption of a "good night's sleep" in the world.

Sanitation and Energy—Energy from Waste in Ghana

Sanitation is a huge problem in many poor countries and for many poor-country governments. When most governments can't find the financial resources to pay teachers, doctors, and other public servants, how are they supposed to fund sanitation? As such, waste management is often a significant problem in poor countries, and, with recent urbanization trends, it doesn't look like it'll get better. Not only is it a deadly health hazard for the local population, but it is also very costly to the economy. That's where Safi Sana comes into the picture.

Safi Sana has built a waste-to-energy factory in Ghana that has been delivering a huge impact for the local people and government. The company's business model is simple. Safi Sana collects fecal and organic waste from toilets and food markets in urban slums, and then converts it to organic fertilizer, irrigation water, and bio-gas in their factory. The biogas is then used to produce electricity, while the organic fertilizer and water are used to grow seedlings. Safi Sana is thus able to offer a viable solution to Ghana's fecal waste problem, while also providing much-needed fertilizer for farmers and a source of clean energy for the people.

In addition, to ensure scalability and long-term sustainability, Safi Sana runs a locally owned model—90 percent of its factory staff are members of the community who go through an intensive training program before being hired. It has already provided jobs and training to more than a thousand Ghanaians who otherwise had limited economic prospects.

Automotive—Mexican Electric Cars . . . for Mexicans

Of the $374 billion worth of exports Mexico shipped in 2016, roughly $88 billion (23.4 percent) was cars, trucks, or other vehicle components.[10] A majority of those cars are foreign brands, such as Ford or BMW, and they run on gasoline. So, when Zacua, a Mexican company, began designing and manufacturing electric cars, many Mexicans felt a sense of national pride. Finally, one of their own. One journalist put it this way: "As Mexicans, we want Zacua to continue to grow and become a relevant brand in terms of electric cars." Zacua plans to sell its base model for just under $25,000.

That model will not have an airbag and is not compliant with international standards. The company plans to sell only three hundred by the end of 2019.[11]

But what if Zacua, instead of entering an already crowded and very competitive electric car market, decided to leverage Mexico's expertise in automotive manufacturing and went after nonconsumption instead? If the company did that, it would not be competing with the likes of Nissan, Renault, BMW, and Ford, companies that are most likely going to win against Zacua, but would find itself competing against nonconsumption.

It is clear that, while Mexicans can make cars, trucks, and other vehicular products, the average Mexican cannot afford most of the cars on the market. For every thousand persons in Mexico, there are about 280 cars.[12] Compare that with the United States' approximately 800, Australia's 740, and Canada's 662.[13, 14] As such, a market that serves Mexican nonconsumption, and then the nonconsumption in Latin America, is just waiting to be created. Whoever targets this market is bound to reap significant returns. What might this resemble? Perhaps Mexico, and more specifically Zacua, can take a page out of the Chinese electric car playbook.

Over the past several years, I have been fortunate to travel to China a few times, and I am amazed every time at the small electric cars all over the place. In 2017 alone, the market for electric cars in China grew by more than 50 percent, and there seems to be no sign of slowdown. Roughly one in three Chinese consumers say they are leaning toward purchasing an electric car, and the country is now responsible for 40 percent of the investment in the industry.[15]

What if, instead of Zacua trying to compete with the incumbents, the company developed small, inexpensive, and just-good-enough electric cars, like its Chinese counterparts? Consider that the average vehicle occupancy in many countries is fewer than two people, so a two-seater could work, for starters.[16] In addition, we should look at the average miles driven per passenger when many of today's rich countries were poorer, as that number has been going up since countries have become wealthier. In the United States, for instance, the average miles driven per year per passenger has increased by 39 percent since 1950. The implication here is that cars in emerging markets may not have to travel as much as cars in rich countries. In essence, instead of starting with what a car is, we focus on what the purpose of a car is, who uses it in what circumstance, and what the nonconsumers can afford. This exercise can help innovators think differently about cars and mobility. In fact, Zacua may end up selling miles as opposed to selling cars. After all, the primary functional purpose of a car is to enable people to travel from one place to another.

Rethinking the automobile could drastically reduce the cost of the car and open it up to the average Mexican consumer. Consider what might happen if Mexico is able to increase its auto ownership rate from about 280 cars per 1,000 people to 350 cars per 1,000 people. That represents an increase of 25 percent. Imagine all the jobs in production, distribution, sales, marketing, and servicing. It is possible. But it would require a different kind of thinking.

Food—Nigerian Tomato Paste

Nigerians love tomatoes. From the internationally popular dish *jollof rice*, to the country's many soups that use tomatoes as a base, Nigerians have become the largest importers of tomato paste in the world. The West African country imports 100 percent of the tomato paste it consumes, amounting to approximately $1 billion of tomato paste imports annually. At the time of this writing, no single can of tomato paste is produced in the country, which is populated by 180 million people. What's particularly striking about the Nigerian tomato market today is that Nigerian farmers grow over two million metric tons of tomatoes annually, but more than half their harvest rots before getting to the customer. This goes back to our point about the fact that a product must be both *affordable* and *available* in order to adequately target nonconsumption and create a new market.

Also, the average Nigerian spends more than half their income on food, making access to tomatoes somewhat of a luxury, with more than half the Nigerian market for tomatoes underserved.[17] Considering Nigeria's low per capita income, infrastructure challenges, and the fact that the country's middle class isn't growing as fast as experts thought, conventional wisdom suggests there is either no opportunity here, or whatever opportunity exists is too risky. But when we use a different lens to assess the landscape, we see vast market-creating opportunity that can be addressed.

One Nigerian company, Tomato Jos, has begun capitalizing on this opportunity. Mira Mehta, CEO of Tomato Jos and Harvard Business School graduate, understands the significant potential of this market. First of all, Nigeria need not import tomato paste. That by itself represents a $1 billion opportunity. Second, improving the affordability and availability of tomatoes will increase the actual size of the market as more people, especially nonconsumers, will get access to fresh tomatoes and tomato paste. At the moment, this production gap between what the country can consume and what is produced is valued at more than $1.3 billion. Third, Nigeria is a microcosm for other African and low-income countries. If Mehta's Tomato Jos is able to capitalize on this opportunity, she will transform the lives of many people in Nigeria and will also make her investors very happy. In 2018, the company closed a $2 million investment round.

Leisure/Entertainment—Disney World in Detroit

Disney in Detroit? It's hard to imagine a less likely location. Detroit has mostly made headlines in recent decades for its urban decay, its depressing battles with crime and drugs, and its dubious future. The city filed for bankruptcy in 2013 after accumulating an estimated $18 billion in debt.

This is in striking contrast to Detroit just a few decades ago. In the 1950s Detroit was the bedrock of innovation in the United States. Home to approximately 1.8 million people, the city was bustling with motors and Motown. Today, Detroit is a fraction of that size, with just 700,000 residents. Although the city is working hard to stage a comeback, it is still replete with abandoned buildings, vacant lots, broken streetlights, and broken dreams. Since 2008, more than half the city's parks have closed.[18] But where people might see a destitute Detroit, we see a Detroit that presents new opportunities in leisure and entertainment.

Many people might think that notion is daft. Shouldn't Detroit focus on getting its basics in place first? But that is similar to how one may have assessed Nollywood, the Nigerian movie industry, when it began. Today, measured by volume of movies produced annually Nollywood is the second-largest movie industry in the world, second only to Bollywood. The industry is worth more than $3 billion and employs upward of one million people, according to the Nigerian Bureau of Statistics.[19] Disney could do the same in Detroit.

But the company would have to think differently. Replicating the Disney World in Orlando would likely be too expensive to build and maintain. An average family of four is advised to budget roughly $3,500 for hotel, park passes, and food for a one-week trip to the Florida park, not including plane tickets. A single-day pass for an adult can cost as much as $124.[20] And those of us who have been there know it's impossible to limit yourself to just one day. You surrender to the Disney experience. The average Detroiter, however, isn't likely to be able to afford that. This is where new market creators excel, seeing opportunity differently.

We do not profess to be experts in entertainment, but we do have our own family memories and experiences to call upon. We can begin to imagine a new type of entertainment that would serve the same Job that Disney in Florida does for so many of its patrons. An escape from the everyday stresses of life into a magical world where everyone is happy and dreams do come true. Disney is the place we go when we want to spend quality time with our families. That desire is in all of us, whether we are wealthy or poor. It is a Job to Be Done.

The point is not that Disney has to replicate the Disney World of Orlando in Detroit. But it can replicate the Disney magic so that Detroiters, and people in many small towns for whom a Disney vacation is out of reach, can experience the magic that is Disney. Because for many Detroit residents, Detroit Disney would be competing with nothing.

Housing—Flooring in Rwanda and Sub-Saharan Africa
More than half of Africa's 1.2 billion people live in rural areas. Although that in and of itself is not a problem because of the benefits of living away from the often highly populated and polluted cities, the problem is the living conditions experienced by many people. On almost every development metric, from access to electricity to access to clinics, Africans living in rural areas are struggling compared to their urban counterparts. One such metric that is often overlooked but presents significant opportunity is the lack of affordable hard and sanitary flooring in rural homes. In Rwanda, where approximately 80 percent of the roughly two million homes have dirt floors, the situation is particularly troublesome.[21] This means that when it rains, puddles of water can easily become breeding grounds for mosquitoes in people's homes. In addition, dirt floors are simply uncomfortable to sleep on and often leave one's clothes and belongings dirty, which can further adversely impact people's health.

The alternative solution, concretizing one's floors, is too expensive for many in Rwanda and sub-Saharan Africa, where the annual per capita income is approximately $705 and $1,461 respectively.[22] In Rwanda, for instance, converting dirt floors to concrete for the average home costs more than two months' wages. How can there be opportunity in a country where the average annual per capita income is less than the price of a new iPhone? But where conventional wisdom sees poverty and risk, we see struggle, non-consumption, and the opportunity to create a sizable new market. One company, EarthEnable, is already targeting this opportunity, and if it is successful in executing an innovative business model in Rwanda and then in other African countries, it could become a multibillion-dollar company with tens of thousands of employees.

For roughly $4 a square meter, EarthEnable is able to provide affordable flooring made from gravel, laterite, sand, clay, and water—all locally sourced materials. The average Rwandan home is just twenty square meters (sixty-five square feet). If the company is able to provide flooring for just 20 percent of the Rwandan population, it will generate more than $25 million in revenue.[23] Now imagine what that number becomes as the company scales to Uganda, Kenya, Burundi, Botswana, Zimbabwe, Nigeria, and Cameroon. EarthEnable will not only generate superior revenue, but also need to hire tens of thousands of people to make, market, distribute, sell, and service its products. In addition, consider the health implications of its products. Indirectly, this company might help reduce incidences of tetanus, malaria, and other illnesses propagated by dirty environments.

Electricity—Power in Bangladesh

Bangladesh is economically poor. With a GDP per capita of $1,359, approximately 20 percent of the country's 163 million people live in extreme poverty, on less than $2 a day. Approximately 75 percent of rural households, where most of those in poverty live, do not have access to electricity. This means that at sundown, either they have to purchase very expensive and polluting kerosene for lighting, or they do nothing. In other words, once the sun sets, so do they. They must close their small businesses, their children must stop studying or playing, and they must take safety measures in order to prevent theft. Life for these tens of millions of Bangladeshi citizens is made more precarious by the lack of electricity. This, we believe, represents an opportunity for a big market to take root.

Over the past few decades, we have seen the price of renewable energy plummet. What's particularly interesting is that entrepreneurs can leverage this technology to develop specific solutions for nonconsumers. In other words, people don't necessarily want electricity, they want what electricity affords them. They want to be able to turn on a light, to watch a show on their televisions, computers, or phones, and to keep their food cold and fresh. If entrepreneurs develop cost-effective solutions that help these nonconsumers overcome their struggles, they are more likely to succeed.

Consider how Infrastructure Development Company Limited (IDCOL) is creating a market by capitalizing on this opportunity in Bangladesh.[24] Over the past decade, IDCOL has successfully installed more than 3.5 million solar home systems (SHS) in rural Bangladesh. The solar systems are not complicated and come in three flavors. One of the systems powers just a lamp and a mobile phone charger. Another powers a lamp, a television, and a mobile phone charger. The third one powers a fan as well as everything the second one powers. According to IDCOL, getting the SHS to millions of homes has created over seventy-five thousand jobs and has impacted more than sixteen million people. By 2018, the program was on track to install six million SHS across the entire country. Instead of looking at Bangladeshi citizens as too poor to enjoy the benefits of electricity, the innovators at IDCOL developed a solution that targeted their nonconsumption. The results speak for themselves. The changed lives speak for themselves.

Just like Bangladesh, many countries in sub-Saharan Africa also struggle with access to steady electricity. Those who have it often pay a significant premium for it by purchasing and using diesel generators. While it is relatively easy to see the nonconsumption of electricity in a rural village, it is more difficult to see it in a thriving African city. But the sound of every generator providing electricity to a home, an office building, or a hospital represents struggle. And in essence this is a clue to a big market creation opportunity. Some citizens in Nigeria, for instance, pay as much as 25 cents per kWh for electricity, more than twice the rate (12 cents) the average American pays.[25] Consider that the per capita income in the United States is roughly 25 times that of Nigeria. Electricity is unavailable for most in Africa, and for those for whom it is available, it is expensive.

Aspire Power Solutions (APS) is an African company targeting those who currently pay exorbitant rates for electricity through diesel-powered generators. The company installs solar panels for its clients and provides information about usage so customers can better optimize their energy consumption. In so doing, APS provides more reliable and less expensive energy for its clients. In Chapter 3, we noted that nonconsumption isn't limited to just the poor or those who are unable to afford existing products. Nonconsumption is often characterized by struggle and workarounds, and APS is tapping into that struggle and creating opportunity.

Agriculture—Moringa in Ghana

Moringa is a rich and sturdy tree that grows across tropical regions of the world. It is known as a "miracle tree" because almost every part of the tree has value. The foliage can be cooked and served as greens; the roots can be used as a substitute for horseradish; the leaf can be dried and pulverized and added as a nutritional supplement to meals; the seeds can be roasted and eaten as nuts, and they can also be processed into cosmetic oils that are good for the skin. But even as miraculous as the moringa tree might seem, money still does not grow on it. Cultivating it however, does present us with a significant economic opportunity in Ghana and West Africa.

Ghana is home to millions of farmers, most of whom earn less than $70 a month. Ghana's annual per capita income is around $1,513. Nutrition, or more accurately malnutrition, is known as a silent killer in Ghana. More than one in five children are stunted.

More than half the children under the age of five are anemic.[26] But Ghana's climate is very well suited for growing the miracle tree. In fact, decades ago an aid organization planted hundreds of moringa trees in Ghana in an effort to spur development. Unfortunately, while the trees grew, development didn't, because the trees were only one component of the solution.

Considering the nutritional and economic benefits of the tree, it is clear that an opportunity exists to create a market for moringa products. If an innovator capitalizes on this, it could be significant. First, the innovator could help Ghanaian farmers more efficiently grow and harvest moringa by providing capital for seeds, fertilizer, and equipment. Second, the innovator would also have to connect the farmers to a market for their products. How can a rural Ghanaian farmer connect to a moringa market in the city? Or even in the next village? These are some of the questions the aid organization failed to ask when it planted hundreds of moringa trees in the country. But these are the hard questions that must be asked when trying to create a new market. These are the questions that MoringaConnect, a young Ghanaian company, is asking.

Founded in 2013 by an MIT-trained engineer and a Harvard-trained development economist, MoringaConnect has set its sights on creating and growing a market for moringa oils and powder. Since its founding, the company has planted more than 300,000 moringa trees and now works with over 2,500 farmers in Ghana. By providing inputs such as fertilizer, seeds, and financing, and by connecting farmers to the market that MoringaConnect is creating for its oils and powder, the company has been able to multiply farmer incomes by as much as ten.[27]

Development Practitioners

One of the joys in writing this book has been learning about different organizations solving specific development challenges—from providing access to safe water to improving access to education—in interesting ways. We have written this appendix to highlight some of the work these organizations are doing in the hope that it not only inspires copycats, but also challenges other organizations in the industry to modify their business models so they can more sustainably solve some of these challenges.

The IDP Foundation

When Irene Pritzker founded the IDP Foundation, Inc. to transform education in some of the poorest parts of our world, she avoided traditional methods of project-based grant-making, and instead set out on a journey to see how she could use philanthropic dollars as catalytic capital to develop a sustainable solution in countries where many children didn't have access to quality education. Pritzker's first stop about a decade ago was Ghana, the West African country where fewer than 40 percent of children finish secondary school. Instead of coming in with a set project in mind, however, Pritzker and her team spent time trying to understand the education landscape and the barriers to providing quality education.

Through the course of their research, they found that, while petty traders who sell yams, tomatoes, and pineapples can very easily access microloans to grow their small businesses, hardworking entrepreneurs who establish low-fee private schools have little to no access to financing. Yams and potatoes, it seems, are better businesses than schools. This makes no sense to the IDP Foundation team because there is extreme demand for these low-fee private schools. The public schools, which are supposed to be "free," are either too expensive (parents still have to purchase uniforms and pay administrative fees), are located too far away, or offer such extremely subpar quality that attending might actually be a setback for a family—with a child wasting precious hours in a school without learning much. Often, classes are overcrowded with up to one hundred children to a room and are taught by heavily union-protected teachers who face few consequences for missing work. Because of the uneven public school offerings, there is enormous demand for privately run schools, even by very poor families.

So after extensive market research, where Pritzker interviewed school owners across urban and rural areas, the IDP Foundation saw an opportunity to fill a gap and address a market barrier for these schools to improve access to capital. IDP Foundation partnered with a Ghanaian microfinance institution (MFI), Sinapi Aba, to create the IDP Rising Schools Program.

Instead of immediately setting up shiny new classrooms, the IDP Rising Schools Program tackled the problem differently by building the capacity of existing *proprietors*—grassroots social entrepreneurs already running private schools in their local communities—through training in financial literacy and school management accompanied by access to capital through small business loans. The funds, coupled with the training, help low-fee schools improve their learning environment and enable them to attract more students. Schools participating in the IDP Rising Schools Program have average class sizes of twenty-two students, and teachers are held accountable. Since the program began in 2009, it has expanded to nearly 600 schools and has helped nearly 140,000 students (as of August 2017).

The IDP Rising Schools Program has already proven to be profitable and scalable, and is helping schools likewise become sustainable and self-sufficient. The IDP Foundation has commissioned a great deal of research on the efficacy and impact of the program. It has also been very active in engaging the government of Ghana to vigorously push for the subsidization of schools serving very poor families using public-private partnerships. As Pritzker sees it: "The IDP Foundation's goal is to see the IDP Rising Schools Program replicated around the world. The program is giving hundreds and thousands of children in Ghana access to quality education and a shot at a bright future. Every development organization, including the IDP Rising Schools Program, must constantly ask itself, 'How can we extricate ourselves, so much so that we have created sustainability, and our programs are no longer needed?'"

That is an important question to ask.

What might have happened if the IDP Foundation went to Ghana and spent millions of dollars to simply build schools for Ghanaians? That would constitute a push strategy, one in which the costs for setup are certain, but the impact after execution is less so. Unfortunately, we have an idea what would have happened. Visit any poor country today and take stock of the public or NGO-funded schools. They are not always signs of prosperity. If anything, they are, too often, symbols of poverty. Those who have visited low- to middle-income countries know what I mean. When you see floods of students crammed into primary and secondary schools, where the education is likely subpar, does it not break your heart? I have yet to meet a person who thinks of this as a sign of prosperity. In fact, it's a visible reminder of the enduring struggles of a country.

Harambe Entrepreneur Alliance

Soon after the IDP Foundation team began experiencing success with the Rising Schools Program, they realized that simply educating children into an economy where there were few opportunities was not enough. What would the newly educated students do *after* they'd completed their schooling? It wasn't as if thousands and thousands of good jobs had gone unfilled waiting for these students to finish their education. Does the value of an education not dissipate precipitously when there are no jobs for the educated?

It turns out, as Pritzker and her team found, that Ghana's "education problem" isn't just an "education problem." It is an innovation problem, one that can be better solved with improved financing, management, and partnerships with entrepreneurs seeking to create viable businesses that can *employ* educated students.

To do this, the IDP Foundation has partnered with **Harambe Entrepreneur Alliance**. Founded by Okendo Lewis-Gayle, Harambe is a growing network of more than 250 highly educated young African entrepreneurs building companies all across Africa. The organization's efforts have been recognized by *The Economist*, *Vanity Fair*, and the queen of England. Harambe entrepreneurs have raised money from Mark Zuckerberg and Priscilla Chan's Chan Zuckerberg Initiative, Pierre Omidyar's Omidyar Network, and YCombinator. They are some of the best that Africa has to offer. In 2016, for instance, the Chan Zuckerberg Initiative invested $24 million in Andela, one of the companies cofounded by a Harambean (entrepreneurs in the alliance). One of Harambe's goals is to help its entrepreneurs create more than ten million jobs in Africa over the next decade. As such, the organization is developing the necessary systems to support innovation and entrepreneurship in Africa. To that end, Cisco Foundation invested $5 million in Harambe and is working with the organization to develop an investment fund for its entrepreneurs. Tae Yoo, Cisco's senior vice president for corporate affairs, who spearheaded this effort at Cisco, is hopeful that this practice becomes more prevalent in the industry.

The IDP Foundation, Harambe, and the Cisco Foundation partnership demonstrates what's possible when we see a problem through a different lens—when we see that the solution to an education problem isn't simply to "build more schools." This is not to say that there will not be difficult days ahead for the partnership and its efforts. These are enormously complex challenges they are trying to solve, and they haven't picked a simple answer. But we are hopeful that, with their different perspective, these organizations can create something that will stand the test of time.

One Acre Fund

One Acre Fund is a similar organization in the sense that it thinks about problems holistically. The organization has developed a market-based solution for farmers in several poor countries because it doesn't see the problems that these farmers, and by extension many people in these regions, face simply as a lack of food. They see it as a lack-of-access-to-a-market problem. So One Acre Fund provides financing (for seeds and fertilizer), distribution (of farm inputs), training (on agricultural techniques), and market facilitation (to maximize profits from harvests) to thousands of farmers in Kenya, Rwanda, Burundi, Tanzania, Malawi, and Uganda. Since its inception in 2006, the organization has made almost half a million farmers more productive and now employs more than five thousand people.

One Acre Fund has seen farmer incomes increase by more than 50 percent and plans to reach over one million farmers by 2020. Andrew Youn, cofounder and executive director of One Acre Fund, wrote in their 2016 annual report that "in 2006, I thought of One Acre Fund solely as an agricultural organization. I didn't account for all the other things farmers needed to improve their lives." It was the organization's focus on improving the life of the farmer that caused it to see the issue facing poor farmers not solely as an agricultural problem. In so doing, the organization has better aligned with the progress farmers are trying to make.

Safe Water Network

Safe Water Network, which is committed to solving the access-to-water problem in poor communities, is an example of an organization working to extract itself from its projects over time. The organization works to ensure the sustainability of its projects in the communities where it works. Safe Water Network understands that the solution to a water problem is not to simply "build a well" or "provide water." The organization has found that there must be a system, or a market, that sustains the water investments it makes.

Instead of viewing people in the communities where it works as beneficiaries, Safe Water Network views them as customers. Christine Ternent of the Inter-American Development Bank (the regional development bank for Latin America and the Caribbean) puts it this way: "We must choose not to see the economically poor exclusively through the lens of their needs, but also through their potential." Safe Water Network lives by that statement, and thus identifies entrepreneurs within the communities where it works, provides them with the necessary equipment for pumping and purifying water, and trains them on how to sell their services. In essence, Safe Water Network goes into a community and builds capacity, and makes it possible for markets to be created.

Although this model takes a lot longer to execute than building a well, it has proven to be more profitable and sustainable. It also has the added benefit of creating jobs for locals. So far, Safe Water Network has implemented its solution in four hundred communities and has provided water to more than one million people. Like the IDP Rising Schools Program, Safe Water Network works with local partners and builds its capacity so as to ultimately extricate itself from the community.

———

One of the benefits of creating a new market is that the market needs are often matched with the capabilities of people in the country. When the capabilities don't exist, the market pulls in what is needed. This is important because one of the things we noticed as we studied some of the development projects being executed across the globe today is that we often don't match the level of the project with the local capabilities. Unfortunately, this practice leaves too many poor countries with very good but highly technical and advanced projects that don't work in their contexts. Hospitals are provided with advanced medical equipment that locals can neither use nor repair; computers are donated in regions without electricity; schools are built without trained teachers and contextual curriculums; and perhaps all too commonly, wells are built without truly understanding how they will be repaired when they break.

We are not suggesting here the aid spigot be turned off around the world while local economies struggle to right themselves. But those activities must be seen in the local context—they must make sense for the region and they must focus on the goal of helping build capabilities that can help the local economy develop itself, in time. Aid can go a very long way in helping achieve that goal if it's directed to the right place.

Governments

Governments have a critical role to play in ensuring countries remain prosperous over time. Over the past two centuries, however, the responsibilities placed upon governments have grown significantly. Today, governments not only are tasked with ensuring law and order in society—a tall order by itself for many poor countries— but also must see to it that citizens have access to quality education and health care, roads, rails, and other public infrastructures, and a plethora of social programs. In fact, governments are now tasked with doing it all, and many poor-country governments are trying to do it all. But few governments have the financial, technical, and managerial resources to provide the myriad of services they are now responsible for. As such, year after year, governments find it harder to both meet their budgets and provide these services.

By studying the responsibilities placed on many governments across the world, we have learned that there is often a gap between what many low- and middle-income country governments are *expected* to do and what they are *able* to do. So with this section we seek to offer hope to the many governments that are trying. Once a government understands the progress the people it serves are trying to make, governments can become more effective at performing their responsibilities. By providing several case studies from different countries—from the Philippines to Rwanda—we will highlight the ways in which governments are supporting innovative programs with the limited resources they have. We hope you find these helpful and inspiring.

Nigeria—The Task to Create Jobs

There are few jobs in the world more difficult than that of a public servant in a poor or under-resourced country. But there are also few that are more important. Millions of lives literally depend on them. When Akinwunmi Ambode decided to run for governor of Lagos State in 2015, by his own admission, he did not appreciate "the numbers." By some estimates, more than twenty million people live in Lagos, with roughly eighty-five people moving to the state every hour. The rapid urbanization of Lagos has led to a severe dearth of housing, employment, and many public services, including schools, health care, and good roads.

To his credit, Governor Ambode understood that he couldn't possibly fix everything all at once, and certainly not all by himself. With a keen understanding that the role of government is to develop an environment that supports entrepreneurs looking to solve many of society's problems, Governor Ambode created the Lagos State Employment Trust Fund (LSETF) soon after taking office.

The vision of the $70 million LSETF is simple: to create employment and entrepreneurship opportunities for all Lagos residents. The fund has a goal to enable the creation of more than six hundred thousand jobs and to achieve financial sustainability by 2019. Although the program focused extensively on research and strategy during its first year, to date the fund has disbursed more than $11 million of long-term, low-interest loans to thousands of entrepreneurs in Lagos. The program has even gotten the attention of the United Nations Development Programme (UNDP), which has committed $1 million to providing vocational training to thousands of Lagos State residents.

Governor Ambode handpicked a team of young, ambitious, and high-potential Nigerians to manage the fund. The board, which reports directly to the governor, is chaired by Ifueko Omoigui-Okauru, a Harvard-trained professional who once led the nation's internal revenue services and serves as an adviser on several other influential boards in the country. Another board member, Bilikiss

Adebiyi-Abiola, is a respected MIT-trained entrepreneur who has been honored by several prominent organizations including Intel, Cartier, Oracle, and many others. To lead the day-to-day operations Governor Ambode selected Akintunde Oyebode, a renowned economist known for his unflinching integrity, with over a decade of experience working in some of Nigeria's major financial institutions.

The verdict is still out on whether the LSETF will meet its ambitious goals of helping Nigerian entrepreneurs create hundreds of thousands of jobs, but so far it seems to be on the right track. As we have noted repeatedly throughout this book, just as one company cannot single-handedly develop Nigeria, a country of more than 180 million people, one LSETF initiative also cannot develop Nigeria. But the principles and processes cultivated by one LSETF initiative can have significant impact in the trajectory of the nation.

Philippines—The Business of Water

Water may be life, but unfortunately water is not free. In fact, far from being free, safe water is quite expensive and often subsidized in prosperous countries. With a GDP per capita less than $3,000, however, the Philippines is not a prosperous country, and as many as ten million citizens did not have access to safe water in 1995. In the eastern region of Manila, the world's most densely populated city, barely a quarter of people living there had access to safe and potable water. The situation got so bad that the government was compelled to enact a National Water Crisis Act, paving the way for innovators to work with the government to solve this problem. Through this crisis, Manila Water, a public-private partnership between the Metropolitan Water Works and Sewerage System and the Philippines' oldest conglomerate, Ayala Corporation, was born.

When Manila Water was formed, the organization didn't simply look to serve only its existing customers more profitably. Instead, their mission was to sustainably and profitably get water to as many people as possible. Fundamentally, they understood what consumers wanted: easy and convenient access to water at an affordable price. In order to accomplish this, the organization focused on developing its workforce and reshuffling the existing organization structure. The organization was able to increase access to safe water from around a quarter of the residents to 99 percent of residents. In 2016, Manila Water served more than 6.5 million customers. In doing all this, they built the necessary infrastructure to support their work, increased efficiency, and tripled the volume of water delivered from 440 million liters a day to more than 1.3 billion liters a day.

The interesting facts about water and Manila are that the water has always been there, the people have always been there, the technology has always been available, and the need for water has always been there. But the partnership between the government and the private sector hadn't been there. If residents and the government in Manila had still seen the provision of water as exclusively a public-sector function, there would be no Manila Water today. Thankfully, they didn't. And as a result, Manila Water has transformed the lives of millions of people in the Philippines.

When governments make decisions that are targeted at providing solutions for the people they serve by supporting organizations that are technically, financially, and managerially more capable to provide the services, lives and economies are transformed.

Rwanda—Open for Business Under One Umbrella

Before the creation of the Rwanda Development Board, doing business in the small, twelve-million-strong East African country was incredibly difficult. In order to get a permit, register a company, or pay taxes, investors and entrepreneurs had to interact with multiple agencies that didn't communicate with one another. The system was inefficient and seemed more as if the Rwandan government didn't want people to do business in the country. All that changed, however, after the government began asking itself some simple questions that helped it better understand its role in creating an environment that supported investments. The government began asking questions like: Why do we make those with capital who want to start companies, create jobs, and provide opportunities for Rwandans jump through so many hoops? How can we make the process easier for them? Is there a reason we can't streamline the process of investing in Rwanda? These were simple questions that led to the creation of the Rwanda Development Board (RDB).

Created in 2009, the RDB is now one of the most important organizations in the country and reports directly to the president. The job of the RDB is to simplify the investment process for those looking to do business in Rwanda. To accomplish that, the organization brought all the agencies and departments with which investors had to interact under one roof. It is a one-stop shop for investors, and provides access to information such as taxes, licenses, immigration, utilities, mortgage registration, and many other services. The RDB reduced processes that could take weeks and months to days and has made the business environment more transparent in the process. So far, the RDB has been a remarkable success.

In 2017, the RDB registered total investments (domestic and foreign) of approximately $1.7 billion, up about 50 percent from 2016. Foreign direct investments totaled just over $1 billion, up from around $8.3 million in 2000. The government of Rwanda, through the RDB, hopes to create tens of thousands of jobs annually. It is well on its way. In 2017, more than 38,000 jobs were registered by the RDB, a 184 percent increase from 2016.

It was only twenty-five years ago that Rwanda experienced a painful genocide where, estimates suggest, up to one million people lost their lives. There seemed to be little hope for this small, poor, and landlocked country. Many deemed it too poor, but the government has turned things around by prioritizing its service and support role in the economy. Although Rwanda is still a poor country today, there is hope that if the country continues on its current trajectory, its future will be bright. Perhaps it can be a beacon of hope for many other African countries as Singapore was, and still is, for many Asian countries.

Singapore—Jobs Through Innovation

"We inherited a heart without a body" is how Lee Kuan Yew, Singapore's first prime minister, described the birth of his country. "[Singapore] faced tremendous odds with an improbable chance of survival. Singapore was not a natural country." By all rights, the small island nation of Singapore should not exist at all, and sixty years ago, few would have predicted that Singapore would become one of the richest sovereign nations in the world. With just 5.6 million people, Singapore's GDP of $300 billion is one-fifth that of sub-Saharan Africa's. Singapore was successful by prioritizing jobs, through innovation.

Decades ago, Dr. Goh Keng Swee, one of Singapore's ministers, would get heartbroken whenever he saw hundreds of children streaming out of schools, because he knew his government had to figure out a way to support companies that would provide jobs for them. Dr. Keng Swee and the government understood that going to school was not enough. What would students do after school? That was the question the government was trying to answer. Singapore found its answer in prioritizing innovation, which is no easy feat. One of the ways Singapore did this was by setting up the Economic Development Board (EDB), which is still functional and influential to this day.

The job of the EDB was to attract foreign investment to Singapore in order to create employment, which at the time was in very short supply. Singaporean government officials visited investors in Chicago, New York, and many other American cities, with the goal of convincing them that Singapore was open for business. Americans loved the fact that Singapore was not begging for handouts—they were asking for investments. They constantly met with American executives and not with the aid community. They did this to send a message that, though Singapore was poor today, it did not in-tend to remain poor indefinitely. Once word got out that Singapore was a safe and profitable place to invest, capital flowed—or rather gushed—into Singapore. In 1970, FDI to Singapore was around $93 million. By 2017, Singapore was attracting more than around $60 billion worth of FDI, more than the FDI attracted by the whole continent of Africa.[28]

It is also important to note that Singapore's FDI has not only in-creased, but the nature of the FDI has changed as well. Today, Sin-gapore isn't attracting investments to focus on job creation in the garments, textiles, toys, and lumber industries, like it did fifty years ago. Instead, it is attracting investments in biotech and pharma, aerospace, electronics, and other advanced industries like clean technology. Apple, Microsoft, Bosch, Novartis, and many other companies have their regional headquarters in Singapore. What this shows is that Singapore focused on innovation, not just indus-trialization or exports. It didn't focus on simply creating jobs, but jobs through innovation, which is a more dynamic and sustainable way to develop an economy.

We have said throughout this book that prosperity is a process. The case of Singapore shows that we must continually learn new things if we want to keep making progress.

Mexico—Exchanging Trash for Food

As more and more countries urbanize, many governments not only have to deal with a significant influx of people into cities, but also have to deal with the waste the newcomers generate. While Mex-ico City has always struggled with managing its waste, the situa-tion worsened when, in 2012, the city shut down the Bordo Poniente landfill site, one of its largest. As a report in the *Guardian* put it, the closure of the plant "highlighted the absence of a comprehen-sive policy for urban waste collection, disposal, and processing" in the country.[29] Residents of Mexico City didn't all of a sudden stop generating waste because the landfill was closed. Instead the waste they generated simply found its way to the city's streets. That is, until the local government created Mercado de Trueque, or Barter Market.

At Mercado de Trueque, Mexicans can exchange their recyclable trash for food vouchers. These food vouchers are good at many of the city's farmers' markets, which patronize local Mexican farmers. Since inception, the program has been wildly popular. One smallholder farmer, Alex Castañeda, noted about the program, "It's great for us [farmers]. The price is good, and the volume is great." The program is also popular with a growing number of Mexicans who now recycle by exchanging their waste for food vouchers. Erika Rodriguez, a regular, said, "It is really worth the effort. Once you start, it is difficult to stop."

The program has been responsible for recycling hundreds of thousands of pounds of waste since the landfill was closed in 2012. By providing a ready market for recyclable products and produce from farmers, the program is both creating jobs for recyclers and improving the lives of Mexican farmers. While this program alone will not solve Mexico City's trash problems, it illustrates a different way of approaching a problem that can create immense value for city officials and local citizens.

India—Fintech

On November 8, 2016, an unexpected shock wave hit India. With no advance warning, Prime Minister Narendra Modi's government declared the 500- and 1,000-rupee notes obsolete, a move that almost brought the Indian economy to a standstill. At the time, both the 500- and 1,000-rupee notes made up approximately 86 percent of the cash in circulation in India, and about 98 percent of consumer transactions in the country were done with cash.[30] The ban of those notes caused an economic tsunami, which led to reduced GDP growth and industrial output, and the loss of jobs for many Indians. Tens of millions of Indians stood in line for hours as they tried to convert their old notes so they would not lose value. There are mixed reactions to the demonetization policy, but most would agree that it created significant struggle in India, a struggle that caused many Indians to innovate.

Although the policy was fraught with several execution issues, from limiting the amount of cash people could collect from their banks and ATMs to not having enough new notes in circulation, the policy has also led to several innovations in payments that would have otherwise taken much longer to come to fruition. Even Google capitalized on this struggle and launched a digital payments app, as analysts project the digital payments market will reach $500 billion by 2020.[31] Digital payments rose by more than 80 percent after the policy took effect.[32]

The demonetization policy and the follow-on digitization of the economy are also impacting other aspects of the Indian economy. For example, before the demonetization policy, approximately 3 percent of Indian workers paid taxes. But the number of filed tax returns went up by 25 percent the year after the policy took effect, as millions of Indians were pulled into the digital economy, where they would now have a digital profile.[33] In some localities, tax collection increased by more than 250 percent. In addition, part of the reason for the policy was to disrupt the human trafficking and terrorism networks in the country. Estimates suggest the policy has been effective, at least for now, in curbing these bad behaviors.[34]

The point here isn't that other governments should also enact a sweeping demonetization policy that is bound to have adverse effects on the economy, in the hopes of spurring some innovation that could make it all worth it. The circumstance in which every country finds itself is different. Instead, the broader point is that sometimes the government has the power to create just enough struggle in the system, which can catalyze innovators to develop products and services that will ultimately make life easier for people. In large part, that is what India's demonetization policy—intentionally or unintentionally—has done.

None of the initiatives profiled in this appendix can single-handedly change a country, but we hope they are helpful to you as you continue to think of ways to generate prosperity in the corners of our world that need it the most.

Conclusion

In the class I teach at Harvard Business School, I tell my students that my hope is that they are able to put on the theories and frameworks I teach them as a set of lenses to enable them see the world differently. That was the purpose of this appendix: to present enough opportunities in different parts of the world that are often written off in the hopes that you would begin to see them differently. Investing in innovation, and, more specifically, creating a new market, is one of the most important things we can do to not only reap outsized returns, but to also sustainably develop these regions. The world is full of opportunity, if you just know what you are looking for.

NOTES

1.   Break-bulk cargo is a process by which goods are loaded into a truck and driven to a port warehouse where workers, called longshoremen, unload the goods from the truck and store them in a warehouse or in a shipping vessel, if one is available.

2.   Charles Duhigg, Aaron Bird, and Samantha Stark, "The Power of Outsiders," *New York Times,* video, accessed January 29, 2018, https://www.nytimes.com/video/business/100000004807604/the-power-of-outsiders.html.

3.   At the time, to grow the bacteria longer than forty-eight hours would have been inefficient. Existing rules, conventional wisdom, and accepted science suggested that the specimens would have been useless for their purposes. As such, there was good reason for the experts to grow the bacteria for no more than two days.

4.   Marshall Barry and Paul C. Adams, "*Helicobacter Pylori*: A Nobel Pursuit?" *Canadian Journal of Gastroenterology* 22, no. 11 (2008): 895–896.

5.   "Sales of washing machines in India from 2007–2016," Statista, accessed January 29, 2018, https://www-statista-com.ezp-prod1.hul.harvard.edu/statistics/370640/washing-machine-market-size-india/.

6.   "Electronic Devices: Washing Machine Market Share & Size, Industry Analysis Report, 2025," Grand View Research, December 2016, https://www.grandviewresearch.com/industry-analysis/washing-machine-market.

7.   "Press Room: Washing Machine Market Size to Reach USD 42.16 Billion By 2025," Grand View Research, December 2016, https://www.grandviewresearch.com/press-release/global-washing-machine-market.

8.   An Indian company, Metro Electronic Lab, has developed a portable washing machine that retails for roughly $40. The machine attaches to a bucket, weighs less than 5 pounds (2.2kg), and can wash 6.6 pounds of clothes in six-minute cycles. See more here: http://www.waterfiltermanufacturer.in/handy-washing-machine.html#handy-washing-machine.

9.   "The World Bank in Cambodia," The World Bank, last updated October 2017, http://www.worldbank.org/en/country/cambodia/overview.

10. "Exports: Mexico," Observatory of Economic Complexity, accessed January 29, 2018, https://atlas.media.mit.edu/en/profile/country/mex/#Exports.

11. Mau Juárez, "Analizamos a Zacua, la marca mexicana de autos eléctricos: ¿Buena idea o proyecto sin rumbo?," Motorpasión México, September 18, 2017, https://www.motorpasion.com.mx/autos-mexicanos/analizamos-a-zacua-la-marca-mexicana-de-autos-electricos-buena-idea-o-proyecto-sin-rumbo.

12. "Data: Road Safety, Registered vehicles, Data by country," World Health Organization, last updated November 11, 2015, http://apps.who.int/gho/data/node.main.A995.

13. "National Transportation Statistics," Bureau of Transportation Statistics, accessed January 29, 2018, https://www.rita.dot.gov/bts/sites/rita.dot.gov.bts/files/publications/national_transportation_statistics/html/table_01_11.html.

14. "Motor Vehicle Census, Australia, January 31, 2018," Australian Bureau of Statistics, last updated July 27, 2017, http://www.abs.gov.au/AUSSTATS/abs@.nsf/Lookup/9309.0Main+Features131%20Jan%202017?OpenDocument.

15. Anjani Trivedi, "China's Electric Car Market Has Grown Up," *Wall Street Journal*, updated January 7, 2018, https://www.wsj.com/articles/chinas-electric-car-market-has-grown-up-1515380940.

16. "Indicators: Occupancy rate of passenger vehicles," European Environment Agency, last modified April 19, 2016, https://www.eea.europa.eu/data-and-maps/indicators/occupancy-rates-of-passenger-vehicles/occupancy-rates-of-passenger-vehicles.

17. "Global Consumption Database: Nigeria," The World Bank, accessed January 24, 2018, http://datatopics.worldbank.org/consumption/country/Nigeria.

18. Monica Davey and Mary Williams Walsh, "Billions in Debt, Detroit Tumbles Into Insolvency," *New York Times*, July 18, 2013, http://www.nytimes.com/2013/07/19/us/detroit-files-for-bankruptcy.html?pagewanted=all&_r=0.

19. Jake Bright, "Meet 'Nollywood': The second largest movie industry in the world," *Fortune*, June 24, 2015, http://fortune.com/2015/06/24/nollywood-movie-industry/.

20. Brad Tuttle, "What It Really Costs to Go to Walt Disney World," *Time*, May 15, 2017, http://time.com/money/4749180/walt-disney-world-tickets-prices-cost/.

21. "Fourth Population and Housing Census 2012," *National Institute of Statistics of Rwanda* (January 2014): 79, http://www.statistics.gov.rw/publication/rphc4-atlas.

22. "GDP per capita (current US$)," The World Bank, accessed January 23, 2018, https://data.worldbank.org/indicator/NY.GDP.PCAP.CD.

23. $80 per home multiplied by 20% of the 1.6 million homes that have dirt floors.
"Fourth Population and Housing Census 2012," *National Institute of Statistics of Rwanda* (January 2014): 79, http://www.statistics.gov.rw/publication/rphc4-atlas.

24. "Infrastructure Development Company Limited (IDCOL) was established on 14 May 1997 by the Government of Bangladesh. The Company was licensed by the Bangladesh Bank as a non-bank financial institution (NBFI) on 5 January 1998." Find out more about IDCOL here: http://idcol.org/home/about.

25. Jess Jiang, "The Price of Electricity in Your State," NPR, October 28, 2011, https://www.npr.org/sections/money/2011/10/27/141766341/the-price-of-electricity-in-your-state.

26. "Health and Nutrition: Nutrition, a silent killer," UNICEF, accessed January 30, 2018, https://www.unicef.org/ghana/health_nutrition_7522.html.

27. "Our Story," MoringaConnect, accessed January 30, 2018, http://moringaconnect.com/our-story/.

28. "Foreign Direct Investment, net inflows (BoP, current US$)," The World Bank, accessed January 23, 2018, https://data.worldbank.org/indicator/BX.KLT.DINV.CD.WD?locations=SG.

29. Emilio Godoy, "The waste mountain engulfing Mexico City," *Guardian*, January 9, 2012, https://www.theguardian.com/environment/2012/jan/09/waste-mountain-mexico-city.

30. Rishi Iyengar, "50 days of pain: What happened when India trashed its cash," CNNMoney, January 4, 2017, http://money.cnn.com/2017/01/04/news/india/india-cash-crisis-rupee/.

31. "Google Just Launched a Digital Payments App in India," *Fortune,* September 18, 2017, http://fortune.com/2017/09/18/google-tez-digital -payments-app-launch-india/.

32. Rajeev Deshpandel, "Demonetisation to power 80% rise in digital payments, may hit Rs 1,800 crore in 2017-18," *Times of India,* November 4, 2017, https://timesofindia.indiatimes.com/business/india-business /demonetisation-to-power-80-rise-in-digital-payments-may-hit-rs-1800 -crore-in-2017-18/articleshow/61500546.cms.

33. Special correspondent, "Number of income tax returns filed goes up 24.7%," *The Hindu,* August 7, 2017, http://www.thehindu.com/busi ness/Economy/number-of-income-tax-returns-filed-goes-up-247/article 19446415.ece.

34. Michael Safi, "India currency note ban sparks 'dramatic fall' in sex trafficking," *Guardian,* December 22, 2016, https://www.theguardian .com/global-development/2016/dec/22/india-currency-note-ban-sparks -dramatic-fall-sex-trafficking.

Acknowledgments

Clayton Christensen: Beyond Prosperity

South Korea was a very poor country when I left it to return to the United States in 1973. The mortality rate for children under the age of five was very high, and people simply didn't live into a ripe old age. I remember friends and acquaintances struggling to provide even the most meager living for their families. I was profoundly changed by my years in South Korea; I left half of my heart in South Korea, determined to find a way to help my friends rise out of the desperate poverty to which they had become accustomed.

But as unrelentingly grim as that picture of the country is, my most lasting impression was something very different. It was one of happiness. I remember running into one of our friends, we called him Brother Yoo, high in the hills of Ulsan, pulling a small cart behind him. He told us that he was in the process of moving apartments, and we offered to roll up our sleeves and help him. With a smile, he gestured to the cart behind him, saying, "This is all we have." In that cart were all of his family's possessions, so few that he could easily manage moving his wife and baby on his own. So many of the people I met seemed to have this inexplicable joy that did not rely on how much they had. They had a few material possessions, but their lives were rich with friends and family.

These days, when I visit South Korea, there are almost no visible signs of the pervasive poverty that I originally associated with the country. I'm happy to report that South Korea virtually eradicated child mortality (now just 2.9 per 1,000 births; America's is 5.6) and life expectancy has increased to more than 82 years. Equally stunning is the pure economic growth—between 1973 and 2017, the country's GDP per capita grew by almost 6700% from around $406 to $27,539 in 2016. That's a compounded annual growth of 10.3% over 43 years—a rate of growth, decade after decade, that would thrill any company, much less country. Because of all these improvements, South Korea was able to go from being a "developing" country to one not only hosting the world at the Olympics—twice—but also one now funding aid projects in many low-income countries.

The country is now home to numerous renowned global brands that design and manufacture sophisticated products, from cars to smartphones to big ships. South Korea even successfully exports its culture (ask your teen about K-pop or flip through the pages of a fashion magazine to see the influence of Korean fashion) to countries all over the globe.

South Korea has solved its prosperity problem. But I fear it might have acquired some new ones in the process.

The suicide rate in South Korea is shockingly high: an average of 29.1 people per 100,000 in 2012, about 2.5 times higher than the OECD average. The country also has the highest rate of hospitalization for mental illness among OECD countries, with more than two million people reportedly suffering from depression annually (and even more heartbreaking is the fact that only fifteen thousand choose to seek regular treatment for depression, due to social stigma and family pressures). South Korea is routinely ranked as having one of the best educational systems in the world—and the country has invested heavily in it—but pressure on students to perform has led to a national debate about the human toll of those high expectations.

We want to be clear that we wish prosperity for the world, but prosperity, by itself, does not solve all of a society's problems. And it doesn't solve our personal ones, either. As Robert Kennedy once said: GDP doesn't register "the beauty of our poetry or the strength of our marriages, or the intelligence of our public debate . . ." GDP measures everything "except that which makes life worthwhile."

I hope that in our struggle to make the world a better place, we never lose track of what matters most. For me, that has been building my life around the desire to help people, a goal that has served as the foundation of my role as a teacher, as a colleague, and as a friend. And most important, I continue to seek to know God more deeply.

By sharing our thinking with you here, Efosa, Karen, and I hope we are helping you, too.

Working side by side with Karen Dillon and Efosa Ojomo has been a delightful experience. Truly delightful. We wrote this book as a team, though we each acquired key roles. Efosa's ability to master and synthesize what academia and practitioners have already brought to this puzzle—both deep and wide research—and then understand where our thinking here fits has been the foundation of this book. The role of Efosa has been to understand the hearts and the minds of Africa, Asia, and the Americas, both past and present simultaneously, and bring that knowledge to life, first in his own research and then on these pages. His understanding of parts of the world that I have never known except in a superficial way is quite remarkable. I can still picture exactly where Efosa sat in my class a few years ago —the second to last row on the left, near the back. Nobody has ever occupied that chair with the same delight and understanding that he brought to my class. I believed he was among my most promising students then, and his work on this book has proven how right I was. As a partner and collaborator, he has exceeded all my expectations.

This is the third time I have had the pleasure of collaborating with Karen on a book, and I've come to appreciate her gifts more each time. On this project, Karen defined our meetings by asking me questions, carefully listened to my responses, and poked and prodded at our answers. She then managed to translate complex thoughts into something that is both clear and powerful at the same time. Karen writes by understanding my mind and my heart simultaneously and has done a beautiful job capturing both here.

As a writer, she is unsurpassed. She truly has been an invaluable thought partner, collaborator, and friend. I feel sorry for anyone who doesn't have the chance to work with Karen.

I also want to thank the many people who have helped us with this book. I'll start with my friends in South Korea, back in the 1970s, particularly President Edward and Sister Carol Brown, who helped ignite my initial interest in the questions around prosperity.

As we've discussed and shared these ideas in class, my students have become my greatest teachers. I've been gratified to see how they have used these ideas in their own work (the founders of IguanaFix and Clinicas del Azúcar, for example, both first learned these ideas while students here in Cambridge and used them to help shape their market-creating innovations), and their experiences, in turn, have helped shape and refine our thinking.

My colleagues at Harvard Business School who teach the BSSE course, Willy Shih, Steve Kaufman, Chet Huber, Derek van Bever, Rory McDonald, Raj Chowdhury, V. G. Narayanan, and Ray Gilmartin, have been an invaluable source of support and feedback. Dean Nohria, who leads us all, has been a constant supporter of my research and a dear friend. Professor Roberto Unger, of the Harvard Law School, with whom I have frequently shared thoughts about how we use disruption to raise human potential, has been the source of inspiration and provocative thinking. Howard Yu, my former doctoral student, demonstrated the power of "deep dives," which has influenced this work. Among my original mentors, whose leadership and support I have deeply valued, are Kim Clark, who taught me how to do research, Kent Bowen, who taught me how to teach, and Steve Wheelright, who was a steady guide as I found my path in academia.

The staff of Harvard Business School Forum for Growth and Innovation, led by Derek van Bever, has been an invaluable source of support and thought leadership, including allowing us to work closely with the Forum's Nate Kim, who has provided us with endless hours of research assistance and critical thinking as we've gathered information from all around the world, and Pooja Venkatraman, whose parallel work on market-creating innovations and capital markets played a role in helping shape our thinking here. Clare Stanton has helped organize and coordinate much of the Forum's efforts to present our work on campus, which has helped us immensely.

I also want to thank my colleagues and dear friends at the Christensen Institute and Innosight, particularly my Christensen Institute cofounder Michael Horn and Innosight senior partner Scott Anthony, both of whom put hours of thought into providing us with invaluable feedback for this work. I'm grateful for your support and your friendship, and this book is better because of you. Both TCS and Li & Fung have also been valued supporters of our larger research efforts at the Christensen Institute, for which I am truly thankful.

I have been fortunate, indeed, to have the support of a stellar team here at the Harvard Business School, including my tireless chief of staff, Cliff Maxwell, who has been my partner in so much important work over the past year. Cliff's sharp mind, deft editing touch, and sincere desire to do work that makes the world a better place has been an enormous gift to us on this project. His predecessor, Jon Palmer, who is now pursuing his own doctorate at HBS, was one of the strongest original supporters of this work, and we're grateful for the hours and hours of thought and energy he has put into helping us bring this book to life. My assistant Brittany McCready has somehow magically kept all of the balls in the air, and I'm grateful for her support on this and all the other projects that she has quietly enabled to run smoothly. Before Brittany, there was Emily Snyder, who continued to be a cheerleader for this work even after she left HBS to pursue her own MBA at Columbia Business School. And now I'm grateful to have the wonderful Erin Wetzel by my side.

I have been fortunate to work with a terrific team at Harper-Collins over the years, including my longtime editor and collaborator, Hollis Heimbouch, who has truly made everything I've ever published better. My longtime agent, Danny Stern, and his top-notch team at Stern Strategy, including Ned Ward, Kristen Soehngen Karp, and Ania Trzepizur, have provided us with constant support and able guidance.

The Christensen family have been among my most important partners in thought and support—on this book and all of my work in past decades. I want to thank Matthew and Liz, Ann, Michael, Spencer and Channing, and Katie for their tireless interest in helping me refine my thinking and do work that will help make the world a better place. My wife, Christine, and I are proud of their success in their own lives and careers—in part because they have used the theories about management that were honed in discussions at home. Beyond this, however, Christine and I are most proud that every day they remember why God sent us to this earth.

And finally, to my wife, Christine, who has truly been my most important partner in everything that has ever mattered in my life. She has read and edited every book I've ever written, but on this one I think she's gone the extra mile. Both her head and her heart have been truly engaged in this work, and her touch is reflected on every page. And she's done all that while helping me through some challenging health problems in recent years. I consider myself fortunate indeed to have Christine by my side, and my work—and my life—has been all the better for it.

Efosa Ojomo: Beyond the American Dream

Twenty years ago I failed the entrance exam into university in Nigeria. Twice. But as God would have it, I was fortunate to gain admission into a college in the United States. And so, in August 2000, I came to America for college, and to get my own slice of the American Dream. I never intended to return to Nigeria, and for the longest time, I didn't even visit. I graduated, got a job, and bought myself a house and an SUV. I was well on my way to realizing this American Dream I had heard so much about. Then, in 2008, in the pages of NYU professor William Easterly's *The White Man's Burden*, I met Amaretch.

On a cold February night in Wisconsin, I read about Amaretch—a ten-year-old Ethiopian girl—whose story instantly changed the trajectory of my life. After learning about how she had to wake up every morning at three a.m., fetch firewood, and sell in the market, I asked some friends to help me start Poverty Stops Here. What we lacked in skill and expertise, we made up for in dedication and passion. After raising a couple hundred thousand dollars, however, I realized the problem was much more complex than I had originally thought. And so, in 2013, I headed to Harvard Business School to learn how business could play a role in eradicating poverty. It was there I met Professor Clayton Christensen.

CLAY: There are few people I have met who are as brilliant and as kind as Professor Christensen. He has the ability to change not just how you see the world, but also how you see yourself and your potential. I first met Clay when I took his course Building and Sustaining a Successful Enterprise and was instantly fascinated by his willingness to help everyone he encountered become a better version of themselves. His dedication to teaching is only surpassed by his genuine affection for his students. After taking his class, making the decision to work for him was easy. For me, this book is the culmination of a three-year process of thinking, writing, and refining our ideas. For him, it represents a three-decade journey to make this world a better place. Clay believed in me enough to take me on this special journey and for that I am eternally grateful. He stretched my thinking when I thought we had found an answer to a pressing question. He showed me patience as we worked on fine-tuning the message of the Prosperity Paradox. And every day we met, he was simply kind. Thanking a person like this is not easy. Outside of my family, Clay has had the most profound impact on my life. He is my professor and my mentor, but, most of all, he is my friend. And to Christine, thank you so much for the countless hours you spent reading and giving us invaluable feedback.

KAREN: Writing a book is akin to running marathon in that it can take a while. Through this process, in between moments of excitement and discovery, there were moments of self-doubt and anxiety. Karen's partnership was absolutely essential in getting this book and the ideas in it to the finish line. Her ability to ask questions, simplify concepts, and emphasize parts of a story that would resonate with readers is truly second to none. She was always ready to give of her time and of herself for the benefit of the book. She has been a true partner through this process, but more important, she has become "fam." I am very grateful for her.

NATE KIM spent countless hours providing excellent research and edits that have made this book stronger. He has a keen ability to simplify complex concepts to make them accessible for all audiences. Nate's help on this project was truly instrumental in helping us write the best book possible.

ANN CHRISTENSEN, my manager, has a question she has asked me every week since I started working at the Christensen Institute: "How can I be most helpful to you?" Ann has not only made writing this book pleasurable, but she has also made working a joy. For the many ways you sacrifice for us, thanks, Ann.

CLIFF MAXWELL, who serves as Professor Christensen's chief of staff, has read this book almost as many times as we have and has provided us with invaluable feedback. Up until the final hour, Cliff was still helping us refine our thinking. We affectionately refer to him as our fourth author.

BRITTANY McCREADY, Clay's faculty assistant, has been pivotal in helping us keep all the balls in motion as we wrote this book. She was encouraging throughout the process and always kept our spirits high.

JON PALMER had the brilliant idea of "recruiting" Karen to join us on this project, and he also graciously read early manuscripts. Jon's editorial prowess is truly second to none. Thanks for helping us improve this book.

Although EMILY SNYDER left to pursue her MBA at Columbia, the culture and structure she created to support Clay's work lives on and was instrumental in ensuring we did our best possible work.

SCOTT ANTHONY and MICHAEL HORN provided feedback that practically changed the direction of this book. They read very early drafts of the entire book (including our many footnotes ☺) and were kind enough to spend time explaining their feedback to us. We are in your debt.

MY CHRISTENSEN INSTITUTE COLLEAGUES—Ruth Hartt, David Sundahl, Horace Dediu, Spencer Nam, Ryan Marlin, Alana Dunagan, Aroop Gupta, Subhajit Das, Jenny White, Rebecca Fogg, Julia Freeland Fisher, John George, Tom Arnett, Chandrasekar Iyer, Richard Price, John Riley, Meris Stansbury, Parthasarathi Varatharajan—working with you all is truly one of the joys of my life. Your dedication to making the world a better place encourages me to improve every day.

I'd like to especially thank HAYDEN HILL and CHRISTINA NUNEZ for reading early manuscripts and providing us with excellent feedback.

POOJA SINGHI and TERRENS MURADZIKWA, two of the most brilliant college students I've ever interfaced with, provided insightful feedback and did excellent research which helped improve the ideas in the book.

MY POVERTY STOPS HERE FAMILY—Jeremy and Amanda Akins, Ranjit and Sneha Mathai, Donald and Grace Ogisi, Terry and Mary Claire Esbeck, Jeff Meisel, Ese Efemini, Femi Owoyemi—ten years ago you took a chance on creating PSH. Your belief that we could create a better world for many who have been dealt a difficult hand continues to fuel me to this day.

MY CHURCH FAMILY—Pastor Chris and Becky Dolson, Jason and Veronica Zhang, Lee-Shing Chang, Bright Amudzi, and my City on a Hill Community Group—you supported me through some of the toughest days I've had in recent time. You prayed for me, you hoped for me, and you helped me become a better version of myself. You reminded me of the role of the body of Christ. Thank you. To Priscila Samuel, who has changed my life in more ways than she can imagine, thank you for always being kind.

MY HBS FORUM FOR GROWTH AND INNOVATION FRIENDS— Derek van Bever, Pooja Venkatraman, Clare Stanton, Bryan Mezue, Tom Bartman, Katie Zandbergen, and Tracy Horn—thank you for your support, your intellectual rigor, and for helping get the word out. I also want to thank Taddy Hall, who introduced us to several entrepreneurs we profile in the book.

HOLLIS HEIMBOUCH, our publisher at HarperCollins, thank you. You not only believed in us when our ideas weren't yet fully formed, but also helped us make them better.

AMY BERNSTEIN at *Harvard Business Review,* thank you for believing in me. You have been instrumental in my growth as a writer.

To our friends at the CENTER FOR INTERNATIONAL PRIVATE ENTERPRISE (CIPE) and their colleagues—Toni Weis, Kim Bettcher, Brian Levy, and Katrin Kuhlman—thank you for reading drafts, providing feedback, and helping us improve our ideas. A very special thanks to Philip Auerswald, who read our whole manuscript and provided invaluable feedback and references.

To my family—DAD, MOM, ESOSA, FEYI, EDEFE, EDEMA, GIGI, and UYI—thank you. Everything I am, I owe to the enduring love and ceaseless encouragement you have shown me. Thank you to my parents for always believing in me. Esosa and Feyi (my brother and his wife), you are as generous as you are brilliant, and, through countless conversations, you have helped me think more critically about many ideas in this book. Your beautiful kids—Gigi and Uyi— are a constant source of inspiration for us all. My two sisters—one of whom has a PhD and the other who is currently working on one—know all too well what it takes to write. Through this process, the two of you have helped me ask better questions and have reminded me to think of the book as an invitation to a conversation. You have always supported me, even when it has come at a cost to you. Thank you.

Most of all, I am thankful to God, the One from whom all my blessings flow.

Twenty years ago, I came to the United States in search of the American Dream. I came to find personal prosperity. But all that has changed now. Life, I have learned, cannot simply be about oneself. Life necessarily has to be about helping as many people as we can in the short time that we all have here on earth. It is my deepest hope that you find the words in *The Prosperity Paradox* helpful in your cause to make the world a better place. Thank you.

Karen Dillon: Beyond Caring

Two years ago, my daughter Rebecca was given an assignment to invite a speaker with a "unique and innovative perspective" on the world to address her high school class. When she asked me if I knew of anyone who fit that description, I immediately thought of Efosa Ojomo. I was aware that Efosa was doing interesting research on innovation and prosperity at the Christensen Institute, though only enough to recommend that Rebecca reach out to him. Having done my "mom duty," I then stepped out of the situation. The day that he came to her class, however, I was sucked right back in. The conversation at our family dinner table that night was animated by what Efosa had discussed with the students. Did I know how rough things were in America just a few generations ago? Did I know about Efosa's wells? Did I know about the innovation happening in the most unlikely places around the world? My sixteen-year-old daughter had been captivated by his ideas, and now, so had I.

In early 2018 the journal *Nature* published the findings of two separate research studies into the progress being made on poor child nutrition and low education levels across fifty-one countries in Africa. The studies assessed, in extraordinary detail, how close each country in Africa is likely to get to the UN's target of ending childhood malnutrition. The findings in *Nature* were grim:

not only had no African country met the initial 2015 Millennium Development Goal of eradicating hunger, but none was expected to meet it by 2030. Simon Hay, one of the authors of the papers published in *Nature*, suggested that the UN global goal was merely an "aspirational" target. And the particular aspiration to eradicate childhood malnutrition, he said, "is very, very far away."

That conclusion is heartbreaking to me. More than thirty years ago, I was one of millions of teenagers glued to the television for the live broadcast of the Live Aid concert, featuring an unprecedented assembly of the world's biggest rock stars who raised millions of dollars to help feed starving people in Africa. We memorized all the lyrics to "Feed the World," we phoned in our pledges, and we convinced ourselves that if we cared enough, we could help change the world.

My two daughters are now roughly the same age I was during that time and it's painfully clear that the needle hasn't moved. But I refuse to watch my daughters' generation slowly sink into the same despair—or, worse, indifference—that has washed over previous generations. Caring isn't enough. We need new tools, new weapons. With this book, Clay, Efosa, and I have joined the fight. By sharing our best ideas, by poking and prodding conventional wisdom, and by encouraging a new lens on old problems, we hope we've spurred you to do the same.

It has been one of the privileges of my life to collaborate with Clayton Christensen. This is now our third book together, and I never fail to appreciate the gift I've been given in working closely with one of the most respected academics in the world. But far more important than that, I have had the chance to collaborate with the truly good man behind that much-deserved reputation. Our work together and the deep friendship we have developed over these years have been priceless to me. You've truly changed my life.

Efosa Ojomo: It has been an unmitigated joy to be your partner on this book. You have inspired me in so many ways throughout the course of our collaboration. Not only are you brilliant, but you are truly kind, an exceedingly rare combination in this day and age. For me, one of the best things to come out of this project is the wonderful friendship we have forged in the days, weeks, and months of working so closely on something that we both cared deeply about. You've been more than a partner; you've become family. I know that the wells you so desperately wanted to give back to Nigeria did not last, but I hope in some way this book becomes your first enduring "well"—one of ideas that may help many more people. I cannot wait to see the great things you have to offer the world in the years ahead.

To Clay's chief of staff, Cliff Maxwell, we couldn't have asked for a more supportive partner in this process. You cared as much as we did about this book; you offered us your best thinking, you challenged us, and your edits helped raise this work to another level. We are all indebted to you. Christine Christensen, who is kindness and class personified, was one of our strongest supporters of this project, and I'm so grateful for your work here. And to the extraordinarily resourceful Brittany McCready, a hearty thank-you for just always stepping up when we needed you, whether being ready with hair spray on a photoshoot, keeping all the balls in the air, or just making us laugh. You were a soul sister throughout this project. Nate Kim, I knew your research for this book would be invaluable, but the wonderful surprise was what a terrific editor and writer you are, too. If we could go through this book with a highlighter and mark all the sections in which you played a critical role, this book would be covered in yellow. Thank you for truly giving this book your all.

To Jon Palmer, who gently coaxed me to have a look at Efosa's work in the early days and then devoted hours of your own time to providing feedback on this book, I owe you an enormous debt of gratitude. You have been a true partner and friend. Scott Anthony and Michael Horn, two of the sharpest minds I know, gave us invaluable insights on early drafts of this work, and the book is much stronger for it. We had the benefit of many other first-class minds along the way, including Ann Christensen, Pooja Venkatraman, Hayden

Hill, Christina Nunez, Karen Player, Khuyen Bui, and Stephanie Gruner. Mallory Dwinal-Palisch was a deeply valued early reader, enthusiastically working through the entire manuscript in between the hours she helps make the world a better place at Oxford Day Academy. Charlene Bazarian, you have been one of my secret weapons these past few years, inspiring me daily with your indefatigable spirit. This may not be our trip to the Ritz yet, but consider it my heartfelt thank-you. To my friends, near and far, who have cheered me on as I dove headlong into this book, I thank you for your unconditional support.

Danny Stern, Ania Trezpizur, Ned Ward, Kristen Soehngen Karp, and the entire team at Stern Strategy have offered steady guidance and encouragement throughout this process and I am so grateful you're on our team. We are extremely fortunate to have had the guidance of the gifted Hollis Heimbouch, our longtime editor at HarperCollins, who took a leap of faith with us on this book. Hollis is the perfect balance of pushing and pulling as an editor, ensuring that we will want to give her our best work. Her colleague Rebecca Raskin was also an invaluable ally as we worked our way through the final days of creating a book.

To Rob Lachenauer and all my colleagues at BanyanGlobal Family Business Advisors: you have been the source of much happiness as you've welcomed me into the fold, challenged me to learn and grow, and reminded me that working closely with world-class colleagues is a gift. It's an honor to be a Banyanite.

To my parents, Bill and Marilyn Dillon, who instilled in me a sense of compassion for others, I continue to owe you an enormous debt of gratitude for your unstinting, lifelong support. My beloved mother, Marilyn, has edited every book I've ever written, and I've come to count on her eagle eye to make my work better. My brother, Bill Dillon, and my sister, Robin Ardito, have been among my most ardent supporters, clearing the way for me to focus on this book while they stepped up to the plate for our family responsibilities. I love you all more than words here can capture.

To my daughters, Rebecca and Emma, who I know will find their own ways to make the world a better place in the years ahead, I am grateful for your support and interest as I've enthusiastically discussed each new nugget of research for this book. Being your mother has been the greatest joy of my life. You've continually inspired me to do work that matters, and I hope with this book I've done you proud. And to my husband, Richard, who has been, day in and day out, an avid scout of insights and examples for this book, my most trusted thought partner, and my best friend: we may not solve all the problems of the world on our long walks, but we sure give it a good try. I can think of no better partner with whom to walk through life.

Index

Page numbers of figures and charts appear in italics.

About the Authors

CLAYTON M. CHRISTENSEN is the Kim B. Clark Professor at Harvard Business School, the author of twelve books, a five-time recipient of the McKinsey Award for *Harvard Business Review*'s best article, and the cofounder of four companies, including the innovation consulting firm Innosight. He is repeatedly recognized by Thinkers50 as one of the most influential business thinkers in the world, who have noted that "his influence on the business world has been profound."

EFOSA OJOMO works side by side with Christensen as a senior fellow at the Christensen Institute for Disruptive Innovation, where he leads the organization's Global Prosperity Practice. His work has been published in the *Harvard Business Review*, the *Guardian*, *Quartz*, CNBCAfrica, and the *Emerging Markets Business Review*. He graduated with an MBA from Harvard Business School in 2015.

KAREN DILLON is the former editor of the *Harvard Business Review* and coauthor of the *New York Times* bestseller, *How Will You Measure Your Life?*, and *Competing Against Luck*. A graduate of Cornell University and Northwestern University's Medill School of Journalism, she is also the editorial director of BanyanGlobal Family Business Advisors. She was named by Ashoka as one of the world's most influential and inspiring women.